FAIR AND FOUL

FAIR AND FOUL

Beyond the Myths and
Paradoxes of Sport

Seventh Edition

D. STANLEY EITZEN
COLORADO STATE UNIVERSITY

CHERYL COOKY
PURDUE UNIVERSITY

ROWMAN & LITTLEFIELD
Lanham • Boulder • New York • London

Senior Acquisitions Editor: Alyssa Palazzo

Sales and Marketing Inquiries: textbooks@rowman.com

Rowman & Littlefield
Bloomsbury Publishing Inc, 1385 Broadway, New York, NY 10018, USA
Bloomsbury Publishing Plc, 50 Bedford Square, London, WC1B 3DP, UK
Bloomsbury Publishing Ireland, 29 Earlsfort Terrace, Dublin 2, D02 AY28, Ireland
www.rowman.com

Copyright © 2025 by The Rowman & Littlefield Publishing Group, Inc.
First edition 1999. Second edition 2003. Third edition 2006. Fourth edition 2009. Fifth edition 2012. Sixth edition 2016.

All rights reserved. No part of this publication may be: i) reproduced or transmitted in any form, electronic or mechanical, including photocopying, recording or by means of any information storage or retrieval system without prior permission in writing from the publishers; or ii) used or reproduced in any way for the training, development or operation of artificial intelligence (AI) technologies, including generative AI technologies. The rights holders expressly reserve this publication from the text and data mining exception as per Article 4(3) of the Digital Single Market Directive (EU) 2019/790.

British Library Cataloguing in Publication Information Available

Library of Congress Cataloging-in-Publication Data Available
ISBN 978-1-5381-9779-0 (cloth : alk. paper) | ISBN 978-1-5381-7566-8 (pbk : alk. paper) | ISBN 978-1-5381-7567-5 (ebook)

For product safety related questions contact productsafety@bloomsbury.com.

∞™ The paper used in this publication meets the minimum requirements of American National Standard for Information Sciences—Permanence of Paper for Printed Library Materials, ANSI/NISO Z39.48-1992.

BRIEF CONTENTS

Preface xii
Foreword by *Michael A. Messner* xv

1 **Paradoxes of Sport: An Introduction** 1

PART ONE SPORT IS FAIR, SPORT IS FOUL 27

2 **Sport Unites, Sport Divides** 29

3 **Sports Includes, Sports Excludes: Sex/Gender in Sports** 55

4 **Sport Is Healthy, Sport Is Destructive** 77

5 **The Organization of Youth Sport: Issues and Consequences** 103

PART TWO SPORTS AS A MICROCOSM OF SOCIETY 117

6 **Are Sports Played on a Level Playing Field? Issues of Race, Class, and Gender** 119

7 **Media and Sport: Changing Sports, Changing Media** 137

8 Big-Time College Sport: Commercialized Sport Within Academia 151

9 Professional Sports Franchises: Public Teams, Private Businesses 171

10 The Challenge: Changing Sport 195

Photo Credits 205
Index 206
About the Authors 219

CONTENTS

Preface xii
   New to the Seventh Edition xiii
   Acknowledgments xiv
Foreword by *Michael A. Messner* xv

1 Paradoxes of Sport: An Introduction 1
   Theme I: Sport Is Fair; Sport Is Foul 3
   Theme II: Sport as a Microcosm of Society 6
   Common Characteristics of Sport and Society 6
      High Degree of Competitiveness 6
      Emphasis on Materialism 7
      Pervasiveness of Racism 7
      Male Dominance as the Norm 7
      Domination of Individuals by Bureaucracies 8
      Unequal Distribution of Power in Organizations 8
      Caveat: Sport Can Also Be an Agent of Change 8
   Variation on the "Sport as a Microcosm of Society" Theme: The Super Bowl 9
   Variation on the "Sport as a Microcosm of Society" Theme: What Football and Baseball Tell Us About Our Society 11
   Overview 14
   Paradoxes of Sport 16
   Organization of the Book 17
      Part I: Sport Is Fair, Sport Is Foul 17
      Part II: Sports as a Microcosm of Society 19

PART ONE SPORT IS FAIR, SPORT IS FOUL 27

2 Sport Unites, Sport Divides 29
The Role of Sport in Unity and Division Among Nations 32
   Sport Unites 33
   Sport Divides 36
Unity and Division Through Sport in the United States 39
   Social Class 40
   Race 43
   Gender 45
   Sexuality 46
Caveats 49
   Are the Expressions of Patriotism by Sport Organizations at Sporting Events Always Real? 49
   Is the Unity Achieved Through Sport Always Good? 49

3 Sports Includes, Sports Excludes: Sex/Gender in Sports 55
Title IX, Participation, and Opportunity 56
Barriers to Girls' and Women's Sports 61
   Structural Barriers 61
   Cultural Barriers 64
   Political Barriers 64
   Policy Barriers 66
Media Coverage of Women's Sports 66
Impact on Society of Girls' and Women's Sports Participation 68
Conclusion 68

4 Sport Is Healthy, Sport Is Destructive 77
Sports and Girls' and Women's Health 78
The Destructive Aspects of Sport 80
   Physical Injuries to Children and Youth from Sport 80
   Sports Injuries: The Case of Men's Professional Football 83
   Injuries in Other Sports 87
   Relative Energy Deficiency in Sports (RED-S) 87
   Drug Use 88
   Mental Health and Sports 92

Contents

      Sexual Abuse of Athletes 93
      Sports and the #MeToo Movement 95
  Conclusion 97

5 The Organization of Youth Sport: Issues and Consequences 103
  Two Fundamentally Different Forms of Play for Young Children 103
      Organization 105
      Process 106
      Impetus 107
      Analysis of Differences 107
  The Dark Side of Adult-Centered Play 108
      Beginning Too Early 109
      Specialization 110
      The Costs—Familial and Financial—of Youth Sports 110
      Out-of-Control Parental Behavior 111
      Untrained Coaches 112
      Intrusion of Organizations on Children's Sport 112
      Excessive Parental Demands 113
  Conclusion 114

PART TWO SPORTS AS A MICROCOSM OF SOCIETY 117

6 Are Sports Played on a Level Playing Field? Issues of Race, Class, and Gender 119
  Racial Inequities 120
  Class Inequities 127
  Gender Inequities 129
  Conclusion 133

7 Media and Sport: Changing Sports, Changing Media 137
  Shifts in the Media Landscape 138
  Televised Sports as a Window on Reality or a Social Construction? 141
  Commercial Interests 141
  Sport as a Male Preserve 144
  Television as a Game Changer 146
  Conclusion 147

8 Big-Time College Sport: Commercialized Sport Within Academia 151

The Case That Big-Time Sport Promotes Education 154
The Case That Big-Time Sport Compromises Educational Goals 154
    Avoiding Education 156
    Taking the Easy Route: Clustering in Easy Majors 156
    The Excessive Time Demands of Big-Time Programs Diminish the Student Role 157
    The "Jock" Subculture 158
    Scandals Involving the Education of Athletes 158
    "One and Done" 159
    Diverting Education Funds to Subsidize College Sports 159
    The Resulting Educational Performance of Athletes 159
    NIL and Pay-to-Play 160
College Sport as Big Business 161
    Consequences of Money in College Athletics 163
Summary: The Contradictions of Big-Time Sport in Academia 166

9 Professional Sports Franchises: Public Teams, Private Businesses 171

Professional Sport as a Monopoly 172
Public Subsidies to Professional Team Franchises 177
    Case Study: Two Stadiums, One for the Cincinnati Bengals and One for the Cincinnati Reds; a Sweetheart Deal for the Owners and "the Worst Stadium Deal" for the Taxpayers 179
    Case Study: Dallas Cowboys Stadium, an Ostentatious Edifice Subsidized in Part by Taxpayers Who, for the Most Part, Have Limited Access to the Excess 180
    Case Study: The Funding of the Milwaukee Bucks Basketball Arena: The Business-Politics Nexus 182
    Other Examples of Egregious Subsidies to Team Owners 182
The Rationale for Public Subsidization of Professional Sports Teams 184
An Alternative Structure 189

Contents

10 The Challenge: Changing Sport 195

    Is Change Possible? 196

        The Racial Integration of Baseball 196

        Free Agency for Athletes 197

        Gender Equity 198

    Should We Change Sport? 199

    How Do We Go About Making Changes? 201

Photo Credits 205

Index 206

About the Authors 219

PREFACE

The first edition of *Fair and Foul* was published in 1999. Over the past twenty-plus years there have been a number of significant changes in both sport and society that have been integrated throughout the seventh edition. Conversations around the social meanings and implications of sports are no longer confined to academia and progressive or niche media outlets. The emergence of social media for example has expanded the voices writing on sports and has diversified the perspectives and viewpoints. There are a growing number of writers, journalists, platforms, and outlets who offer critical insights into the sports world. Social media has shifted the production and consumption dynamics such that athletes and fans have access and means to create content. As a result, many of the myths of sports, often reproduced and upheld in legacy media outlets, are now challenged by journalists, fans, and athletes. Athletes and fans can "talk back" to legacy media and legacy media often incorporates those views into their own content and coverage (the coverage of sexism in sports broadcasting and commentary is a good example of this). This shift not only changes how scholars and researchers study sport media, but more importantly it also impacts how students (and other readers) consume sports and thus how they see and understand sports. The new edition takes these shifts into consideration.

The book opens with the chapter "Sport Unites, Sport Divides" and begins with a discussion of 9/11. While students will not have personal experience with 9/11, in many ways 9/11 marks a pivotal point in American history. In his book, *The Heritage: Black Athletes, a Divided America and the Politics of Patriotism*, sports journalist Howard Bryant draws on historian David Halberstam to illustrate the significance of 9/11. Halberstam examined what he called "intersections of history." Bryant describes these intersections as "crucial pivot points where decisions or indecisions made by a handful of key people at key times altered the arc of history" (100). Bryant asserts that 9/11 is one of those intersections: "As sports fractured along the lines of the protest and politics, race and patriotism, 9/11 was that intersection. . . . Nothing about the current state of the sports world can be explained *without* the context of September 11, 2001." COVID-19 is perhaps another "intersection." Indeed, media outlets proclaimed March 11,

Preface

2020, as "the day everything changed," when the World Health Organization declared a global pandemic in the wake of *118,000 cases in 114 countries and 4,291 deaths.* Several months later in the summer of 2020, the Black Lives Matter social movement went global after the death of George Floyd, catalyzing changes in both society and in sports. In many ways, both 9/11 and the COVID-19 pandemic fundamentally shifted sports role in society, both events united many, yet also further deepened divisions in our society.

New to the Seventh Edition

The table of contents for the seventh edition has been revised to collapse chapters and to include new and/or expanded chapters. The new edition includes ten chapters; each organized around one of the two themes identified in the book (paradoxes of sport or sport as a microcosm of society).

New to the seventh edition of the text, we introduce students to the framework of the book by posing the question: "Can you be a 'fan' and a critic?" This section primes students to think critically about sports and demonstrates how critical thinking is not oppositional to "loving sports" (either as an athlete, fan, or aspiring professional/practitioner). The text has also been updated to reflect the current state of politics in the United States; in particular, the increased polarization and divisiveness reflected not only in the responses to athlete activism as it relates to social justice/racial justice, but also in the wave of anti-trans bills in the United States and beyond, which exclude trans athletes from participating in sports. We continue to situate 9/11 in the contemporary context of sports even though students will not have experiential knowledge of that day. As Howard Bryant has argued, contemporary athlete activism (and much of what is happening in sports in the United States) continues to be informed and shaped by 9/11. The importance of 9/11 for understanding the contemporary context of sports in the United States is now included in the new edition.

A new chapter 3, "Sports Includes, Sports Excludes: Sex/Gender in Sports," consolidates the discussion of sex/gender binary into one chapter. It focuses on Title IX as expanding opportunities and access. It also discusses how sports excludes in terms of the barriers girls and women encounter despite access and opportunity. Chapter 4, "Sport Is Healthy, Sport Is Destructive," retains the discussion of the physical benefits of sports, and in particular the benefits to girls and women who participate in sports. The chapter now includes a brief discussion of mental health, specifically the increased visibility of mental health issues and attention given to mental health among elite and professional athletes. The book's discussion of sports media now integrates the role of social media and streaming platforms in sports content/coverage and takes into consideration the shifts in media production/consumption on sport. It also integrates the recent Name Image Likeness (NIL) Supreme Court ruling, recent conference realignments, and the role of the media (e.g., ESPN and Fox Sports television contracts) and what that might mean for the future of college athletics.

Acknowledgments

I would like to thank my editor, Alyssa Palazzo, and the editorial staff at Bloomsbury Publishing for the invitation to revise and update the book. I appreciate the support and constructive feedback. Thank you also to Alyssa for sending pictures of her cute dogs attached to email messages. This kind gesture reminded me of what matters, especially as we were emerging from the COVID-19 pandemic and into a "new normal." Thank you to the entire Bloomsbury team for all your assistance in seeing this book through to publication.

Thank you to the reviewers who provided insights and suggestions for the revisions to the new edition:

Duane Aagaard, Catawba College
Sheila Alicea, St. Edward's University
Chris Bolsmann, CSU Northridge
Deborah Buswell, Austin State University
Umer Hussain, Texas A&M University
Suzanne Parker, Coker University
Demetrius Pearson, University of Houston
Brenda Riemer, Eastern Michigan University
Christine Wegner, University of Florida

I appreciate your feedback and am thankful for the time you invested in this project.

A special thank you to Kelly Eitzen Smith and Florine Eitzen for entrusting me with the task of continuing Stan's work now that he is no longer with us. I am truly honored and profoundly humbled to carry the torch and hope I have kept true to Stan's vision for the book.

Thank you to Michael Messner, for introducing me to Stan, your mentor, and for your continued support, guidance, mentorship, and friendship over the past twenty-five-plus years.

Finally, thank you to all the instructors for assigning this book and to all the students for engaging with the research, arguments, examples, and ideas we present. We hope it is helpful in your understanding of sport as a participant, fan, as well as in your professional career wherever it may take you. This book is for you.

FOREWORD

Michael A. Messner

When a right-handed batter rips a line drive down the left field line, the umpire immediately makes a clear call: if the ball lands to the left of the white line, it's a foul. If the ball hits on or to the right of the line, it's fair. Baseball, "a game of inches," promises fans a sense of clarity: ball or strike; out or safe; win or lose; fair or foul. But life outside of baseball rarely offers such an either-or sense of clarity; instead, there is a ton of gray zone in everyday life. Stan Eitzen, the author of the first six editions of this book, knew that sports too are a gray zone of social life: whether we are athletes or spectators, sports mesh with our lives, our health, our schools, families, communities and politics in complicated and often contradictory ways.

    D. Stanley Eitzen (1934–2017) was a prolific author of many books—on social problems, crime, inequality, poverty, homelessness, and families. Stan was also one of the founding scholars of the sociology of sport, a field that started in the 1970s and blossomed in the subsequent decades. I also was fortunate to know Stan as a generous mentor, and as a warm friend. I cherished our ritual lunch at the annual meetings of the North American Society for the Sociology of Sport (NASSS)—an organization for which he had served as president—where he would patiently listen and offer sound advice to my questions about how to navigate my early career, my first years as a father, and eventually the minefield of administrative work at my university.

    Eventually, I would ask Stan what he was working on. He'd casually note that he was currently revising two or three of his textbooks. And, even in the years after his retirement, he normally had some new book idea that he was excited to share. Somewhere in the mid-1990s at one of our lunches, he was unusually enthused about an idea for a new book that would simultaneously examine the upsides and the downsides of sport. He even had a working title. "It's not either-or," he explained with a gleam in his eyes, "not Fair *or* Foul. It's Fair *and* Foul."

    Stan could feel this "both-and" perspective about sport in his bones. He loved the game of basketball, and he'd continued to play well into his adulthood, including pickup games at the University of Kansas where he'd started his academic career. At one NASSS meeting in the late 1980s, we joined a group of colleagues attending an NBA game. Stan and I marveled at the sweet shooting touch of all-star guard Rolando Blackman, as we also shared some critical observations about how NBA games were becoming increasingly commercialized in ways that reduced the pure pleasure of watching talented athletes like Blackman. Stan lived the reality that one could love sports, and simultaneously examine sports as a critical sociologist. Stan could see with his own eyes, and could document with systematic research, that sport was not all rosy, not for everybody, not all of the time. In fact, sport could simultaneously unite and divide, promote health and injury, could represent the best of democratic principles and be exclusive, hierarchical, and xenophobic. This dual understanding of sport, this both-and perspective, is the brilliant insight at the core of *Fair and Foul*, and the reason that through several editions the book has been so useful for stimulating lively discussion in classrooms.

I cherish a memory of Stan Eitzen, alongside his good friend the late sociologist George Sage—both a bit bent with age, their long and lanky bodies still speaking of their past as basketball players—standing in the book display area of a NASSS conference talking with younger scholars. Eitzen and Sage had been instrumental in gestating the field of sociology of sport and continued to contribute to the field until the end of their lives. But neither of these senior scholars ever gave the impression that they somehow owned the field, nor did they express any desire to dictate its future. Instead, Stan and George remained genuinely interested and delighted to learn what younger scholars were coming up with, and where the field would move next.

It's for this reason that I am certain that Stan Eitzen would be delighted that Cheryl Cooky has accepted Stan's torch and is running with this new edition of *Fair and Foul*. Cooky is a next-generation star scholar of sport. Like Stan, she is a past president of NASSS. And Cooky has produced some of the most important research and public sociology around the hottest issues in sport today, including gender equity in girls' sports and in sports media, feminist social movements and sport, and transgender inclusion in sport. Like Stan, Cheryl deploys a critical lens that illuminates the unhealthy, unfair, and oppressive aspects of sport. And like Stan, Cheryl also appreciates that this "foul" dimension of sport always exists alongside the "fair" elements of sport, which, when deployed with good data and analytic insights from the social sciences, can be mobilized by athletes, coaches, community members and fans to nudge sport into more just, equitable, and healthy directions.

It was Stan Eitzen's hope, and I am certain Cheryl Cooky shares this vision, that students of sport can use this book to broaden and deepen our understandings and conversations about sport. And as we do so, we can expand and celebrate the life-affirming, fair, and democratic impulses in sport, while also building a more peaceful and just world.

1
PARADOXES OF SPORT: AN INTRODUCTION

Can you be sports fan and a critic? It is a question often posed to professors and researchers who teach and study sports as a social phenomenon. The pairing of critical academic inquiry and sports fandom is seemingly contradictory. Academic inquiry identifies significant social, cultural, and economic issues in sports. Yet, sports fandom often requires of participants an unwavering loyalty and allegiance to one's team, coach, or favorite player. That unwavering loyalty can lead us to either ignore, diminish, or dismiss any questions that are critical of sports. Most sociologists who study sports do so through a critical lens. We pose questions whose answers expose what some might refer to as the "dark side" of sports. Yet many sociologists, ourselves included, are avid sports fans, current and/or former athletes, or coaches. Some have worked in the sports industry, as journalists for example. The question of whether one can be both a sports fan and a critic taps into these contradictions.

Some might see incongruity or disingenuousness by sociologists who offer a critical window into the sports world while simultaneously participating in or being a fan of that very institution. Murray Sperber, a retired professor of English who wrote several books on college sports, considered the tensions in being a fan and a critic in some of his writing, suggesting that being such is not oppositional or contradictory. He argued that to reform sports, in other words to ensure sports are equitable, inclusive, and fair for those who participate, critics "will have to understand the power that it has over its fans—a significant percentage of the population—and how deep its roots are in the American psyche."[1] Extending Sperber's perspective, as athletes or as fans, we use our lived experiences and perspectives to help in our scholarly inquiry. Our sport experiences inform how we approach the study of sport in ways that improve our analyses. Lived experience alone cannot substitute for theoretical frameworks, rigorous research, empirical evidence, and statistical data. We suggest, however, that it enhances our understanding of sport. Our experiential knowledge and personal connections to sport allow us to consider the emotional connections and deeply held meanings and investments we have as individuals and as a society. It is our love for the game that motivates our research and teaching. We hope it is through our shared experience as athletes and as fans that we are able to connect with audiences we most want to reach, you, the reader.

Perhaps you are an undergraduate student reading this book as an assigned text for a sports management course or a sociology course. If you are like the students in our courses, most likely you have some connection to sports. You are studying sports either because you are (or were) an athlete, because you are a fan, because you aspire to a career in the sports industry, or perhaps you envision yourself as a university professor writing about and researching sports, or some combination of the above. A few of you may not consider yourself a fan, may have never participated in organized sports, and are reading this book because it was assigned in a class that you registered for because it fit your schedule or fulfilled some curricular requirement. Perhaps you are not reading this book for a class at all; you came across this book because it received stellar reviews on Amazon, and you had to see what the hype was about! For whatever reason you are reading, we hope this text will offer novel insights, expose you to differing ways of viewing sports and pose questions that you had not yet considered.

The subject of this volume is sport in US society. To guide this inquiry, we have organized the book around two themes. The first theme is that sport has positive and negative consequences—that is, sport is both fair and foul. The second theme is that sport is a microcosm of society. Each theme brings into sharper focus the paradox that, on the one hand, as a society, we love sport and are fascinated by its magical qualities, yet sport has troublesome qualities as well. In their book, *Loving Sports When They Don't Love You Back: Dilemmas of the Modern Fan*, sports journalists and authors Jessica Luther and Kavitha A. Davidson describe how this paradox is experienced by many sports fans; perhaps this resonates:

> Sports are a big business and with that comes the dirtiness of any major moneymaking thing that holds cultural significance. You know that college athletes are exploited for their labor, but you also really love the roller coaster of March Madness. You are aware that violent hits to the head on the football field mean the players are sacrificing their bodies and brains—and sometimes they carry that violence off the field into their personal lives. Still, you love the tailgating, and a good, hard tackle is, well, a good, hard tackle. You get that the mascot of your team is a racist caricature of a Native person, but you've loved this team your whole life—long before you became aware of the mascot's problems. You understand why athletes are using their platforms to advocate for change within and beyond sports. But couldn't they just play the game you came here to see and give you a break from the ills of the world for a couple of hours?[2]

Theme I: Sport Is Fair; Sport Is Foul

Sociologist Jay Coakley observes that Americans believe in what he calls the "Great American Sports Myth," which is "the widespread belief that all sports are essentially pure and good, and that their purity and goodness are transferred to those who participate."[3] This is the message given at a typical high school sports banquet honoring the school's athletes. The guest speaker, with examples, humor, and sincerity, extols the many virtues of sports participation. The implications of the "Great American Sports Myth" are, foremost, that sports participation builds character. Second, if there are problems, they are because of a few "bad apples," not the system. And third, acceptance of the system makes critical thinking about sport difficult.[4] The primary goal of the essays in this book, to the contrary, is to examine the world of sport from a critical perspective: to see how the system works sometimes in beneficial ways *and* sometimes not. As Coakley explains,

> Critical research often deals with *why* physical activities and sports are organized, controlled, and played in certain ways; *who* is advantaged and disadvantaged in different sports systems; and *how* the prevailing forms of

sports influence ideas and beliefs that maintain the status quo or inspire structural changes in society. ... Critical research tends to make some people uncomfortable as it exposes negative personal and social outcomes related to sports, inequalities related to gender and race, corruption, and forms of deviance, such as cheating and taking performance-enhancing substances. At the same time, it supports athletes and others who speak out and act on behalf of those who are excluded or disadvantaged in or by sports.[5]

On the "sport is fair" side, there are countless examples of athletes' philanthropy for such public goods as providing college scholarships for poor children, subsidizing public school budgets to keep sports programs alive, and HIV/AIDS research. There are also numerous examples of athletes who have supported their teammates when they were faced with racial and/or gender bias or homophobia. Or on a wider scale, they can put themselves in the national spotlight drawing attention to the hate and prejudice that plague society. Since the mid-2010s, there have been numerous instances of athletes supporting anti-racist protests and social movements in impactful ways. During the 2015 season, the University of Missouri's football team boycotted all football-related activities to join the student-led protests on campus.[6] The protests were the result of numerous instances of racism experienced by students of color on campus and the lack of response to those incidents by university administrators. The student-protests and the football team's boycott took place in the aftermath of the deaths of Trayvon Martin and Michael Brown, who were killed by a self-proclaimed neighborhood watch member and a police officer, respectively. The extrajudicial police shootings of unarmed black individuals throughout the mid- to late 2010s precipitated the #BlackLivesMatter movement. Many leagues and athletes throughout the sports world including the WNBA, NBA superstars Lebron James, Dwayne Wade, and Stephen Curry (to name a few), US Women's National Team soccer player Megan Rapinoe, and most notably NFL San Francisco 49ers quarterback, Colin Kaepernick and his teammate Eric Reed came out in support of the anti-racist movements and to support protests against police brutality. Athlete support for social justice movements also includes support for LGBTQIA+ activism. In 2021, when NFL Raiders defensive end Carl Nassib came out as gay on Instagram, he donated $100,000 to the Trevor Project, an advocacy organization offering mental health services to LGBTQ youth. The NFL followed suit, donating an additional $100,000.[7] Many NFL players, coaches, and owners publicly asserted their support of gay and bisexual team members in the league,[8] signaling a shift in the acceptance of these athletes—who had for decades prior been excluded, marginalized, and ostracized in one of the most masculine (and homophobic) cultural institutions in the United States.

Theme I: Sport Is Fair; Sport Is Foul

Conversely, the "sport is foul" side of the equation can be observed in the sports section of any news outlet or social media site. Chances are you will find one or more examples of athletes accused or found guilty of rape, spousal abuse, illegal substance abuse, and other criminal activities. You'll learn about coaches and institutions of higher education that have either explicitly or implicitly ignored reports of sexual abuse among athletes or minors, reproducing cultures of silence around abuse. You will find athletes, coaches, and occasionally referees who cheat. Similarly, you might find examples of scandals where schools are accused of illegal recruiting, enrolling athletes in "phantom" courses, failing to enforce regulations that promote gender equality, shielding their accused athletes from court actions that would make them ineligible to play, and protecting the school's image rather than seeking justice.[9] Or you will see examples of the governing organization of college sport enforcing rules of amateurism that serve to enrich some individuals and organizations while restricting the money of the workers—the athletes.[10] There are also professional sports leagues that have avoided taking responsibility for failures to protect or compensate their athletes for the long-term effects of head injuries.

But just as we are ready to condemn sports and vow to never watch another football game or *SportsCenter* on ESPN, there are numerous examples of athletes and sports inspiring and uplifting people and communities. Often this happens behind the scenes. Many athletes volunteer their time and donate their income to support their communities. Athletes and coaches utilize their platform to advocate for causes that are close to their hearts. For example, the LGBTQI advocacy organization, Athlete Ally, which advocates for inclusive LGBTQI athletic environments, was started by former college wrestler, Hudson Taylor. In some cases, professional leagues, like the WNBA, invest in social justice causes and organizations and support anti-racist and pro-LGBTQ efforts. The US Women's National Team reinvigorated discussions around gender equity and equal pay in their 2016 discrimination lawsuit against US soccer. In 2022, Megan Rapinoe, who won two World Cup titles and two gold medals, and Simone Biles, who as of the time of this writing has seven Olympic gold medals, thirty world championship titles, and five gymnastics moves officially named after her, were presented the Presidential Medal of Freedom by President Joe Biden. Rapinoe earned the medal for her advocacy for gender pay equality, racial justice and LGBTQIA+ rights. Biles earned the medal for her advocacy for athletes' mental health, children in foster care, and sexual assault victims.[11]

What are we to make of this contradiction of sport and its actors having elements of the good and the bad—of being fair and foul? That is what this book is about.

Theme II: Sport as a Microcosm of Society

Analysts of society are inundated with data. They are faced with the problems of sorting out the important from the less important and with discerning social patterns of behavior and their meanings. They need shortcuts to ease the task. To focus on sport is just such a technique for understanding the complexities of the larger society.

Sport is an institution that provides scientific observers with a convenient laboratory within which to examine values, socialization, stratification, and bureaucracy, to name a few structures and processes that also exist at the societal level. The games people choose to play, the degree of competitiveness, the types of rules, the constraints on the participants, the groups that do and do not benefit under the existing arrangements, the rate and type of change, and the reward system in sport provide us with a microcosm of the society in which sport is embedded.[12]

Common Characteristics of Sport and Society[13]

Suppose an astute sociologist from another country were to visit the United States with the intent of understanding its values, the system of social control, the division of labor, and the system of stratification. Although the answers could be found by careful study and observation of any single institution, such as religion, education, polity, economy, or family, an attention to sport would also provide answers. It would not take long to discern the following qualities in sport.

High Degree of Competitiveness

Competition is ubiquitous in US society. Competition is the essence of sport. The downside is that competition divides participants into winners *and* losers. As Jon Wertheim observes, "If there weren't losers, it wouldn't be competition."[14] Americans demand winners. In sports (for children and adults), winning is the ultimate goal, not pleasure in the activity. The adulation given to winners is incredible, while losers are maligned. Example: Popular locker room slogans exemplify this divergence: "Show Me a Good Loser and I'll Show You a Loser" and "Lose Is a Four-Letter Word." Consider, for example, the difference in how the winner and the loser of the Super Bowl or the World Series are evaluated. Clearly, to be second best is not good enough. "Nobody remembers who came in second" is the conventional wisdom. The goal of victory is so important for many that it is laudable even if attained by questionable methods. "Whatever you can get away with" is another conventional maxim.

Emphasis on Materialism

Examples of the value that Americans place on materialism are blatant in sport: for example, players signing multiyear, multimillion-dollar contracts, with the highest contracts in (men's) professional sports ranging between $300 and $700 million dollars; universities leaving conferences for others where the economic rewards are greater (as seen most recently with several major moves, including UCLA and USC to the B1G Ten conference); professional teams being moved to more economically lucrative cities (the move of the Oakland Raiders to Las Vegas, for example); and lavish stadiums being built mostly at public expense.[15]

Pervasiveness of Racism

Although conditions have improved in meaningful ways since the civil rights movement and other social upheavals of the 1960s, recent social movements of the 2020s including Black Lives Matter generated national conversations about the continued systemic racism and its impacts on BIPOC (Black, Indigenous, People of Color) communities. Racism and racial bias continue to shape who coaches, who plays what positions, and the futures of racialized minorities after their sports career. Just as in the larger society, racialized minorities in sport are rarely found in positions of authority. In the NFL, for example, although 53.5 percent of NFL players are Black, only 18.8 percent of coaches, and 3.1 percent of team owners are Black. This is despite the league's efforts to increase diversity through the "Rooney Rule," which requires teams to interview at least one person of color when hiring for a head coaching position.[16]

Male Dominance as the Norm

Men control sport. Almost every major professional, amateur, and educational sport organization in the United States is under the management and control of men. The proportion of women in leadership and decision-making positions—those with power and influence—in sport is quite small; far smaller, certainly, than would be expected based on the number of women in sports. Significant shifts in the balance of gender dominance in major professional and collegiate sports are difficult to find. And although we are seeing more "firsts" of women in various coaching, staff, and administrative positions in sport, when women do enter sports as either athletes, coaches, administrators, medical staff, or journalists/reporters they often encounter discriminatory treatment, limited opportunities for advancement, unequal pay, a "glass ceiling," "revolving door," and in some instances workplace sexual harassment or assault.

Sport perpetuates male dominance by defining sport as a male activity; by men occupying positions of power and decision-making positions in sports, even women's sport; by giving most media attention and the most resources through community and school budgets, facilities, and the like to men's sports; and by trivializing women's sports and women athletes.[17]

Domination of Individuals by Bureaucracies

Conservative bureaucratic organizations, through their desire to perpetuate themselves, curtail innovations and deflect activities away from the wishes of individuals and from the original intent of these organizations. Many sport organizations—the NCAA, intercollegiate athletic conferences, professional sport leagues—pride themselves on having adopted bureaucratic business practices.

Unequal Distribution of Power in Organizations

The structure of sport in the United States is such that power is in the hands of the wealthy (e.g., boards of regents, corporate boards of directors, each professional league, corporate media entities, wealthy entrepreneurs, the United States Olympic Committees, and the National Collegiate Athletic Association). Evidence of the power of these individuals and organizations is seen in the exemptions allowed to them by state governments and the federal government in dealing with athletes and owners, in tax breaks, and in the concessions that communities make to entice professional sports franchises to relocate or to remain, and, incidentally, to benefit the wealthy of that community.

Caveat: Sport Can Also Be an Agent of Change

While sport is a microcosm of society, it's not just a passive reflection. Sports are social constructions, that is, as part of the social world they are created by people in interaction, and they can be changed by people. Conflict, in the forms of lawsuits, strikes, and demonstrations, historically and presently has been used by the less powerful in the sports world to change sport. As sportswriter and author Dave Zirin explains: "Sports has often acted as a reflection of the national life. At different times it has also been a fetter holding back the tide of change. In other instances, it has been a Taser, sending an electric jolt into the body politics."[18]

Variation on the "Sport as a Microcosm of Society" Theme: The Super Bowl

Football is the most telegenic of all team sports, and the Super Bowl is the quintessential US sports event, being the most watched single network broadcast (sport and non-sport) in the United States. In 2023, with over 115 million viewers, it became the most watched television program in US history.[19]

Super Bowl Sunday is unique—a shared, nationwide social event organized around a single stage at a single time. It is colloquially referred to as an unofficial national holiday; one of the biggest days for online betting and gambling, and the second-biggest day in the year for food consumption (trailing only Thanksgiving). The Super Bowl provides a "monoculture" in an era where digital streaming and social media algorithms have created personalized and customized content that has nearly eliminated the opportunity for us to connect with one another over a shared experience. The Super Bowl is one of the remaining entertainment-based cultural events wherein a vast majority of Americans participate simultaneously and in real time.

The Super Bowl brims with the potential for great drama, heroics, disastrous errors, and excellence in performance, all of which are heightened by an uncertain outcome. For these and many other reasons, the game embodies all sport—and shows why the excitement of sport is so infectious to so many.

But there is another side to the Super Bowl, a side that diminishes sport. A sports contest, a physical competition between opponents, is decided by differences in abilities, strategy, and chance. The effort to win under these conditions is the essence of sport, whether a playground basketball game, a church league slow-pitch softball game, a college rivalry, or the Super Bowl. But as the level of sport becomes more sophisticated, sport shifts from play to work and from pleasurable participation to pageantry—pageantry wedded to militarism (e.g., flyovers, a giant flag, precision parachutists landing on the fifty-yard line, military honor guards, and military personnel honored).[20]

Sport has become a spectacle ruled by money, and the Super Bowl is the exemplar, where we celebrate a league valued at $163 billion (more than the NBA and MLB combined)[21] and owned by the wealthy elite. Television networks pay billions for the broadcasting rights to the Super Bowl. In 2023, the total amount of the NFL's television/streaming deals was $125.5 billion.[22] The networks in turn sold advertising time to corporations, who paid $7 million for a thirty-second spot.[23] Social media such as X (formerly known as Twitter), YouTube, and Meta (formerly the Facebook company) share profits on Super Bowl advertising with the NFL. The NFL has an estimated $1 billion marketing contract with Nike, with Nike supplying the NFL with uniforms, shoes, and other gear for its thirty-two teams.[24] The NFL's revenue for the 2022 season was $11.9 billion, shared equally among the teams, with each of the thirty-two teams earning $372 million from "national media rights, league sponsorships, merchandising and licensing."[25] The NFL commissioner made $63.9 million a year in the 2020– 2021 season.[26] Despite the billions generated in revenue, since 2000, "public funds diverted to helping build professional sports stadiums and arenas have cost taxpayers $4.3 billion."[27] While the leagues and local politicians will assert the benefit to the communities, economists and urban planners' research illustrates the benefits are often short-lived, and recommend public monies instead be diverted to more pressing community needs like education, housing, and health care, which would provide long-term benefits to a broader collective. Moreover, the NFL as a league gets a tax break because it has been deemed a *nonprofit organization*.[28]

The expenses involved in attending the Super Bowl mean that most attendees are affluent. The face value of a ticket to the 2024 Super Bowl ranged from $950 for nosebleed seats to $9,500 for seats behind the bench on the fifty-yard line.[29] Most fans however will not have the ability to purchase a ticket at face value. According to an analysis by Yahoo Finance, this is because the tickets are distributed within the league and its season ticket holders. The two teams in the Super Bowl share 35 percent of the tickets available, and those are distributed to either players or season ticket holders. The team of the stadium where the Super Bowl is played receives 5 percent, and the other twenty-nine teams share about 35 percent of the tickets. The league itself also keeps most of the remaining tickets to distribute to partners, sponsors, and the media. This means that most fans will have to purchase tickets on the secondary market. For the 2023 Super Bowl (LVII), the average ticket available for fans cost $8,837. For one ticket! According to the 2022 census, the median household income was $74,580.[30] The cost for a family of four to attend the Super Bowl is over $35,000, well beyond what would be an affordable budget for entertainment. After the cost of tickets, the cost of parking, souvenirs, and food/drink is outrageous. Airfares, lodging, and food costs escalate dramatically during Super Bowl week. In other words, the Super Bowl is not for the average fan. It is for the rich and famous who engage in conspicuous consumption such as renting a mansion for $250,000 a week.[31]

Violence is glorified in the Super Bowl. During the course of the game, there are cheap hits aimed at intimidating and perhaps injuring an opponent. Injuries are commonplace. Moreover, there are instances of rule breaking, such as placing silicone on jerseys to make the player harder to grab and the alleged deflating of game balls in the Conference Championship game leading to the Super Bowl in 2015 (i.e., "Deflategate") to give the New England Patriots and their quarterback, Tom Brady, an advantage in gripping and throwing the ball.

Racism is evident at the Super Bowl. About 54 percent of the players in the NFL are Black, yet there is a dearth of Black coaches, coordinators, owners, general managers, trainers, publicists, and media personnel. Likewise, the Super Bowl represents the sexist side of sport as it glorifies team and media personnel, all but a small fraction of whom are male. Historically, women have only provided supporting roles. Their bodies are used to heterosexualize the festival as cheerleaders, dancers, halftime performers, and promotional sex objects.[32] Those who provide sideline or half-time entertainment do not receive compensation for their talent/labor and in some cases encounter sexual harassment and assault in their work promoting the teams and the league.[33]

Winning the Super Bowl is vitally important. We Americans emphasize the outcome of games rather than the process. We glorify winners and vilify losers. As John Madden, Hall of Fame coach and broadcaster, has said, "The biggest gap in sports is between the winner of the Super Bowl and the loser in the Super Bowl."[34]

The Super Bowl symbolizes the fundamental sports paradox: it is both compelling and materialistic, unifying and divisive, inclusive and exclusionary, expansive and exploitive. These agony-and-ecstasy elements of sport are the subjects of this book. And these dualities remind us that sport reveals so much about ourselves and our society.

Variation on the "Sport as a Microcosm of Society" Theme: What Football and Baseball Tell Us About Our Society[35]

An important indicator of the essence of a society is the type of sport it glorifies. Football and baseball are the two preeminent sports in American society. Examining these sports, we find there are a few similarities, most notably that both are played mostly by boys and men. Women are involved in supportive roles.[36] Although there are other similarities between the two (e.g., rule breaking and rule bending are common in both), the two sports are basically opposites, and these differences provide insightful clues about Americans and American society.

Baseball was once America's most popular sport. Now football is the people's favorite, with more Americans watching football on Sundays than attending church. The NFL is the richest sports venture, with about $20 billion in total annual revenue in 2022. An estimated 50.4 million Americans bet on Super Bowl LVII, with $16 billion wagered.[37] When baseball was the national pastime, the United States was a pastoral, agrarian nation.[38] Farmers and small-town craftsmen, merchants, and laborers worked alone or with their families to achieve success. But then America became an industrial nation, with people moving to the cities to work in factories and to large bureaucracies associated with a large industrial society. These bureaucracies require "elaborately choreographed cooperation among large groups: success for the team is success for everyone."[39] In effect, part of football's appeal is that its structure is similar to the structure of the contemporary workplace.

These two sports have fundamentally different orientations toward time. Baseball is relatively unbounded by time while football must adhere to a rigid time schedule. "Baseball is oblivious to time. There is no clock, no two-minute drill. The game flows in a timeless stream with a rhythm of its own."[40] (In September 2022, however, MLB announced several rule changes, including a "pitch clock," which has reduced the average time of a baseball game from just over three hours to approximately just over two and a half hours. This illustrates how MLB is shifting the structure of the game to better accommodate contemporary US society.) In this way, baseball reflects life in rural America as it existed in the not-too-distant past compared to football's emulation of contemporary urban society, where persons have rigid schedules, deadlines, appointments, and time clocks to punch.

The innings of baseball have no time limit, and if the game is tied at the end of the nine innings, the teams play as many extra innings as it takes to determine a winner. Football, on the other hand, is played for sixty minutes, and if tied at the end, the game goes into sudden death. The nomenclature of the two sports—"extra innings" compared to "sudden death"—illustrates a basic difference between them. There are other semantic differences. A baseball player makes an "error," but a football team is "penalized."[41] The object of baseball is to be "safe at home" while the goal of football is to penetrate deep into the opponent's "territory, crossing the enemy's goal line." In baseball, there is no home territory to defend; the playing field is shared by both teams. In football, there is "clipping," "hitting," "spearing," "piling on," and "personal fouls." Baseball, in sharp contrast, has the "sacrifice," and players commit "errors." There is no analogue in baseball for the militaristic terms of football, for example, "blitz," "bomb," "trap," "trenches," "field general," "aerial attack," and "ground attack." Such linguistic differences imply a basic difference between baseball and football. Baseball, as seen in its benign verbs (home run hitters *trot* around the bases; pitchers "toe" the rubber),[42] is essentially a calm and leisurely activity while football is intense, aggressive, and violent. A baseball player cannot get to first base because of strength, aggression, or ability to intimidate. The only way to get there is through skill or an opponent's lack thereof. In football, however, survival (success) belongs to the most aggressive. Clearly, the source of football's appeal is violence.[43]

Baseball is a game of repetition and predictable action played over a 162-game schedule. The players must stay relaxed and not get too excited. They

Variation on the Sport as a Microcosm of Society Theme

must pace themselves and not let a loss or even a succession of losses get them down. In football, though, losing is intolerable because of the short season (seventeen games). Thus, football players must play each game with intensity. The intensity that characterizes football resembles the tensions and pressures of modern society, contrasted with the more relaxed pace of agrarian life and baseball.

The two sports differ in their orientation to change. Baseball today is much like it was decades ago. Managerial actions are relatively predictable for the various situations that arise because there is a time-honored way of doing things. Football, on the other hand, is constantly changing as coaches devise new offenses and defensive coaches design new ways to counteract these changes as well as creating new defenses to confound offenses. Football is also more reliant on technology than baseball. Baseball does use the speed gun, videotaping, computers, analytics, and other forms of technology but not nearly as much as football where computers are used to evaluate player performance on each play, to discover opponent's tendencies in play calling by situation, and the like.

An interesting contrast between these two sports is the equality of opportunity each offers. Baseball promotes equality while football is essentially unequal. This difference occurs in several ways. First, the usual route to become a professional football player is to first play in college. Some baseball players do also, but they have the option of working up through the minor leagues. A second way that baseball is more egalitarian than football is that it can be played by players of all sizes. Football, however, is for big people (with a few exceptions). Baseball is also more equal than football because everyone has the opportunity to be a star. Except for designated hitters, all players play offense and defense, giving each the chance to make an outstanding defensive play or to bat in the winning run. In football, stardom is essentially reserved for those who play at the positions that score points. Others labor in relative obscurity. This is similar to American society, where the elite few score the points, call the plays, and get the glory at the expense of the commoners.

Another dimension on which the two sports differ is individualism. Baseball is highly individualistic. It is "a team sport, but it is basically an accumulation of individual activities. Throwing a strike, hitting a line drive or fielding a grounder is primarily an individual achievement."[44] Elaborate teamwork is not required except for double plays, defending sacrifice bunts, and being in position for cut-off throws. Each player struggles to succeed on his own.

As Gerald Cavanaugh has written:

> Baseball is each [player] doing the best . . . within a loose confederation of fellow individualists. . . . This reflects a society

in which individual effort, drive, and success are esteemed and in which, conversely, failure is deemed the individual's responsibility.[45]

Football, in sharp contrast, is the quintessence of team sports. Every move is planned and practiced in advance. The players in each of the eleven positions have a specific task to perform on every play. Every player is a specialist whose actions are coordinated with the other specialists on the team. Each player's personality must be subordinate to the team's goals as set by a demanding coach. The parallel between the organization of a football team and a factory or a corporation or other bureaucracies is obvious.[46] In each, the intricate and precise actions of all members doing different tasks are required for the attainment of the organization's objective.

In summary, baseball represents what we were. It continues to be popular because of our longing for a relaxed, simpler time. Football, on the other hand, is popular now because it symbolizes what we now are—an urban-technological-corporate-bureaucratic society. Thus, the two sports represent cultural contrasts: rural vs. urban, stability vs. change, harmony vs. conflict, calm vs. intensity, and equality vs. inequality. Each sport contains a fundamental myth that it elaborates for its fans. Baseball represents an island of stability in a confused and confusing world. As such, it provides an antidote for a world of too much action, struggle, pressure, and change. Baseball provides this antidote by being individualistic, relatively unbounded by time, nonviolent, leisurely in pace, and by perpetuating the American myths of equal opportunity, egalitarianism, and potential success for everyone.

Football represents what we are. Our society is violent. It is highly technological. Change is rapid. It is highly bureaucratized, and we are all caught in its impersonal clutches. Football fits contemporary urban-corporate society because it is team oriented, highly technological, highly militarized, and dominated by the clock and because it rewards aggressive behavior, celebrates dominance, and perpetuates inequality.

Overview

We begin with a central paradox: Sport, a seemingly trivial pursuit, is culturally (and economically) important. Sport is a fantasy—a diversion from the realities of work, relationships, and survival. Sport entertains. Why then do we take it so seriously? First and foremost, sport mirrors the human experience, as noted by the *Nation* in its introduction to a special issue on sport:

Sport elaborates in its rituals what it means to be human: the play, the risk, the trials, the collective impulse to games, the thrill of physicality, the necessity of strategy; defeat, victory, defeat again, pain, transcendence and, most of all, the certainty that nothing is certain—that everything can change and be changed.[47]

Second, sport mirrors society in other profound ways. It shares with the larger society the basic elements and expressions of bureaucratization, commercialization, racism, sexism, homophobia, greed, exploitation of the powerless by the powerful, alienation, and ethnocentrism. American sport embodies American values—striving for excellence, winning, individual and team competition, and materialism. Parents want their children to participate in sport because participation presumably teaches them the basic values of American society and builds character.

Third, sport is compelling because it combines spectacle (a universal human social tendency to combine sport and pageantry) with drama (an outcome that is not perfectly predictable), performance excellence, and clarity (exactly who won, by how much, and in what manner). We also know who lost and why.

Fourth, there is something transcendent about sport. Fans celebrate. Fans high-five strangers. Fans emote with cheers, jeers, screams, and tears. As Scott Simon of National Public Radio puts it: "You can tell yourself: it's just sports, nothing real; it has nothing to do with your life, no resonance in the real world of living, dying, and struggling. And you'd be right. Then, something [magical] happens. . . . And inside, where your body cannot kid you, something takes over and it feels real."[48]

Finally, there is the human desire to identify with and connect to something greater than oneself. For athletes, this is being part of a team, working and sacrificing together to achieve a common goal. For fans, identifying with a team or a sports hero bonds them with others who share their allegiance; they belong, and they have an identity. Esteemed analyst of sports, Frank Deford puts it this way: "In today's world, where we are so fragmented, an arena is one place left where we come together to share. . . . That's why the creeps at games who shout loud obscenities are not merely being offensive. They're breaking a compact, which is that all us sports fans must sacrifice a little of our individuality to, for one rare modern moment, commune."[49]

Sport is a pervasive aspect of US society. According to the CDC, in 2020 54.1 percent of children between ages six and seventeen participated in sports. Most children are involved in organized sport at some time in their lives. Sport is the subject of much conversation, media content, leisure activity, and discretionary spending. There is a growing number of broadcast networks, online news sites, social media accounts, and streaming platforms devoted to covering sports. Most professional athletes and many college athletes have social media accounts and create sports-related content. For example, Lebron James (NBA) has over 235 million followers across several social media sites.

We sports fans consume sports media content with a keen interest in the latest scores, win-loss records, favorite athletes, and possible new college recruits or trades that improve our beloved professional teams. We know a great deal about sport. We know point spreads, current statistics, playoff probabilities, biographical information about athletes and coaches, and more. As children, many of us learned sports information, memorizing incredible amounts of trivia. Moreover, most of us play sports, whether as individuals or on organized teams, throughout much of our lives.

But do we truly understand sport? Can we separate the hype from the reality and the myth from the facts? Do we question the way sport is organized? Unfortunately, many fans and participants alike have a superficial, uncritical attitude that takes much for granted.[50] The purpose of this book is to examine sport critically and to ask probing questions.

As sociologists, we examine all social arrangements critically. A sociologist asks questions such as: How do we know what we know about sport? Is our knowledge based on personal experience or opinion, news media coverage, social media content? Is it based on academic research, statistical evidence? How does sport really work? Who has power and who does not? Who benefits under the existing social arrangements and who does not? These questions scrutinize existing myths, stereotypes, media representations, and official dogma. The answers to these questions enable us to demystify sport and truly understand it. We examine sport and the beliefs surrounding it, holding them to the light of current research findings and critical thinking to demythologize them. We focus on showing how sport really works, and in the process, we identify a duality in it, which exists in all human institutions. In other words, sport has positive and negative outcomes for individuals and society, as we have already discussed. Our approach will probably raise questions, doubts, resistance, and even anger among some readers, which in important ways demonstrates the power of myth. In the process, though, we hope readers will see sport from a new angle, one that brings new interpretations and insights to their experiences in and with sport.

Paradoxes of Sport

The subtitle of this book refers to the paradoxes of sport. *The Random House Dictionary of the English Language* supplies the following definition of paradox:

(1) "any person, thing, or situation exhibiting an apparently contradictory nature"; and (2) "any opinion or statement contrary to commonly accepted opinion."[51]

This book is titled *Fair and Foul*[52] because sport in the United States is beset by a number of contradictions (definition 1 above), and the common understanding of sport is often guided by myth. Our goal is to demythologize sport by calling into question the prevailing beliefs about this phenomenon (definition 2 above). These two dimensions of the term "paradox" constitute the organizing principle—the essence—of this book.

Sport is inherently contradictory. On the one hand, sport provides excitement, joy, and self-fulfillment for the participants. As former Olympic athlete Kenny Moore puts it: "To celebrate sport is . . . to celebrate sheer abandon, to savor moments when athletes surrender themselves to effort and are genuinely transformed. This is when sport takes loneliness, fear, hate and ego and transmutes them into achievement, records, art, and powerful example."[53]

But there is also a dark side, as Moore concedes: "[Sport also presents us with] cocaine deaths, steroid cover-ups, collegiate hypocrisies, gambling scandals, criminal agents, and Olympic boycotts. Such failings show that sport's civilizing, freeing effect on us is incomplete. Not everyone is following the rules. Not everyone is trying."[54]

Put another way, sport provides examples of courage, superhuman effort, extraordinary teamwork, selflessness, and sacrifice. Yet the images conveyed through sport—violence, greed, exploitation, selfishness, cheating, and contempt for authority—are not always uplifting.[55]

Sport is clearly appealing. We are fascinated by the competition and the striving for excellence. Sport is compelling because it transcends our everyday routine experiences with excitement, heroics, and unpredictability. But much about sport is also appalling. Paradoxically, fans often find the appalling appealing—the violence, the incredible amounts of money, the cheating, and the outrageous behaviors by some athletes, coaches, and owners.

Organization of the Book

Part I: Sport Is Fair, Sport Is Foul

Each chapter in this book takes up a particular paradox of sport. Chapter 2 focuses on the paradox of sport as both unifying and divisive. Chapter 2 shows how sport can unite during times of national trauma and suffering, such as during the COVID-19 pandemic or immediately following 9/11, unite warring factions, and bring different social classes and racial groups together. However, it can also reinforce the barriers that divide people along race, social class, and gender.

This paradox is certainly illustrated in athletes who have embraced the Black Lives Matter movement and the resistance to integrating social movements into sports contexts by fans, owners, the leagues, and even the former president of the United States.

In chapter 3, we continue the discussion of the influence of social movements and politics in sports by examining another paradox as it relates to gender, sport both includes and excludes. This chapter focuses on sport's role in the maintenance of male dominance, of the sex/gender binary, and in particular how the sex-segregated nature of most sports includes certain girls and women while excluding others. It focuses on Title IX and its impact on gender equality and equitable distributions of resources. We also discuss sex testing policies in sports, trans-inclusion policies in sports, and the status of nonbinary athletes (how the very structural organization of sports excludes those who do not conform to the sex/gender binary).

Chapter 4 considers the paradox of "sport is healthy, sport is harmful." Sport encourages good physical health. Obviously, the physical exercise that sports participation requires is beneficial because it promotes endurance, coordination, weight control, muscle strength, strong bones, joint flexibility, and increased aerobic (lung and heart) capacity. The benefits of sport participation are particularly strong for girls who experience positive physical and psychological health outcomes. At the same time, however, participants get hurt during sporting activities. Sport can damage the health of athletes through overtraining, rapid weight loss to meet weight requirements, excessive weight gain for competitive advantage, and the use of drugs that promote muscle mass, strength, and endurance. Demanding coaches may expect too much from their athletes. Parents may drive their child athletes too hard, too fast. Elite young athletes are especially vulnerable to excessive training and even sexual abuse from adult authorities. Athletes who are subject to eligibility policies for women's competitions may be required to take medically unnecessary hormones or engage in medically unnecessary surgeries, both of which have been shown to have negative health outcomes. The NFL's history of denying the existence of a link between playing football and chronic traumatic encephalopathy (CTE), one which the NFL admitted in the 1990s and subsequently buried, has cost the lives of not only professional football players, but also for college and high school athletes. In addition to physical harms, more and more athletes, from elite-level athletes to athletes in youth sports are publicly speaking about the toll that sports have on their mental health and well-being.

Chapter 5 discusses the organization of youth sports, the issues and consequences. It examines two forms of children's play—peer centered and adult centered. Since the latter dominates the sports experience of children today, we focus on the dark side of this phenomenon. This chapter considers whether and in what ways sports can positively develop youth.

Part II: Sports as a Microcosm of Society

Chapter 6 demythologizes the prevailing notion that sport is played on a level playing field, where talent, strategy, and luck determine winners and losers. This is not the case when it comes to the participation of minoritized athletes in some sports (e.g., automobile racing, bowling, golf, and tennis). Similarly, gender, sexuality, and social class issues illustrate how athletes encounter (or do not) barriers to their sports participation. Social advantages (or disadvantages) are not distributed evenly across athletes. Intersectional identities and social locations shape ways athletes' participation is facilitated or constrained.

In chapter 7 we examine the role of the media in what we see and how we interpret what we see. Most significant, legacy media historically have acted as the "conductor" of sports—influencing the scheduling of games, changing rules, and infusing great amounts of money into sports, with consequences for sustaining big-time college sport, college league realignment, increased coaching salaries, and other manifestations of an arms race. Legacy sports media have focused primarily on men's sports, and the "big three" in men's professional and collegiate sports: football, basketball, and baseball. This focus has eclipsed the coverage of women's sports and sports outside of the big three. Emergent media, such as online, social, and streaming platforms as well as niche media have offered viewers and fans expanded opportunities to consume and follow athletes and sports beyond legacy media. The stories sports journalists and commentators tell about sports have shifted. The proliferation of media sites, platforms, and "feeds" has created a diversity of voices and perspectives, some of which provide critical insights into the sports world. The emergence of social media sites such as Facebook, X (formerly Twitter), Instagram, TikTok, and others allows athletes, journalists, fans, conferences, organizations, and leagues to produce their own content unfiltered by legacy media outlets.

Chapter 8 investigates the contradictions of big-time college athletics. Sport is an integral part of higher education in the United States. Big-time college sport supplies full-ride scholarships to athletes and generates millions of dollars for their institutions, their communities, the NCAA, and corporate America. Big-time college sport unites its supporters, provides free publicity for the schools, and gives good athletes from economically disadvantaged backgrounds the chance for a college education. And it serves for the development of future Olympic and professional athletes. Does it, however, fit with the educational mission of these universities? A strong case can be made that sport is detrimental to academics (as chapter 8 explores). For example, most of these schools actually lose money, since scholarship money and other economic resources are channeled away from academics and toward athletics. And athletes admitted to these schools tend to perform below the student body average on test scores and graduation rates; they are often athletes first and students second. In addition, occasional scandals hurt the image of the schools involved; the programs and resources are disproportionately geared toward the male athletes in the revenue-producing sports; gender equity has yet to be achieved despite Title IX's passage over fifty years ago; and despite the recent Supreme Court ruling allowing athletes to be compensated from their "Name, Image, and Likeness" (NIL), athletes continue to be exploited under the guise of amateurism. The overarching contradiction is that big-time school sport is organized as a commercial entertainment activity within an educational environment. This arrangement may have certain positive consequences, but it compromises educational goals.

Chapter 9 examines the link between private ownership of professional teams and public subsidies for them. Large cities either have professional sports franchises or actively seek them. In either case, the cities subsidize or offer to subsidize the teams and their wealthy owners, typically by providing arenas or stadiums, refurbishing these venues as needed, charging little or no rent, providing access roads, and giving generous percentages on concessions and parking. The rationale for such largesse is that professional teams benefit their host cities economically.

This raises some interesting questions: Who benefits financially from professional teams and who does not? Do women and men and the members of all social classes share in the benefits? Should wealthy owners and affluent athletes be subsidized by taxpayers, many of whom are not interested in sport? Do men and women in the community gain more or less equally from the arrangements? Does a city actually benefit economically from having professional teams? Is the profit margin so low for professional teams that they can only survive if subsidized by taxpayers? Is there a better alternative to professional teams being owned by affluent individuals or large corporations who threaten to move the team to a city that offers more generous subsidies?

These paradoxes are considered in this book. Although each chapter focuses on a central issue, the book also explores related contradictions and myths. Issues of class, race, ethnicity, and gender are also considered in each chapter.

Do these contradictions and questions pique your interest about how sport really works? Or does their critical orientation make you defensive about sports? Both are likely reactions, indicating once again the contradictory nature of sport. Our point is that anyone who truly wants to understand sport in American society must accept its inherent paradoxes.

Too often we focus on "sport is fair," letting myths guide our perceptions and analyses. As a counterpoint to the myths and misperceptions, we emphasize "sport is foul," to demythologize and demystify it. At the same time, we keep in mind the elements of sport that are so captivating and compelling. Overcoming this basic contradiction—being critical of sport while retaining a love for it, while being a fan—will enable us to examine the paradoxes of sport with the goal of seeking alternatives to improve this vital, interesting, and exciting aspect of social life.

Finally, sports organizations can be changed, but this requires a plan, a strategy, and an organized effort (the topic of chapter 10). Sociologist Jay Coakley puts it this way:

> The growing importance of sports in society makes it more necessary for us to take a closer and more critical look at how sports are defined, organized, and played. As we do this, some of us will call for changes in dominant forms of sports or reject those forms and call for new and alternative sports. However, we should not expect widespread, revolutionary changes to occur overnight. Social transformation is always a challenging and tedious process. It requires long-term efforts and carefully planned strategies, but it does not occur without a clear vision of possible futures and strategic efforts to turn visions into realities.[56]

In chapter 10, we consider how sports can be a site for change in society. We include a discussion of the recent iterations of athlete activism, particularly around racial justice, equal pay, trans inclusion, and other issues. Understanding sport must precede any effort to change it for the better. That is the goal of this book.

Notes

1. Murray Sperber, "On Being a Fan," *Chronicle of Higher Education*, October 5, 2007, 5.
2. Jessica Luther and Kavitha A. Davidson, *Loving Sports When They Don't Love You Back: Dilemmas of the Modern Sports Fan* (Austin: University of Texas Press, 2020).
3. Jay Coakley, *Sports in Society: Issues and Controversies*, 11th ed. (New York: McGraw-Hill, 2015), xii; J. Coakley, "Assessing the Sociology of Sport: On Cultural Sensibilities and the Great Sport Myth," *International Review for the Sociology of Sport* 50 (June–August 2015): 4–5.
4. In the early 2010s, Stan was approached by an administrator from a nearby high school asking if he would speak at the school's end-of-the-year banquet honoring their athletes. He agreed to do so but said that he would include both the positives *and* negatives of high school sports and what a school and community might do to ameliorate the problem areas. The school principal withdrew his offer, saying that they really only wanted to hear the positive side of sports.
5. J. Coakley, "Sociology of Sport: Growth, Diversification, and Marginalization, 1981–2021," *Kinesiology Review* 10 (2021): 292–300.
6. Rohan Nadkarni and Alex Nieves, "Why Missouri's Football Team Joined a Protest Against School Administration," *Sports Illustrated*, November 9, 2015.

7   "NFL Renews Support of The Trevor Project, Donates $100,000," *NFL News*, https://www.nfl.com/news/nfl-renews-support-of-the-trevor-project-donates-100-000.

8   Cyd Zeigler and Jim Buzinski, "These 61 Current NFL Players, 13 Owners, and 9 Head Coaches Support Gay and Bi Athletes," *Outsports*, October 22, 2022, https://www.outsports.com/2022/10/27/23425352/nfl-gay-bi-players-straight-support-lgbt-rk-russell.

9   See, for example, Ben Cohen, "The College Football Grid of Shame," *Wall Street Journal*, August 27, 2014, http://online.wsj.com/articles/the-college-football-grid-of-shame.

10 The current state of college athletics is in flux given the recent 2021 Supreme Court decision in the anti-trust case, *NCAA v. Alston*. In the 9–0 decision, Justice Kavanaugh said, "It is highly questionable whether the NCAA and its member colleges can justify not paying student athletes a fair share of revenues." Dennis Dodd, "NCAA Amateurism Is Effectively Dead, and the Association Itself May Not Be Far Behind," *CBS Sports*, June 21, 2021, https://www.cbssports.com/college-football/news/ncaa-amateurism-is-effectively-dead-and-the-association-itself-may-not-be-far-behind/.

11 ESPN News Services. "Simone Biles, Megan Rapinoe among Recipients of Presidential Medal of Freedom," July 1, 2022, ESPN, https://www.espn.com/olympics/story/_/id/34179511/simone-biles-megan-rapinoe-recipients-presidential-medal-freedom.

12 Consider Finland, for example, an isolated country with a relatively rural population. The solitude of this country is revealed when we find that it is not particularly good at team sports but excels in individual sports with world-class javelin throwers, hockey goalies, Formula One drivers, and cross-country skiers. See Chris Koentges, "The Puck Stops Here," *Atlantic*, March 2014, 51–63.

13 This section draws on characteristics identified in chapter 1 of George H. Sage and D. Stanley Eitzen, *Sociology of North American Sport*, 10th ed. (New York: Oxford University Press, 2015).

14 L. Jon Wertheim, "Losing Power," *Sports Illustrated*, June 30, 2014, 15.

15 Darren Geeter, "Taxpayers Are Paying Billions for the Renovations and Construction of NFL Stadiums: Here's How," *Chicago Tribune*, December 22, 2022, https://www.cnbc.com/2022/12/22/taxpayers-are-paying-billions-for-nfl-stadiums-heres-how.html.

16 Adrien Bouchet, Bryson Turner, Jacquelyn Rollins, Roberta Pascotto Martire, and David Zimmerman, *The 2023 Racial and Gender Report Card: National Football League*, The Institute for Diversity and Ethics in Sport (Orlando: University of Central Florida, 2023).

17 Lois Bryson, "Sport and the Maintenance of Masculine Hegemony," *Women's Studies International Forum* 19 (1987): 349–60.

18 Dave Zirin, *A People's History: Sports in the United States* (New York: The New Press, 2008), 268.

19 Bill Shea and Richard Dreitsch, "Super Bowl LVII Sets Viewership Record: Examining Updated Numbers and Why They Matter," *The Athletic*, May 2, 2023, https://theathletic.com/4478840/2023/05/02/super-bowl-57-tv-ratings-record/.

Notes

20. Dave Zirin, "The NFL: Where Dr. King's Dream Goes To Die," *The Nation*, January 21, 2013. https://www.thenation.com/article/archive/nfl-where-dr-kings-dream-goes-die/.

21. Mike Ozanian, "The NFL's Most Valuable Teams," *Forbes*, August 30, 2023, https://www.forbes.com/sites/mikeozanian/2023/08/30/the-nfls-most-valuable-teams-2023-dallas-cowboys-remain-on-top-at-a-record-9-billion/?sh=511999db362c.

22. Ozanian, "The NFL's Most Valuable Teams."

23. Greg Lee, "The Rise in the Cost of a Superbowl Commercial," *Front Office Sports*, February 17, 2023, https://frontofficesports.com/the-rise-in-the-cost-of-a-super-bowl-commercial/.

24. Ahiza Garcia, "NFL and Nike Sign 8-Year Contract for Uniforms," *CNN Business*, March 27, 2018, https://money.cnn.com/2018/03/27/news/companies/nike-nfl-gear-contract/index.html.

25. Mike Ozanian, "NFL National Revenue Was Almost $12 Billion in 2022," *Forbes*, July 11, 2023, https://www.forbes.com/sites/mikeozanian/2023/07/11/nfl-national-revenue-was-almost-12-billion-in-2022/?sh=7c6cf412d74b.

26. ESPN News Services, "NFL Commissioner Roger Goodell Receives 3-Year Extension," ESPN, October 18, 2023, https://www.espn.com/nfl/story/_/id/38687143/nfl-commissioner-roger-goodell-receives-3-year-extension.

27. Geeter, "Taxpayers Are Paying Billions."

28. Kristen Steele, "The Super Bowl of Subsidies," *Common Dreams*, February 1, 2014, http://www.commondreams.org/view/2014/02/01-0?. See also, Richard Crepeau, "Sport and Society for Arete: Super Bowl XLIX," January 30, 2015, *Huff Post*, https://www.huffpost.com/entry/sport-and-society-for-are_b_6581028.

29. Graham Kates and Cara Tabachnick, "Why Do Super Bowl Tickets Cost So Much? Inside the World of NFL Pricing, Luxury Packages, and Ticket Brokers with Bags of Cash," *CBS News*, February 12, 2024, https://www.cbsnews.com/news/superbowl-2024-ticket-prices-nfl-brokers/.

30. "Income in the United States: 2022," US Census, September 12, 2023, https://www.census.gov/library/publications/2023/demo/p60-279.html.

31. Martin Rogers, "Rich, Famous Gladly Spend," *USA Today*, January 27, 2015, 3C.

32. Josh Peter, "Sex Sells, But Is It Out of Bounds?" *USA Today*, January 29, 2015, 1A.

33. Cheryl Cooky, "At Super Bowl 2022, the NFL, Rams, Bengals Rake in Money, Cheerleaders Get Pennies," *NBC Think*, February 12, 2022, https://www.nbcnews.com/think/opinion/super-bowl-2022-nfl-rams-bengals-will-rake-money-cheerleaders-ncna1289003.

34. From Brainyquote.com, https://www.brainyquote.com/quotes/john_madden_461835.

35. What follows is taken primarily from D. Stanley Eitzen, "The Structure of Sport and Society," in *Sport in Contemporary Society: An Anthology*, ed. D. Stanley Eitzen (New York: St. Martin's, 1979), 40–46. See also, Gregg Easterbrook, *The King of Sports: Football's Impact on America* (New York: St. Martin's, 2013), 262–78.

36. Mariah Burton Nelson, *The Stronger Women Get the More Men Love Football: Sexism and the American Culture of Sports* (New York: Harcourt Brace, 1994), 8.

37. Wayne Parry, "Super Bowl Betting Estimated to Reach $16 Billion," PBS News, February 7, 2023, https://www.pbs.org/newshour/nation/super-bowl-betting-estimated-to-reach-16-billion.

38. This rural/industrial thesis to explain the changing popularity of baseball and football is argued by Michael Mandelbaum, *The Meaning of Sports* (New York: Public Affairs Books, 2005).

39. Easterbrook, *The King of Sports*, 265.

40. Richard C. Crepeau, "Punt or Bunt: A Note on American Culture," *Journal of Sport History* 3 (Winter 1976): 205–12.

41. This paragraph is paraphrased from the classic take on football and baseball by comedian George Carlin, ed., "Baseball and Football," in *3 X Carlin: An Orgy of George* (New York: Hyperion, 2008), 60–63.

42. Joe Posnanski, "Prose Football," *Sports Illustrated*, September 12, 2011, 72.

43. Nathaniel Rich, "The Super Bowl: The Horror & the Glory," *New York Review of Books*, March 5, 2015, https://www.nybooks.com/articles/2015/03/05/super-bowl-horror-glory/.

44. David Brooks, "Baseball or Soccer?," *New York Times*, July 10, 2014, http://www.nytimes.com/2014/07/11/opinion/david-brooks-baseball-or-soccer/.

45. Gerald J. Cavanaugh, "Baseball, Football Images," *New York Times*, October 3, 1976, 25S.

46. Easterbrook, *The King of Sports*, 265.

47. "Why Sports?" *Nation*, August 10–17, 1998, 3.

48. Scott Simon, *Home and Away* (New York: Hyperion, 2000), 15.

49. Frank Deford, "Why We Love Sports," CNN Sports Illustrated, December 29, 1999. See also David Shaw, "The Roots of Rooting," *Psychology Today* 11 (February 1978): 48–51; Eric Miller, "Why We Love Football," *Christianity Today* 51 (September 2007): 26–30; William S. Nack, "Behind the Thrill of Victory," *Time*, January 17, 2005, A44–A45; Michael Elliott, "Hopelessly Devoted," *Time*, June 20, 2005, 76; and Michael Rosenberg, "Innocent until Proven Innocent," *Sports Illustrated*, September 21, 2015, 64.

50. David L. Andrews, "Rethinking Sports in America," *Center News* 14 (Spring 1996): 3. *Center News* is published by the Center for Research on Women at the University of Memphis.

51. Jess Stein, ed., *Random House Dictionary of the English Language*, unabridged edition (New York: Random House, 1966), 1046.

52. For an examination of another social institution using paradoxes as an organizing theme, see Judith Lorber, *The Paradoxes of Gender* (New Haven, CT: Yale University Press, 1994).

53. Kenny Moore, "Uplifted, Gently, by Sport," *Sports Illustrated*, November 15, 1989, 234. See also George H. Sage, "Sports Participation as a Builder of Character?" *The World & I* 2 (October 1988): 641.

54. Moore, "Uplifted, Gently, by Sport," 234.

Notes

55 John Meyer, "Great Escapes . . . and Other Fantasies," *Rocky Mountain News*, January 9, 1982, 2B.

56 Jay J. Coakley, *Sport in Society: Issues and Controversies*, 7th ed. (New York: McGraw-Hill, 2001), 504.

PART ONE

SPORT IS FAIR, SPORT IS FOUL

2
SPORT UNITES, SPORT DIVIDES

On March 11, 2020, after 118,000 cases in 114 countries and 4,291 deaths, the World Health Organization declared COVID-19 a global pandemic.[1] It has been referred to as "The Day Everything Changed."[2] That evening the Oklahoma Thunder were scheduled to play the Utah Jazz. The game was canceled right before tipoff as Utah Jazz Center Rudy Gobert tested positive for COVID-19. NBA Commissioner Adam Silver would later cancel the remainder of the 2019–2020 season; it was the first major sports league in the United States to do so. A serendipitous meeting at an NBA game earlier that year between Silver and world-renowned infectious disease expert, Dr. David Ho led Silver to reach out to Dr. Ho for advisement. Silver's decision sent shockwaves throughout the world of sports and society. COVID-19 cases had emerged in the United States as far back as January of 2020 and various attempts were taken including proposed travel bans to limit the spread of the virus within the United States. The country had undergone increased political polarization since the 2016 election, along with a lack of trust in institutions and a questioning of the validity of scientific knowledge and experts. COVID-19 was caught in the middle of this perfect storm of a polarized nation; many in the United States were skeptical of both the government and of science. Questions were raised as to whether we should mask up, lock down, work from home, or whether such "extreme" measures were effective or even necessary. It was in this context of uncertainty that, when the NBA season was canceled, things got real for many. Shortly after the NBA's announcement, other professional leagues, including the NHL and MLB, postponed (and later canceled) their seasons. The NCAA announced basketball games would be played but without fans. The very next day (March 12) the NCAA shifted course, announcing the cancelation of the remainder of the season, including the men's and women's March Madness tournaments, which were set to begin the following week. The WNBA would announce in April the postponement of its 2020 season and held a "virtual draft," on April 17, which was the second most-watched draft in ESPN's history. During a time when there were no live sports, fans were eager to tune in. While President Trump and other politicians ignored medical and scientific experts and downplayed the severity, threat, and risk of the disease for political gain, by late March hospitals were overwhelmed with COVID-19 cases. In the United States and elsewhere, many in need of nonurgent medical attention either had their treatment delayed or received treatment in sports stadiums or other "surge sites," which took on patients when hospitals were still overflowing with cases. During this hiatus, the significant economic impact on sports became evident, with an estimated $12 billion in lost revenue and hundreds of thousands of jobs lost.[3] Yet many sports fans were desperate to "return to normal" and yearned for sports to help escape from the horrors (or for some, boredom) caused by the pandemic.

Several months later, during the summer of 2020, when much of the United States was "shut down," in a "stay-at-home" work/school arrangement, or unemployed due to the lack of ability to operate business under the conditions imposed by the pandemic, millions took to the streets to protest the extrajudicial police killing of George Floyd. Seemingly overnight, BlackLivesMatter transformed into a global social movement and became the largest social movement in US history, with approximately 4,700 protests in late May and throughout June.[4] On June 11, the NFL announced it was donating $250 million to "combat systemic racism and support the battle against injustices faced by African Americans,"[5] a significant departure from just a few years earlier when the NFL turned its back on Colin Kaepernick, who played his last game on January 1, 2017, just a few months after he began kneeling during the national anthem to protest the recent killings of Black and Brown people by police officers. Many professional athletes joined in the summer of 2020 BLM protests, continuing the march of athlete activism of the 2010s, amplifying social justice issues and protesting police brutality and systemic racism. And despite the millions of Americans, the vast majority of whom were white, who marched in the streets that summer, the backlash against athlete activism of Black athletes was immediate. Sport was used to further divide an already politically polarized country. As sports journalist Michael Weinreb observed,

> The pushback to this pandemic-enhanced wave of athlete activism was sometimes fierce, rooted in the ever-present notion that athletes should just shut up and play—that sports should be a respite from the real world. An emotional safe space. A bubble of a different kind. Why, some wondered, should we have to view everything through the prism of activism? Why can't we just enjoy something in this otherwise dire moment? For opportunistic conservative talkers, and for the president himself, sports became a useful cudgel, a handy metaphor for the political battles raging over the restrictive public health measures enacted to fight the virus, and when and how to resume business as usual. Canceling games meant you lived in fear. Canceling games meant you might as well have been canceling America itself.[6]

Nearly two decades earlier, on the morning of September 11, 2001, four commercial planes were taken over by hijackers who piloted the planes to new destinations, and the course of history was fundamentally altered. Two of the planes flew into the World Trade Center in New York City, another plunged into the Pentagon. The fourth plane, on course to hit the nation's capital, Washington D.C., failed in its mission, presumably because of the heroism of the passengers, several of whom were former high school and collegiate athletes, who learned of the attacks on the World Trade Center Towers and the Pentagon through cell phone calls with family members. The passengers coordinated to storm the cockpit in an attempt to retake the plane, crashing instead in a field in rural Pennsylvania. About three thousand people were killed on September 11, 2001, roughly the same number of Americans who died in the attack on Pearl Harbor on December 7, 1941.

After 9/11, the stunned nation came together, rallying around the flag. Sports played an important role in building this patriotic unity. At first, the various sports leagues and teams postponed games out of respect for those who died. Then, as the rescheduled games began, from high school to professional games, each was preceded by a variety of unifying symbolic acts—moments of silence to reflect on the fallen and the heroic, patriotic songs such as God Bless America were sung before games, the presentation of the American flag (some nearly the size of a football field), military flyovers, and spontaneous chants of "U-S-A!

U-S-A!" among fans. These patriotic displays brought the people in the stadiums and in the television audiences together in a cause larger than themselves.

The first Super Bowl after the September attack, on February 3, 2002, in New Orleans, outdid itself in nationalistic fervor. For the gathering of 131 million US households, the largest assemblage of Americans since 9/11, television networks and the NFL took the opportunity to celebrate all things American. Fox's three-hour pregame show had as its theme "Hope, Heroes, and Homeland," which it advertised in *USA Today* as a "celebration of football and the American spirit." Included in the event was a reenactment of the signing of the Declaration of Independence with famous athletes reciting words from that document, former presidents reading passages of Abraham Lincoln's speeches, Barry Manilow singing "Let Freedom Ring," and Paul McCartney singing his song "Freedom," with military personnel, firefighters, police holding flags, and young women dressed as Statues of Liberty. The pageantry before the game also included a huge flag, and Mariah Carey sang the national anthem. At halftime, the NFL presented the band U2, whose set list included "Where the Streets Have No Name," performed on a stage set up on the football field in front of a huge unfurling scroll listing all the names of those whose lives were lost on September 11.[7] And to top off this spectacle of football and nationalism, the winning team, in a huge upset, was the New England Patriots! As the Patriots were presented with the Vince Lombardi trophy, the field was inundated with red, white, and blue confetti.

Fast forward ten years to the time when Osama bin Laden, founder of the terrorist group al Qaeda and mastermind of a series of attacks against the United States including the 9/11 attacks, was assassinated. The announcement of the assassination resulted in spontaneous eruptions of patriotic zeal with fans at sporting events joining in chants of U-S-A, U-S-A. This was followed by organized patriotic celebrations at stadiums throughout the country, such as Military Appreciation Nights; displays of football field–sized flags, and military flyovers. As sports commentator Dave Zirin argues: "Sports has been co-opted, exploited, scarred, and turned inside out by the aftermath of 9/11 and the hunt for Osama bin Laden. Some have wondered if now that bin Laden is dead, life will 'go back to normal' But . . . this is the new normal."[8]

The Role of Sport in Unity and Division Among Nations

Two opposing forces are at work throughout the world today: increasing intolerance, ideological purity, exclusion, and conflict, as well as many signs of tolerance, cooperation, compromise, acceptance of differences, and inclusion.

The Role of Sport in Unity and Division Among Nations

Just as the world is moving toward becoming a global community, it is torn by parochial hatreds, dividing nations and regions into warring ethnic enclaves.[9] Sport, too, embodies these contradictory elements as it increasingly pulls people apart on the one hand and pulls them together on the other.

Sport Unites

International events bring together people from different countries and different racial, ethnic, and religious backgrounds, promoting understanding and friendships across these social divides. The US government uses athletes to promote international goodwill. The State Department, for example, sponsors tours of athletes to foreign countries for these purposes. Sport has also been used to open diplomatic doors. In the 1970s, when communist China and the United States did not have diplomatic relations, the leadership of the two nations agreed that their athletes could compete in each country. After this "ping-pong" diplomacy broke the ice, the two countries eventually established normal relations. In 1998, US wrestlers were invited to participate in a seventeen-nation tournament in Iran, the first American athletic team to visit Iran since the 1979 Islamic revolution. Wrestling is Iran's national sport, and Iran's president at that time, Mohammed Khatami, encouraged this breakthrough to crack "the wall of distrust between the two nations." International journalist Thomas Omestad described an important symbolic act that he hoped might help to bridge the antagonism between Iran and the United States that had existed for over two decades:

> It was only a small, spontaneous gesture. But it worked emotional magic. After winning a silver medal . . . American Larry "Zeke" Jones waved a hand-sized Iranian flag, and the 2,000 fans packed into a Tehran arena went wild with delight. "America! America!" They chanted in response—a sudden, unscripted reversal of the ritual "Death to America!" chorus that Iranians usually chant at public events.[10]

Sport was a wedge helping to break down the hostility between these two countries. In June 1998, Iran upset the United States in a first-round World Cup soccer match in Lyon, France.[11] The Iranians celebrated their unexpected victory wildly but not (and this is crucial) with taunts directed at the United States. President Bill Clinton congratulated the Iranians, and the Iranian president was a gracious winner.

Since India was divided into two nations—India and Pakistan—in 1948, they have gone to war three times, with millions killed. The tension between these two nuclear powers is enormous and unrelenting, unleashing religious hatred, as

India is a predominantly Hindu and Pakistan is predominantly Muslim. However, in 2004, the two nations came together in a series of cricket matches, as the team from India, for the first time in fourteen years, toured Pakistan for thirty-nine days. *Sports Illustrated* journalist S. L. Price describes the tensions between the two countries,

> The phrase *sporting event* can't begin to contain the religious extremism, unforgiven deeds, and rabid jingoism that swirl around each India–Pakistan cricket match; the game is haunted by battle dead, and the air is charged with the ongoing dispute between the two countries over control of Kashmir. For generations cricket has been a proxy for war between the two nations.[12]

Temporarily, at least, sport brought these two warring nations together, promising either better relations between the two countries—or an explosion of violence.

Sport can be used to unite groups within one country, but this is not always with benevolent purpose. For example, Adolf Hitler used the 1936 Olympic Games in Berlin to unite the German people through the accomplishments of Germany's athletes on the world stage. According to Richard D. Mandell in his book *The Nazi Olympics*, the Olympic festival was a shrewdly propagandistic and brilliantly conceived charade that reinforced and mobilized the patriotism of the German masses.[13] The successes of the German athletes at those Olympics (they won eighty-nine medals, twenty-three more than US athletes and more than four times as many as any other country) was "proof" of German (i.e., white) superiority and by extension the superiority of the political ideology of Nazism. The use of the Olympic games to advance a government responsible for the systematic genocide of over six million Jews across German-occupied Europe is one horrific way sports have been used to unite a country, albeit in this case toward destructive ends.

Success in international sports competition can trigger pride across divisions within a country. For example, even in war-ravaged Iraq, with its ethnic and sectarian divides, unity was achieved briefly in 2007 when the national Iraqi soccer team, composed of Shiites, Sunnis, and Kurds, won its first ever Asian Cup, defeating Saudi Arabia. Spontaneous celebrations occurred following the victory with people dancing in the streets and waving Iraqi flags.[14]

Cuba provides another example of the great potential that sport has a mechanism for promoting domestic unity.[15] Fidel Castro, Cuba's former leader, decreed that sport is a right of the people. No admission is ever charged to a sporting event. The communist leadership in Cuba uses sport to unite its people through pride in its athletic achievements. The most promising athletes are given the best coaching and training. In the Pan American Games, Cuban athletes, from a country with a third the population of California, win many times more medals than US athletes on a per capita basis. In the 2012 Olympics,

Cuba ranked third in the number of medals per 100,000 people (the United States ranked 48th).[16] Cuban athletes are sports heroes and heroines, evoking intense nationalistic pride in the Cuban people and, indirectly, support for the ruling elite.

Racially, South Africa is a nation deeply divided. Sport has helped to break down this division, at least in part, in two ways. First, when the whites in South Africa held an election to decide whether to dismantle apartheid, 69 percent voted to give up their privilege, marking a rare peaceful transition of power. One reason for the favorable vote was South African president F. W. de Klerk's warning that failure to pass the measure would return the country to isolation in business and sport.[17] South Africa had last participated in the Olympics in 1960 and had been barred since then from international competition. Its apartheid racial policies had made it a pariah country in everything from politics to sports for three decades. With apartheid dismantled, South Africans could once again show their athletic prowess. This was a compelling argument for many whites. Subsequently, South Africa has been allowed to compete in the Olympics and in other worldwide competitions, especially in rugby, which is very important to its people.

After the formal fall of apartheid and the election of Nelson Mandela, the sports world accepted South Africa. The World Cup in rugby was held in South Africa in 1995. President Mandela used the rugby World Cup as an opportunity to bring the races somewhat closer together within his country—to use sport for the greater good.[18] The national rugby team, the Springboks, and rugby itself had symbolized white South Africa, since it had been an all-white team. But Mandela, against the wishes of his advisors, kept the Springbok name and encouraged Black Africans to think of this team as their team. In speaking to a Black audience, Mandela, wearing a Springbok cap, said, "This Springbok cap does honor to our boys. I ask you to stand by them tomorrow because they are our kind." Mandela inspired *Sports Illustrated* to comment:

> *Our kind*. Not [black]. Not white. South African. The rugby team became a symbol for the country as a whole. . . . Given the right time and place, sport is capable of starting such a process in a society. It is only a start, of course. The hard work lies ahead, after the crowds have dispersed and the headlines have ceased. South Africa's racial and economic woes are not behind it. Far from it. But thanks to the common ground supplied by a rugby pitch, those problems appear less imposing than they did only a month ago.[19]

The Springboks went on to win the World Cup, defeating the world's two rugby powers—Australia and New Zealand—in the process. For the first time in South Africa's troubled history, white people and Black people found themselves unified by a sport. Of course, this kind of unity is superficial and temporary, but it is nevertheless an instrument that can help to achieve unity in an otherwise divided country.

South Africans were also brought together through sport when a white South African golfer, Louis Oosthuizen, and his Black caddy, Zaack Rasego also from South Africa won the British Open in 2010.[20] The player and caddy had worked together since 2003 and when Oosthuizen won the Open, he hugged his caddy, not as his employee, but as a partner—a hugely symbolic act to both races in South Africa, and the goal of Nelson Mandela to unify his nation.

Still experiencing deep racial divisions, sport continues to move South Africa toward some semblance of racial unity. In 2010, South Africa hosted the World Cup, the biggest sporting event on the planet. The tournament was a huge success with the country receiving international recognition and a source of pride for its people of all races. As Danny Jordan, the CEO of the World Cup organizing committee, said: "You're talking about the transformation of a country and a society. Our past has been a past of apartheid, a past of separation of people based on discrimination. This project can actually bind the nation."[21]

Sport Divides

But sport also has the capacity to divide people. Phillip Goodhart and Christopher Chataway argue that there are four kinds of sport: sport as exercise, sport as gambling, sport as spectacle, and representative sport. Representative sport often divides rather than unites people. Representative sport refers to sporting events in which representatives from towns, regions, or nations are pitted against each other through the sport event. Each opponent or team represents its own distinct town/region/nation. Spectators are drawn to the event not so much for the competition or the ritual of the game, but primarily because they identify with their representatives. As Goodhart and Chataway explain,

> Most people will watch [the Olympic Games] for one reason only: there will be a competitor who, they feel, is representing them. That figure in the striped singlet will be their man [sic]—running, jumping, or boxing for their country. For a matter of minutes at least, their own estimation of themselves will be bound up with his performance. He will be the embodiment of their nation's strength or weakness. Victory for him will be victory for them; defeat for him, defeat for them.[22]

This keen identification with national athletes frames the contest as a symbolic battleground between "us" and "them." This attitude, of course, is exclusionary rather than inclusionary.

Sport can encourage division rather than unity. Tensions generated in sports matches, such as those that erupted between El Salvador and Honduras and between Gabon and the Congo after soccer matches, have contributed to the outbreak of war. A full-scale war between El Salvador and Honduras followed the clash between fans at the elimination round of the 1970 World Cup and concluded with bombing raids, troop movements, and, eventually, two thousand dead. Obviously, the matches themselves did not start these conflicts since the matches occurred in an already tense context over land disputes and other contentious issues. A sports event between two quarreling countries can (and occasionally does) provide the catalyst for actual war between them.

Losing an international match can cause deep internal division, whereas unity typically accompanies victory. When Colombia lost the 1994 FIFA World Cup, riots occurred in the country because the people were distressed over their team's play. Shockingly, Andres Escobar, who had inadvertently scored a goal for the opposition (the United States) was murdered when he returned to his hometown, presumably for his failure during the match.

In 2008, the Israeli basketball team was to play Turkey's national team in Ankara, Turkey, soon after Israel had bombarded Gaza, including bombing Gaza's Palestine National Stadium. Before the game could begin, Turkish fans chanted "Israeli killers!" and Palestinian flags were unfurled. The police tried to gain control of the crowd, and after ninety minutes, all the fans were expelled from the arena. The referees attempted to get the teams on the court to play before an empty arena, but the Israeli team had no desire to play. The referees declared the Turks as winners.[23]

Israel's actions against Palestinians in Gaza inflamed the Middle East. This was manifested as Islamic athletes demonstrated against Israel. An Egyptian soccer star followed a goal by raising his shirt to reveal the slogan "Sympathise with Gaza." Similarly, a Spanish soccer player raised his shirt to reveal a shirt that said "Palestine" in multiple languages.[24]

The ongoing conflict between the Israelis and the Palestinians erupted again in 2012 when the Israeli Air Force bombed the Palestinian stadium in Gaza, which headquartered the center for youth sports programs throughout the Gaza Strip. This action was justified by the Israeli government as "collective punishment" following Hamas rockets fired on the Israelis. Dave Zirin asks why a sports stadium was the target. Answering his own question, he states:

> Sports is more than loved in Gaza. . . . It's an expression of humanity for those living under occupation. . . . Attacking the athletic infrastructure is about attacking the idea that joy, normalcy, or a universally recognizable humanity

could ever be a part of life for a Palestinian child . . . attacking sports is about nothing less than killing hope.[25]

In 2011, the men's basketball team from Georgetown University was engaged in a "Goodwill Tour" of China. An exhibition game against a Chinese team composed of players from the People's Liberation Army began with rough play that deteriorated into an ugly fight. This fight in Beijing's Olympic Stadium was witnessed by Vice President Biden and his Chinese counterpart Xi Jinping. Biden's trip to China was to lay the groundwork for a reciprocal visit by Vice President Xi. Basketball, in this instance, did not foster friendly relations between the two countries.

Indeed, the tensions between the United States and China would continue throughout the decade. Both Xi Jinping and Joe Biden would ascend to the presidency of their respective nations. In 2022, China was set to host the winter Olympics, the first time a country would have hosted both the summer and winter games. President Biden decided the United States would engage in a diplomatic boycott of the 2022 Beijing Winter Olympics given the administration's concerns over China's human rights record, including China's attempts to limit protests in Hong Kong (which had been advocating for independence from China), for detaining and abusing Uyghurs (a religious minority), which was described by some as "genocide," and for China's policies in Tibet and Taiwan. President Biden and other US political leaders did not attend the Olympic events although US athletes would be able to compete.

Long-standing tensions between nations can keep them from cooperating in common ventures involving sport. In 2014, for example, the International Olympic Committee in an effort to reduce the cost of hosting the Games decided to allow host cities to move some competitions to other cities or countries where existing facilities were available. One idea was to allow South Korea, the host of the 2018 Winter Games, to shift the bobsled and luge events to Japan. South Korea rejected this idea because many Koreans harbored resentment against Japan, its onetime colonial ruler.[26]

Conflicts can arise within Olympic host countries as well. For example, the 2016 games held in Rio de Janeiro, Brazil were rife with citizen protests, both before and after the games. Over $13 billion dollars was spent on infrastructure tied to the games, including the construction of a doping laboratory, a subway line, and clean-up of a polluted bay that had been used for Olympic events. The expenditures happened at a time when Brazil was experiencing its worst recession since the 1930s.[27] Brazilians questioned the investment in construction of Olympic venues, as the government was unable to pay the salaries of police officers and health care workers. Over 22,000 Brazilians, including many who lived in favelas, were displaced to make way for infrastructure and transportation projects tied to the 2016 games.[28]

Unity and Division Through Sport in the United States

Fans of a team, by definition, are united in their fealty to that team. In a sense, they belong to voluntary communities or collectives. They may even call themselves a "nation," as in "Steeler Nation" (Pittsburg Steelers) in pro football or "Buckeye Nation" (Ohio State University). These "nations" are emotionally intense affinity groups, and they are important sources of community.

But, of course, intense identification with a "nation" can have divisive consequences. It may lead to shouted obscenities, booing fans, hanging coaches in effigy, and racial taunts. Such behaviors often result in fights between opposing fans at the arena, in bars, or on the streets. It may lead to riots following a team's victory or defeat. Rivalries may even result in a rabid follower doing something foolish or even dangerous. Indeed, a perceived increase in violence in NFL stadiums was noted during the 2023 season, with several high-profile incidents of physical altercations between home and away team fans generating news headlines.[29] Also consider the case of the attack on the oak trees at Toomer's Corner. Two majestic 130-year-old trees at Toomer's Corner in Auburn, Alabama, were poisoned following Auburn's victory over archrival Alabama in 2010. By long tradition, when Auburn University wins a football game, these oaks are covered with toilet paper. A sixty-two-year-old University Alabama fan, whose children are named Bear (after legendary Alabama coach, Bear Bryant) and Crimson Tyde, admitted to poisoning the trees, the symbols of hated Auburn victories. As a commentator in *Sports Illustrated* opined: "This alleged crime seems an extreme example of the intense partisanship pervading college athletics in general and SEC football in particular. The expression of that animosity straddles the line between passion and pathology."[30]

A keen interest in sports, however, can also break up one's intense feelings for or identification with a sports team. The phenomenon of fantasy sports, such as fantasy football, does just that.[31] In 2022, about 50.4 million football fans aged eighteen and older participated in fantasy sports leagues, with well over half participating in fantasy football. Players in these leagues draft players from NFL (or other professional sports) rosters. Each fantasy player's individual roster then is composed of players from a number of teams, which may or may not include a fan's favorite or "home" team. As a result, the fantasy sports participant cares about the performance of athletes beyond those on his/her/their favorite team. The dynamics of fantasy sports thus shifts fan loyalty and the salience of one's favorite/home team for one's fandom dissipates as a result.

Looking at the effect of sport on unity or division at the societal level, distinguished sports commentator Frank Deford, writing nearly three decades ago, made a strong case that sport divides: "It is time to recognize the truth, that sports in the United States has, in fact, never been so divisive. Uniquely today, sports have come to pit race against race, men against women, city against city, class against class and coach against player."[32] The divisiveness of sports has existed from its very early development to the contemporary context, particularly because sports are a microcosm of society, a social institution and cultural site wherein the larger societal forces and dynamics take shape.

The following sections examine how sport both unites and divides considering the four major hierarchies in society: social class, race, gender, and sexuality. The question: Does sport lead to greater harmony within these systems of social stratification? Or does sport increase division? As we shall see, it has the potential to do both. We emphasize the divisive nature of sport because it counters the "Great American Sports Myth" as we discussed in chapter 1.

Social Class

Money separates. Historically, sport has been pursued mainly by the affluent, who alone had the time and the money for such non-income-producing activities. The notion of the sports "amateur" was a nineteenth-century invention that the affluent used as a mechanism of class separation.[33] The major competitions in Europe, including the Olympics, were limited to those who could afford the necessary travel, equipment, and coaching, and had the leisure to pursue athletic excellence. More than having the ability to participate, class origins precluded international competition for many. John Kelley, a world-class rower, was barred from the 1928 Olympics because as a bricklayer he had a physical advantage over those who either did not work at all or did not do manual labor. Ironically, the well-to-do in this case used their athletic prowess in international competitions as "proof" of their superiority over the lesser classes.

Amateurism was not limited to international competitions and in many ways has been a foundational principle of the development of collegiate athletics in the United States. As former NFL player and English professor Michael Oriard notes, throughout the history of the NCAA, the organization vociferously defended the ideal of amateurism for college athletes, an ideal rooted in British definitions often at odds with "American democratic principles."[34] Restrictions on college students' ability to earn income from their athletic participation throughout the historical development of college athletics limited participation to those athletes who could "afford" to not be paid, or to live off the scholarship support provided by the university. As college sports, and in particular men's football and basketball commercialized, the disparities between what universities "earned" from student-athletic talent and effort and what student-athletes received increased dramatically. According to an ESPN analysis, the highest-paid public employee in forty of the fifty states in the United States was either a college football or college basketball coach.[35] College athletes have challenged the NCAA's restrictive policies regarding amateurism, bringing forward legal cases against the NCAA, including the most recent Supreme Court decision opening up opportunities for college athletes to earn income from their "Name, Image, and Likeness" (see chapter 8).

Does sport provide opportunity for those with athletic ability regardless of class origin? The answer is a little yes, but mostly no. Athletes of humble social origins can become incredibly wealthy. Professional golfer Tiger Woods, for example, was the first athlete to make $1 billion from his achievements, endorsements, and personal appearances. Similarly, tennis superstars Serena and Venus Williams were raised in Compton, California, a city infamously known for its gangs and drugs. Both sisters have experienced significant success both on and off the courts, and Serena Williams consistently tops the "highest-paid" female athlete list. As of the publication of this book she has been the only female athlete to earn enough to make it to the overall highest-paid athlete list, earning $45.3 million in 2022. These athletes not only were incredibly successful despite coming from less affluent communities with fewer resources to succeed, but they also did so in the white "country club" sports of golf and tennis. The visibility of these and other athletes lead many to believe that they too can become professional athletes if they work hard enough. How reasonable is this expectation? In two words, extremely improbable.

Moreover, despite some high-profile athletes like Tiger and Serena, the opportunity for upward mobility is limited to a few sports. Children from families with limited economic resources tend to participate in sports that require little equipment and are publicly funded, such as community youth programs and recreational or school-based sports. The sports that are accessible are often limited to football, basketball, baseball, track, and boxing. Children of the affluent, on the other hand, have access to golf courses, tennis courts, ice rinks, and swimming pools, as well as coaching in those sports, through private country clubs, neighborhood associations, and parental subsidies. Moreover, some sports, such as gymnastics, ice-skating, and hockey require considerable money for coaching, access, equipment, and travel (young elite ice skaters, for example, spend more than $100,000 annually). According to the Aspen Institute, the average family spends $833 on one child's primary sports in a year. Parents in the wealthiest tier of income spent four times as much on youth sports as the lowest-income parents. The wealthiest families spent significantly more on travel than middle- or low-income families, an important disparity given that more competitive opportunities reside in "travel" teams rather than in community, recreational, or school-based sports. The report's "bottom line": Children in the United States are still having different sports experiences based on money.[36]

Ironically, most professional opportunities for women athletes are in sports in which the affluent have a tremendous advantage from childhood.

Athletes may develop friendships with those from different social backgrounds, thus transcending social class in terms of social connections and peer group interactions. There are instances where players from humble origins may be upwardly mobile, increasing their interaction with people across class boundaries. Certainly, obtaining a college education, which athletic participation facilitates, increases interaction across social classes. But sport scholarships are for the very few. And attending college on an athletic scholarship does not necessarily lead to graduation. Athletes in the "revenue-producing" sports are less likely to graduate than their nonathlete peers.

Sports also divide when it comes to being a spectator or fan. Members of differing social classes are not proportionately represented at professional sports events as the cost of attending sports contests is too high for many. According to the Fan Cost Index, in 2023, a family of four attending a major league baseball game paid an average of $256.41 for "four average-price tickets, two small draft beers, four small soft drinks, four regular-size hot dogs, parking for one hour, two game programs and two least-expensive, adult-size adjustable caps."[37] For the NFL, it was $590.64, the NBA $444.12, and for the NHL it was $462.58.[38] Obviously, these amounts are prohibitive for many families since the median weekly income for full-time wage and salary workers in Q4 of 2023 was $1,145 according to the Department of Labor's Bureau of Labor Statistics.

This was not always the case. Over the past four decades, the cost of attending a professional sports event has become increasingly prohibitive by design. According to sports economists, this is a result of two interrelated dynamics.[39] The first is the potential earnings for professional leagues from the sale of televised (and now streaming) rights fees. Leagues and teams benefit financially when fans are at home watching the game (increased ratings equals increased fees leagues can charge to media outlets for TV/ streaming rights). The second is the trend in new and renovated sports stadia, which has expanded the number of corporate/luxury suites, decreasing the space allotted for non-suite seating. Leagues generate significant revenue from corporate and luxury suits and are incentivized to price out the average fan in favor of corporate entities with millions at their disposal to spend on hosting clients and networking with vendors. For example, Major League baseball teams the New York Yankees, Minnesota Twins, Florida Marlins, and Atlanta Braves' new stadiums each have at least eight thousand fewer seats than their previous homes. The reduced seating capacity subsequently drives up prices for non-luxury seating, further pricing out fans from the middle and lower strata of the social class hierarchy.

Among those who do attend professional sporting events, members of differing socioeconomic groups will not have many opportunities to interact across class lines. Stadium seating is segregated by cost, in a very stratified arrangement. The very rich enjoy luxury suites, while the less well-to-do are dispersed by the cost of seating, with the cheapest seats farthest from the action. The lowest income earners, of course, are not in the seats at all. If they do attend, they likely are there as vendors, cooks, janitors, or parking attendants. John Underwood, writing in the *New York Times*, lamented the high cost of attending sports events:

> The greatest damage done by this new elitism is that even the cheapest seats in almost every big-league facility are now priced out of reach of a large segment of the population. Those who are most critically in need of affordable entertainment, the underclass (and even the lower-middle class), have been effectively shut out. And this is especially hateful because spectator sport, by its very nature, has been the great escape for the men and women who have worked all day for small pay and traditionally provided the biggest number of a sport's core support. As it now stands, they are as good as disenfranchised—a vast number of the taxpaying public who will never set foot inside these stadiums and arenas.[40]

Race

Progress in race relations has been slow and, in some instances, seems to be stalling. Cities were more racially segregated in 2019 than in 1990.[41] School children are more racially diverse, yet the schools they attend remain racially segregated, with over a third of K–12 students attending a predominantly same-race/ethnicity school.[42] The gap between white students and Black and Latino students is widening in terms of income, wealth, education, and employment. With growing concerns regarding immigration and challenging economic circumstances for the working poor, racial tensions increase. Racial discrimination in housing, lending policies, job opportunities, and an often-unjust criminal justice system (e.g., racial profiling) continues. Frustrations with these forms of racial injustice reached a tipping point in the summer of 2020 with the Black Lives Matter protests, as discussed at the beginning of this chapter. In response, there were efforts among community leaders, corporations, and schools to create solutions that would foster racial and social inclusion and equality. These efforts, however, were short-lived. The backlash to racial and social justice movements was swift, evidenced in concerns expressed by conservative media outlets and politicians over social justice movements or "wokeness," as it is often described, along with a wave of anti-DEI (diversity, equity, and inclusion) laws across the United States. As of March 2024, thirty states have introduced or passed anti-DEI legislation in higher education and public offices.[43] The question for us, given these racial realities in contemporary US society, is whether sport reduces or exacerbates racial tensions. Does it challenge or does it reinforce racial inequality? Does it create and foster racial harmony or discord?

Regarding racial harmony, sport works both ways. Clearly, teammates make friends across racial lines through sport. Research has found that positive attitudes toward race are enhanced (1) when players from diverse racial backgrounds contribute equally to team success and (2) when the team is successful.[44] Thus, on racially integrated teams in which each participants needs the other to succeed and the team does succeed, teammates have positive feelings toward each other.

In many sports, athletes from racially marginalized backgrounds are heroes cheered by their fans of all races. That is, fans tend to appreciate the athletes on their own teams, regardless of race. According to a 2023 YouGov poll, of the top ten overall most popular athletes in the United States nine are Black athletes, including Muhammad Ali, Michael Jordan, Jackie Robinson, and Serena Williams.[45] But fans who adore their home team or favorite athlete may direct racism toward athletes of opposing teams. It is also the case that appreciating the achievements of athletes from marginalized or minoritized backgrounds does not preclude one from also espousing or holding generalized racist attitudes, beliefs, or stereotypes. In other words, liking a Black athlete is not the same as supporting racial equality or racial inclusion.

A strong case can be made that sport divides the races. Historically, desegregating a sport has intensified racial hostilities. Consider Jackie Robinson's status as being among the most popular athletes today, yet Robinson experienced intense racial hostility when he played for the L.A. Dodgers, from opponents, baseball fans, and the public. Because of America's persistent racial divide, sport sometimes provides the context for episodes of racial hostility (in schools, parks, playgrounds, prisons). Similarly, games that involve teams representing white schools versus teams representing Black or predominantly Latino schools often provide a setting for racial taunts and violence by players and fans. This occurs with some regularity in metropolitan areas when mostly white suburban high schools play against high schools from the inner city that have a mostly Black or Latino student body. It also occurs in small-town America where recent immigration has brought Latinos to once all-white communities.

Race tends to be a factor in the choices that athletes make. That is, on integrated teams, players often segregate themselves voluntarily for meals, travel arrangements, and leisure activities, and they tend to select roommates of the same race. As white and racial minority athletes compete for positions on a team, each group may feel that the other race is getting special treatment, leading to various manifestations of "racial paranoia."

Integrated teams may be segregated by position, which is called "stacking." For example, historically in professional football, white players were more likely to play on offense and at thinking and leadership positions that more often determine the game's outcome. Black players were overwhelmingly on defense and played at positions that require physical characteristics such as size, strength, speed, and quickness. This means that the members of one race spend most of their practice time with players of the same race. Although longitudinal research examining race and player position from 1960 to 2020 indicates certain positions have become racially integrated over time, there has been "hyper-segregation" of Black players in positions at high risk for injury, including defensive back, defensive line, linebacker, running back, and wide receiver. Conversely, hyper-segregation also exists at central positions of quarterback, with very little integration of Black players into this position.[46]

The majority of Black college athletes play for schools that are predominantly white (with Black students sometimes constituting less than 5 percent of the student body). Athletes are often segregated on campus (i.e., dorms, meals, courses, majors, training facilities) and interact with other athletes but rarely with other students. For non-white student athletes at predominantly white institutions (PWIs), the segregation from other aspects of college-life further isolates them from their white peers. Jonathon Howe, an assistant professor in sports management, writing for the *Conversation* describes the realities for many Black male athletes at PWIs, illustrating that in this case, sports serve to reaffirm racial discrimination and stereotypes:

> They are discriminated against for being Black, for being Black males and for being athletes. Although touted for their physical prowess, Black male athletes are often labeled "dumb jocks"—their intelligence somehow discredited by their physical stature. They are sometimes seen by students, faculty, staff and even fans as lacking the intellectual ability and motivation to succeed academically. They are characterized as illegitimate students who undermine the academic mission of the university and receive special treatment.[47]

Gender

The United States is a patriarchal society. Despite the decades-long fight for equal pay, women continue to earn less than men from entry-level to C-suite job positions. Despite more women now earning college degrees than men, women continue to be underrepresented in leadership positions and positions of power in most social institutions. With few exceptions, women occupy secondary roles at home, in corporations, in colleges and universities, and in voluntary associations. Women experience discrimination by lenders, by employers, and by the Social Security system, to name a few.[48]

Does sport reinforce this imbalance, or does it work to break down gender inequities? As with class and race, a case can be made for both sides on this question. In terms of breaking down gender inequities, sports play a significant role in gender equality, in terms of empowering girls and women and shifting conventional expectations. In the United States the passage of Title IX in 1972 is credited with much of the advancements in women's sports. Title IX states that no person in the United States can be excluded, on the basis of sex, from participation in, can be denied the benefits of, or can be subjected to discrimination in any educational program or activity receiving federal financial assistance. As a result of this landmark legislation, there has been a boom in women's participation in high school and college athletics. High school programs for girls went from about 300,000 participants in 1971 to 3,328,180 (4,529,789 boys participated) in 2023. The number of women in college sports has also increased over time from 29,997 in 1971–1972 to 215,486 in 2021–2022, according to a recent Women's Sports Foundation report.[49] Girls and women's participation in sports has been linked to a host of positive social, psychological, health, and educational outcomes. Playing sports also has been linked to positive outcomes in corporate America. An Ernst and Young report found 94 percent of women executives have a background in sports, 80 percent of women Fortune 500 executives played competitive sports, and over 60 percent of executives believed that playing sports contributed positively to their career success and advancement. Thus, participation in sports may help women to successfully navigate workplace dynamics and create more gender diversity.

In terms of sports reinforcing gender inequality, there is compelling evidence. While participation rose substantially since the 1970s, a *USA Today* report[50] published during the fiftieth anniversary of Title IX found 87 percent of colleges and universities do not offer athletic opportunities proportional to their enrollment (proportionality is the primary way schools can demonstrate compliance with Title IX). The report also found inequity in the distribution of scholarship funds, with nearly one half of the 107 schools investigated failing to meet Title IX's requirement for equitable support for women and men's sports, which represented a $23.7 million gap in funding.[51] Moreover, there is a huge gender pay gap among college coaches. According to a 2023 study, between 2014–2021 coaching salaries increased 55 percent for men and only 33 percent for women coaches at Power 5 conference schools.[52]

Gender-related issues, as they pertain to sport, will be more fully elaborated upon in chapter 3.

Sexuality

Heterosexual orientation is the norm in American society. The Williams Institute estimates that the percentage of adults in the United States who identify as lesbian, gay, bisexual, or trans is 5.5 percent or 13.9 million Americans.[53] This estimate is undoubtedly lower than the actual number, primarily because so many LGBTQ+ people do not always disclose their sexuality. LGBTQ+ individuals do this to avoid or escape the marginalization, derision, and contempt expressed by members of society and the interpersonal and institutional discrimination leveled against them. The recent wave of anti-LGBTQ+ legislation in the United States is one such example. The number of state bills targeting LGBTQ+ civil liberties and civil rights tripled in 2022–2023, according to the American Civil Liberties Union (ACLU). Moreover, in 2018, there were 42 anti-LGBTQ+ bills in state legislatures. By 2023, that number was 510, a new record according to the ACLU.[54] Many of these bills seek to ban access to gender-affirming care, ban LGBTQ+ curriculum in schools and universities, require the use of bathrooms and other sex segregated public facilities that correspond with the individuals assigned sex at birth, and target trans inclusion in sports (see chapter 3).

Homophobia pervades the sports world, as it does in wider society. Although hundreds of gay men have doubtless been professional athletes, not one of the 3,500 men who actively play professionally each year in the big four American sports—football, baseball, basketball, and hockey—publicly "came out" (disclosed their sexuality) before 2013. Jason Collins, the first openly gay NBA player, proclaimed in *Sports Illustrated*: "I'm a 34-year-old NBA center. I'm black. And I'm gay."[55] He was followed by Michael Sam who publicly came out and became the first openly gay college football player drafted in the NFL (he was subsequently released by the St. Louis Rams before the season). Historically most gay male athletes did not come out until after their careers ended.[56] Athletes, coaches, and team officials were divided on whether a team should have gay players. The argument in opposition was that this would negatively affect team morale, be a distraction, and disrupt normal locker-room routines. Supporters of inclusion argued that when a player's sexual orientation is known to his teammates it has proven to not be a problem, which was the case for Michael Sam at the University of Missouri and Derrick Gordon of the University of Massachusetts, the first openly gay male NCAA Division I athletes.[57] In 2021, NFL player Carl Nassib made history by becoming the first active NFL player to publicly come out as gay. He did so through a post on social media which in part read,

> I'm a pretty private person so I hope you guys know that I'm not doing this for attention. I just think that representation and visibility are so important. I actually hope that one day, videos like this and the whole coming out process are not necessary, but until then I will do my best and my part to cultivate a culture that's accepting and compassionate and I'm going to start by donating

$100,000 to the Trevor Project. They're an incredible organization, they're the number one suicide-prevention service for LGBTQ youth in America.[58]

For women's sports, homophobia manifests itself in distinct ways. This is in part given the conflation of gender with sexuality and the linkages between masculinity and athleticism. Conventional femininity—the social expectations, norms, and standards of behavior for girls and women—is defined in opposition to masculinity. Yet the expectations and norms associated with athleticism (e.g., aggressiveness, competitiveness, rationality, stoicism, etc.) have historically aligned with masculinity, particularly the forms of athleticism embodied in the sports that dominate American culture (i.e., football, basketball, baseball, and hockey). Women's athleticism runs counter to conventional femininity. Women who embody masculinity are assumed by our society to be a lesbian or to desire women. Conversely, for men participating in sports, and particularly the dominant sports in the United States, the athleticism embodied in these sports aligns with conventional masculinity and therefore heterosexuality. The institutional discrimination, cultural stereotypes, and stigma led many in the world of women's sports to avoid any suspicions of lesbianism, by either remaining in the proverbial closet and/or self-presenting in ways that aligned with conventional femininity. In the contemporary moment, with relatively more cultural acceptance of LGBTQ+ people and more younger generations identifying as LGBTQ+, women athletes no longer "come out." And while women athletes in basketball, soccer, and softball have been openly out, and the leagues like the WNBA and the NWSL themselves have embraced and celebrated both their lesbian and queer athletes and fans, women athletes in the "feminine-appropriate" sport of gymnastics are increasingly coming out. Yet, except for a few male athletes, including those noted above, at the time of this writing, there are no NBA active players who are openly gay, and the one active NFL player retired before the 2023 season. As sports journalist Katie Barnes explains in their book *Fair Play: How Sports Shape the Gender Debates*,

> There has been a significant shift in how athletes in women's sports come out, meaning they don't anymore. They just post photos of their lives on social media. . . . The gains in women's sports have not led to a stampede of sharing in men's sports. . . . The sea change has been in women's sports so far. I think the primary reason why is that for all the angst felt in women's sports about appearing too masculine or being queer, the assumption in men's sports (with a few exceptions) is that masculinity and straightness are the default. It's exactly the opposite in women's sports. If we think of queerness in women as masculine, then I would argue we think of queerness in men as feminine. And in American male sports, femininity is not tolerated.[59]

Caveats

Are the Expressions of Patriotism by Sport Organizations at Sporting Events Always Real?

Expressions of patriotism (e.g., national anthems, unfurling flags, jet flyovers) are a common mechanism to unify a sports crowd. But sometimes we are misled. A Senate oversight report by Republican Senators John McCain and Jeff Flake revealed that the Defense Department, mostly through the Army National Guard and the Air Force, had paid professional sports franchises in the NFL, Major League Baseball, and the National Hockey League, NASCAR, and college programs in exchange for patriotic tributes at sporting events honoring members of the armed services.[60] It is hard to not be cynical when we learn that public relations by the military are used to manipulate fans by tugging at their heart strings.

Is the Unity Achieved Through Sport Always Good?

Most discussions of sport implicitly assume that unity is good and division is bad. This is not always the case.[61] The Nazi Olympics of 1936, for example, unified the Germans in their contempt for Jews, people of color, homosexuals, and non-Germans. This unity was achieved by separating the German people into superior and inferior categories. Soccer wars divide nations precisely because of soccer's ability to unite the people within national boundaries. The infamous statement against racial injustice and poverty made by Tommie Smith and John Carlos on the victory stand during the national anthem in the 1968 Olympics was viewed by most Americans as a divisive gesture pulling white and Black athletes, and by extension white and Black Americans apart. Many of those in anti-racist movements, however, interpreted this symbolic act as a powerful, unifying political statement. Depending on the audience, this act was divisive or unifying, unpatriotic or empowering.

Nearly fifty years later, NFL San Francisco quarterback Colin Kaepernick's kneeling during the national anthem in the 2016 NFL season games was received similarly to the 1968 Olympic protests. While many Americans, including professional athletes in the WNBA, NBA, and NWSL supported Kaepernick and joined him in protesting, just as many Americans, including the then-president of the United States, viewed the protests as unpatriotic and un-American. Kaepernick was essentially banned from the league and although the NFL would eventually support racial justice in its "Inspire Change" initiative, to the date of this publication Kaepernick has not been signed to play for any NFL team, despite his desire to do so. Thus, it is not simply a matter of sport either uniting or dividing but a question of who, how, and under what circumstances does sport unite and/or divide and with what consequences, particularly in terms of who benefits and who pays a cost?

Sport does have a unifying function. This can be accomplished with inclusive consequences if it is organized to make full participants of the members of all social classes, races, genders, and sexual identities. Sport does this to some degree, but for the most part sport reinforces the inequalities in society.

Notes

1. "CDC Museum COVID-19 Timeline," Centers for Disease Control and Prevention, https://www.cdc.gov/museum/timeline/covid19.html.
2. Laurel Wamsley, "March 11, 2020: The Day Everything Changed," *The Corona Virus Crisis*, National Public Radio, March 11, 2021, https://www.npr.org/2021/03/11/975663437/march-11-2020-the-day-everything-changed.
3. ESPN Staff, "Sudden Vanishing of Sports Due to Coronavirus Will Cost at Least $12 Billion, Analysis Says," ESPN, May 1, 2020, https://www.espn.com/espn/otl/story/_/id/29110487/sudden-vanishing-sports-due-coronavirus-cost-least-12-billion-analysis-says.
4. Lawrence Buchanan, Quoctrung Bui, and Jugal K. Patel, "Black Lives Matter May Be the Largest Movement in U.S. History," *New York Times*, July 3, 2020, https://www.nytimes.com/interactive/2020/07/03/us/george-floyd-protests-crowd-size.html.
5. Judy Battista, "NFL Commits $250 Million over 10-Year Period to Combat Systemic Racism," NFL, June 11, 2020, https://www.nfl.com/news/nfl-commits-250m-over-10-year-period-to-combat-systemic-racism.
6. Michael Weinreb, "One Year Later: How COVID-19 Drove and Accelerated Change in Sports—and Beyond," *Global Sport Matters*, April 9, 2021, https://globalsportmatters.com/culture/2021/04/09/one-year-later-covid-19-change-sports-beyond/.
7. Joanne Ostrow, "Patriotism Takes Over Airwaves on Super Sunday," *Denver Post*, February 4, 2002, 11D.
8. Dave Zirin, "Shut Up and Play: Patriotism, Jock Culture and Limits of Free Speech," *Edge of Sports*, May 5, 2011, https://www.edgeofsports.com/column/shut-up-and-play-patriotism-jock-culture-and-the-limits-of-free-/index.html.
9. Benjamin R. Barber, "Jihad vs. McWorld," *Atlantic Monthly* 269 (March 1992): 53–63; and Benjamin R. Barber, "Beyond Jihad vs. McWorld," *Nation*, January 21, 2002, 11–18.
10. Thomas Omestad, "Wrestling with Tehran: U.S., Iran Go to the Mat in a Replay of Ping-Pong Diplomacy," *US News & World Report*, March 2, 1998, 44.
11. For the political background of this event, see Ian Thomsen, "Political Football," *Sports Illustrated*, June 1, 1998, 66–69.
12. S. L. Price, "Diplomacy by Other Means," *Sports Illustrated*, May 10, 2004, 56.

Notes

13 Richard D. Mandell, *The Nazi Olympics* (New York: Macmillan, 1971).
14 Grant Wahl, "What a Ball Can Do," *Sports Illustrated*, August 6, 2007, 23; Stephen Farrell and Peter Gelling, "With Eyes Fixed on a Distant Soccer Field, Iraqis Leap at a Reason to Celebrate," *New York Times*, July 30, 2007, www.nytimes.com/2007/07/30/world/middleeast/30iraq.html?_r=1&oref=slogin&ref.
15 Steve Wulf, "Running on Empty: Cuba Maintains a Rich Sports Tradition Despite Shortages of Everything but Pride," *Sports Illustrated*, July 29, 1991, 60–70.
16 Shaffer Grubb and Michelle Gilcrist, "Which Countries Win the Medals," *San Diego Union*, August 5, 2012, D9.
17 "Rugby over Race," *Sports Illustrated*, March 30, 1992, 10.
18 Charles P. Korr, "Mandela Used Sport's Power," *USA Today*, December 6, 2013, 12c. See also, Gerald Imray, "Mandela Changed Everything with a Jersey," Associated Press, December 6, 2013.
19 E. M. Swift, "Bok to the Future," *Sports Illustrated*, July 3, 1995, 33. See also John Carlin, *Nelson Mandela and the Game That Made a Nation* (New York: Penguin, 2009).
20 Michael Bamberger, "Driving Force," *Sports Illustrated*, July 26, 2010, 32–34.
21 Grant Wahl, "The *New* Face of a Nation," *Sports Illustrated*, April 12, 2011, 68.
22 Phillip Goodhart and Christopher Chataway, *War Without Weapons* (London: Allen, 1968), 3.
23 Dave Zirin, "No Justice, No Play? Gaza Anger Overwhelms Hoop Contest," *Edge of Sports*, January 8, 2009, https://www.edgeofsports.com/column/no-justice-no-play-gaza-anger-overwhelms-hoops-contest/index.html.
24 Dave Zirin, "Politics on the Pitch: When Gaza and Sports Collide," *Edge of Sports*, January 23, 2009, https://www.edgeofsports.com/column/politics-on-the-pitch-when-gaza-and-sports-collide/index.html.
25 Dave Zirin, "Killing Hope: Why Israel Targets Sports in Gaza," *Edge of Sports*, November 19, 2012, https://www.edgeofsports.com/column/killing-hope-why-israel-targets-sports-in-gaza/index.html.
26 Choe Sang-Hun, "South Korea Rejects Sharing Winter Olympics with Japan," *New York Times*, December 12, 2014, http://www.nytimes.com/2014/12-13/world/asia/south-korea-rejects-sharing-winter-olympics-with-japan.
27 Renata Brito and Stephen Wade, "AP Analysis: Rio de Janeiro Olympics Cost $13.1 Billion," AP News, June 14, 2017, https://apnews.com/general-news-d1662ddb3bae4d2984ca4ab65012be78.
28 Bruce Douglas, "Brazil Officials Evict Families from Home ahead of 2016 Olympic Games," *Guardian*, October 28, 2015, https://www.theguardian.com/world/2015/oct/28/brazil-officials-evicting-families-2016-olympic-games.
29 Leslie Marin, "'It's Been Getting Worse': Fans React to Apparent Increase in Fighting at SoFi Stadium," KCAL News, October 18, 2023. See also Alex Prewitt, "Is the NFL Ready for All Its Rowdy Friends?," *Sports Illustrated*, September 10, 2021.
30 Austin Murphy, "All Together at Toomer's Corner," *Sports Illustrated*, February 28, 2011, 15. See also Mike Lopresti, "Tree Mugger Further Poisons Sport," *USA Today*, February 18, 2011, 5C.

31 Brendan Dwyer, "Divided Loyalty? An Analysis of Fantasy Football Involvement and Fan Loyalty to Individual National Football League (NFL) Teams," *Journal of Sport Management* 25 (2011): 445–57. See also, Mike Tierney, "From One Man's Fantasy, a Real Addiction," *New York Times*, December 17, 2014, B10–B11.

32 Frank Deford, "Seasons of Discontent," *Newsweek*, December 29, 1997–January 5, 1998, 74.

33 D. Stanley Eitzen, "The Sociology of Amateur Sport: An Overview," *International Review for the Sociology of Sport* 24, no. 2 (1989): 95–105.

34 Michael Oriard, "Chronicle of a (Football) Death Foretold: The Imminent Demise of a National Pastime?," *International History of Sport* 31, no. 1–2 (2014): 120–33, DOI: 10.1080/09523367.2013.842557.

35 Charlotte Gibson, "Who's Highest Paid in Your State?," ESPN, n.d., https://www.espn.com/espn/feature/story/_/id/28261213/dabo-swinney-ed-orgeron-highest-paid-state-employees.

36 "Project Play: State of Play 2022," Aspen Institute, https://projectplay.org/state-of-play-2022/costs-to-play-trends.

37 Christina Gough, "Fan Cost Index of Professional Sports League in the United States as of 2022," https://www.statista.com/statistics/1318050/fan-cost-index-sports-leagues/.

38 "Fan Cost Index of Professional Sports Leagues in the United States as of 2023," Statista, https://www.statista.com/statistics/1318050/fan-cost-index-sports-leagues/.

39 Nathan Meyersohn, "Why Buying Tickets to a Game Is So Unaffordable," CNN, February 4, 2024, https://www.cnn.com/2024/02/04/business/its-not-just-the-super-bowl-going-to-a-game-is-becoming-unaffordable/index.html.

40 John Underwood, "From Baseball and Apple Pie, to Greed and Sky Boxes," *New York Times*, October 31, 1993, 22.

41 Alana Semuels, "The U.S. Is Increasingly Diverse, So Why Is Segregation Getting Worse?," *Time Magazine*, June 21, 2021, https://time.com/6074243/segregation-america-increasing/.

42 Sequoia Carrillo and Pooja Salhotra, "The U.S. Student Population Is More Diverse, but Schools Are Still Highly Segregated," *Morning Edition*, National Public Radio, July 14, 2022, https://www.npr.org/2022/07/14/1111060299/school-segregation-report.

43 Char Adams and Nigel Chiwaya, "Map: See Which States Have Introduced or Passed Anti-DEI Bills," *NBC News*, March 2, 2024, https://www.nbcnews.com/data-graphics/anti-dei-bills-states-republican-lawmakers-map-rcna140796.

44 J. McKee McClendon and D. Stanley Eitzen, "Interracial Contact on Collegiate Basketball Teams: A Test of Sherif's Theory of Super-Ordinate Goals," *Social Science Quarterly* 55 (March 1975): 926–38.

45 "The Most Popular All-Time Sports Personalities," YouGov US, https://today.yougov.com/ratings/sports/popularity/all-time-sports-personalities/all.

46 G. Marquez-Velarde, R. Grashow, C. Glass, A. M. Blaschke, G. Gillette, H. A. Taylor, and A. J. Whittington, "The Paradox of Integration: Racial Composition of NFL Positions from 1960 to 2020," *Sociology of Race and Ethnicity* 9, no. 4 (2023): 451–69, https://doi.org/10.1177/23326492231182597.

Notes

47 Jonathon Howe, "How Black Male Athletes Deal with Anti-Black Stereotypes on Campus," *The Conversation*, January 31, 2024, https://theconversation.com/how-black-male-college-athletes-deal-with-anti-black-stereotypes-on-campus-220121.

48 See D. Stanley Eitzen, Maxine Baca Zinn, and Kelly Eitzen Smith, *Social Problems*, 14th ed. (London: Pearson, 2021), especially chap. 9.

49 E. J. Staurowsky, C. L. Flowers, E. Busuvis, L. Darvin, and N. Welch, *50 Years of Title IX: We're Not Done Yet*, Women's Sports Foundation, 2022, https://www.womenssportsfoundation.org/wp-content/uploads/2022/05/Title-IX-at-50-Report-FINALC-v2-.pdf.

50 Rachel Axon and Lindsay Schnell, "Title IX: Falling Short at 50: 50 Years after Title IX Has Passed, Most Top Colleges Deprive Female Athletes of Equal Opportunities," *USA Today*, June 3, 2022, https://www.usatoday.com/in-depth/news/investigations/2022/06/03/title-ix-failures-50-years-colleges-women-lack-representation/9664260002/.

51 Kenny Jacoby, Rachel Axon, Lindsay Schnell, and Steve Berkowitz, "Title IX: Falling Short at 50. Female Athletes Stiffed on Scholarships at Some of the Biggest Colleges in the Country," *USA Today*, December 15, 2022, https://www.usatoday.com/in-depth/news/investigations/2022/05/26/title-ix-falling-short-50-exposes-how-colleges-still-fail-women/9722521002/.

52 Amanda Christovich, "The Growing Gender Disparity in Power 5 Coaching Salaries," *Front Office Sports*, February 3, 2023, https://frontofficesports.com/the-growing-gender-disparity-in-power-5-coaching-salaries/.

53 Andrew R. Flores and Kerith J. Conron, "Adult LGBT Population in the United States," Williams Institute, December 2023, https://williamsinstitute.law.ucla.edu/publications/adult-lgbt-pop-us/.

54 Annette Choi, "Record Number of Anti-LGBTQ Bills Were Introduced in 2023," CNN, January 22, 2024, https://www.cnn.com/politics/anti-lgbtq-plus-state-bill-rights-dg/index.html.

55 Jason Collins, "Why NBA Center Jason Collins Is Coming Out Now," *Sports Illustrated*, May 6, 2013. See also, Dave Zirin, "Knocking Out Homophobia," *Progressive* (December 2012/January 2013): 66.

56 John Amaechi, *Man in the Middle* (New York: ESPN Books, 2007).

57 Amanda Terkel, "Derrick Gordon Comes Out as Gay," *Huffington Post*, April 9, 2014, http://www.huffingtonpost.com/2014/04/9/derrick-gordon-gay-umass-player/.

58 Grant Gordon, "Raiders DL Carl Nassib Becomes the First Active NFL Player to Come Out as Gay," NFL, June 21, 2021, https://www.nfl.com/news/raiders-dl-carl-nassib-becomes-first-active-nfl-player-to-come-out-as-gay.

59 Katie Barnes, *Fair Play: How Sports Shape the Gender Debates* (New York: St. Martin's, 2023).

60 Paul Myerberg, "Senator Seeks Answers in Pay-for-Salute at Games," *USA Today*, May 12, 2015, 3C.

61 Our thanks to Mike Messner, who made these points in his review of an earlier edition of this book.

3

SPORTS INCLUDES, SPORTS EXCLUDES: SEX/GENDER IN SPORTS

Historically, girls and women's sports participation in the United States has been characterized by progress toward gender equality alongside continued discrimination, barriers to participation, and inequality.[1] Researchers and women's sports advocates credit Title IX,[2] along with other civil rights laws, for the dramatic increase in participatory sporting opportunities for girls and women in the United States. The influx of girls and women in sports contributed not only to changes in the way our culture thinks about gender and sport, but also in the expectations we have for men and women. Despite the progress made in terms of the increased number of girls and women playing organized sports, participants continue to encounter gender-based forms of discrimination. Sociologists Michael Messner and Cheryl Cooky (second author of this book) have referred to this as the "unevenness of social change." We often hear an understanding of progress in women's sports from students, family members, parents, or journalists in comments such as, "Women weren't allowed to play sports before Title IX," or "There's no professional football league for women," or "Women only played football in the lingerie league."[3] Messner and Cooky rightly point out that progress in women's sports has not (and does not) occur in a linear manner. In other words, progress in some areas (e.g., opportunities, participation) does not always correspond to progress in others (e.g., access, resources, compensation, promotion, media coverage). Indeed, the inequalities that girls and women faced fifty years ago, or even one hundred years ago, continue today. Importantly, not all girls and women, and in particular those individuals who do not conform to the binary gender structure of sports, have benefitted equally from Title IX. As we discuss in subsequent chapters, gender intersects with other social locations, such as race and ethnicity, social class, and sexuality, among others. An intersectional approach to understanding gender discrimination is essential. In fact, one of the criticisms of Title IX as a law is that it only addresses one dimension of identity and thus one dimension of how discrimination operates. As such, Title IX cannot account for the ways in which gender discrimination intersects with other forms of discrimination such as racial discrimination or discrimination based on sexual identity.

This chapter focuses on how sport includes and how sport excludes participants on the basis of sex/gender. Sport is one of the remaining institutions in the United States that segregates individuals based on sex/gender. This sex segregation is legally enforced (through Title IX and other forms of legislation and policy) and culturally accepted. Most people consider it "common sense" that there are separate leagues, teams, and opportunities for boys and girls, and men and women. As such, sex/gender becomes a central organizing principle in sport.

Title IX, Participation, and Opportunity

The year 2022 marked the fiftieth anniversary of Title IX, a significant moment in the history of women's sports in the United States. Title IX of the Education Amendments of 1972 states: *No person in the United States shall, on the basis of sex, be excluded from participation in, be denied the benefits of, or be subjected to discrimination under any education program or activity receiving Federal financial assistance.* Title IX fundamentally changed the landscape of education in the United States by prohibiting sex-based discrimination, which opened opportunities for women to enter historically male-dominated professions such as medicine and law. Although not explicitly stated in the legislation, Title IX also opened opportunities for girls and women in athletics. Prior to 1972, boys and men received the overwhelming majority of sports opportunities. According to data from the National Federation of State High School Associations,[4] in 1971–1972, over 3.6 million boys participated in high school varsity sports, compared to only 294,015 girls. By 2018–2019, the number of girls participating had risen to 3.4 million. Boys' participation rates similarly increased during the same time frame, with over 4.5 million boys participating in 2018–2019. This trend has been identified as the "gender gap" in high school varsity sports participation. This gender gap indicates that boys' and men's opportunities to participate in sports have correspondingly increased alongside girls' and women's opportunities. Women's sports advocates note this is an important data point to counter the myth that Title IX has taken sports opportunities away from boys.

Similar trends are observed in National Collegiate Athletic Association (NCAA) varsity sports participation.[5] According to the Women's Sports Foundation,[6] in 1971–1972 there were 29,977 women competing on teams sponsored by NCAA institutions compared to 215,486 in 2020–2021. The percentage of women college athletes had risen from 15 percent in 1972 to 44 percent during the 2020–2021 academic year. Despite the increased sports participation of girls and women since Title IX's passage, according to the US Department of Education only 8.6 percent of NCAA Division I institutions offered athletic opportunities relative to their enrolment. Moreover, 87 percent of all three NCAA divisions offered disproportionately higher rates of athletic opportunities to male athletes relative to their enrolment.[7] These numbers indicate most NCAA institutions are not in compliance with Title IX, specifically as determined by the "proportionality test."

To assess whether its athletic program is in compliance with Title IX, an institution can demonstrate that the athletic opportunities offered satisfy one of the following of the three-part test: part 1, substantial proportionality; part 2, history and continued practice of expanding opportunities; and part 3, accommodation of interests and abilities. The proportionality part of the compliance test can be met by an institution if it demonstrates the distribution of its athletic opportunities to be proportional to the overall student enrolment. In other words, an institution whose overall student body is 60 percent male and 40 percent female could be in compliance if 60 percent of the athletic opportunities went to men's athletics and 40 percent went to women's athletics. Contrary to popular myths, Title IX does not dictate that boys and girls, men and women receive equal (i.e., 50 percent–50 percent) athletic opportunities.

When institutions are asked to demonstrate compliance most use the proportionality test, yet there are few universities that achieve that threshold. A *USA Today* investigative report found that of the 127 public and private schools in the Football Bowl Subdivision (FBS), 87 percent were not offering athletic opportunities to women proportionate to their enrolment in the 2020–2021 academic year. According to the report, "110 FBS schools would need to add a total of 11,501 female roster spots to close the participation gap. That's an average of 104 (spots) per school—roughly the size of a football team and enough to add three or four women's teams each."[8]

If an institution does not meet compliance based on the proportionality test, they may demonstrate compliance by meeting one of the other two remaining tests. Part 2 of the three-part test is "history and continuing practice of program expansion." To meet compliance based on this test an institution must demonstrate that over a period of time the institution has been adding athletic programs and opportunities for girl/women athletes. Given Title IX was passed fifty years ago, women's sports advocates argue institutions had sufficient time to develop programs and opportunities for women. As stated in a Women's Sports Foundation report on Title IX at fifty,

> As we enter the next half century of Title IX, many of those initial start-up considerations are no longer valid. Schools that have been slow off the mark in providing female athletes equal access to athletic opportunities can no longer claim that they did not have time to plan or to devise a way to accommodate female athletes. A record of long-term non-compliance and/or serial non-compliance is inherently unreasonable, and school administrators should take note of this.[9]

An institution failing to meet part 2 can turn to the third part of compliance. Part 3 "full and effective accommodation of interests and abilities" provides institutions the option to demonstrate compliance by illustrating how the athletic opportunities provided meet the interests and abilities of the female student population. Under this test, institutions would assess participation in club and intramural sports, interest expressed by the female student population in participating in a given sport, the geographic location of the school (e.g., identifying a fast-growing sport in the geographic area of the school and subsequently adding a program in that sport), and sports offerings among other institutions in a conference/district. According to a *USA Today* investigative report on Title IX, the University of Kentucky had been under review and found to be out of compliance with Title IX for not offering women enough athletic opportunities. Moreover, surveys of women students at the University of Kentucky indicated interest in participating in sports like lacrosse, beach volleyball, and equestrian competitions, yet the university had not added any of those sports. Instead, in 2021 the University added "stunt" (competitive cheerleading) to their sports offerings, despite nearly twice as many students indicating interest in equestrian activities, which represented nearly four times as many students needed to field the average

NCAA team. Even after adding stunt, Kentucky was among the top 20 percent of FBS schools with a participation gap.

At the high school level, it is difficult to determine on a systematic basis the extent to which schools are in compliance with Title IX. College sports are mandated by the Equity in Athletics Disclosure Act (EADA) to make gender equity information about athletics programs available. Universities must make available on an annual basis information on participation by gender, distribution of athletic scholarships awarded, recruitment expenses, coaching salaries, revenues, and operating expenses for men's and women's sports. A similar mandate or law does not exist for high school sports,[10] contributing to the lack of data and the ability to determine if a high school is in compliance with Title IX. Based on what data are available, there are indicators that many high schools are not in compliance. For example, the Women's Sports Foundation's analysis of National Federation of State High School Associations participation data[11] found that in 2018–2019, high school "girls in every state were provided proportionately less access to athletic participation opportunities compared to boys relative to enrolment." The analysis also revealed high school girls received 42 percent of athletic opportunities despite representing 48.5 percent of the overall high school student population. To address the proportionality gap, high schools would need to add 1.1 million more sports opportunities for high school girls.

In addition to a lack of mandated reporting, the data collected by the Department of Education's Office of Civil Rights are incomplete and often do not correspond with data compiled by school districts.[12] According to investigative reporting by the Shirley Povich Center for Sports Journalism and Howard Center for Investigative Journalism at the University of Maryland Philip Merrill College of Journalism, in the state of Maryland approximately 40 percent of districts' federal data indicate that when compared to their proportion of enrolment, girls outnumber boys in sports. Yet, examining the school's own data, all the districts had fewer opportunities for girl athletes. The discrepancy was attributed to the Office of Civil Rights' (OCR) own definition of sports participation, which defines participation as that which occurs in single-sex sports. Although many high school sports are single-sexed, a high school boys football team with one girl player would be considered a "mixed" sport, and therefore the participants on the team, mostly boys, would not be included in the school's reporting to the OCR. This leads to overestimates on the number of participation opportunities for girls. Although national data on high school compliance are limited, sufficient indicators in mainstream news sources, women's sports advocacy reports, and small-scale research studies indicate widespread issues with compliance among high school athletics programs.

There are several major challenges to ensuring compliance of Title IX and thus to achieving gender parity in sports. First, there is little to no meaningful oversight or enforcement of Title IX.[13] Should a school or college not be in compliance, the onus is on individual students to file a complaint with the Office of Civil Rights. This is often a lengthy and arduous process with complaints not resolved until well after the students have graduated. According to an investigation into Title IX by *USA Today*, "schools accused of violating Title IX—which bans sex discrimination across all aspects of education, including athletics and sexual harassment— have little to fear from the Office for Civil Rights; they can openly defy the agency, withhold records and fail to heed agreements with impunity."[14] The report notes even when institutions are found to be in violation of the law, sanctions are not issued. Rather the goal is to work with the institution to comply with the law. The only sanction possible under the law is removal of federal funding, a sanction so extreme the Office of Civil Rights has never used it. According to the *USA Today* investigation, "dozens of schools openly skirt the law, continuing to violate Title IX by short-changing female athletes of playing opportunities and scholarships."[15] Second, there is an overall lack of education and awareness of Title IX. This lack of awareness plagues universities and schools, athletic departments, coaches, and parents/caregivers. Specifically, there is a lack of clarity and consistency in the roles, responsibilities, and expectations about who is responsible for tracking participation data and to whom to report that data.[16] Third, Title IX only addresses discrimination based on sex. The law does not take into account the ways in which sex discrimination intersects with other forms of identity-based discrimination; for example, how sex discrimination varies by race, ethnicity, sexual orientation, socioeconomic status, gender identity, disability, immigration status, or the various permutations of these intersecting identities.[17] Girls and women who are white, identify as heterosexual and cisgender, are able-bodied, and are from affluent, suburban communities have benefitted most from Title IX.[18] For example, girls from schools in predominantly minoritized communities had fewer opportunities to participate in sports compared with girls from schools in predominantly white communities. At the collegiate level, Black women tend to be racially clustered into two sports—track and field and basketball. Girls with disabilities have fewer opportunities to participate in adapted sports/parasports than boys with disabilities or girls without disabilities. Girls from low-income or underserved communities also have fewer opportunities to participate. As noted in the Women's Sports Foundation report on Title IX at fifty:

> Research over many years confirms that the access girls and women have to sport opportunity is directly connected to their environment. Community recreational resources and neighborhood population size affect how often girls and women participate in physical activity and sports. Whether a school offers athletic opportunities to females in compliance with Title IX requirements is another contributing factor. If the opportunity is not there, participation does not happen.[19]

Barriers to Girls' and Women's Sports

Despite the increases in athletic opportunities in high school, college, and professional sports, there are significant barriers to girls' and women's participation. The ways in which barriers manifest and impact girls and women varies based on social identities and social locations (e.g., gender, race, sexual orientation, etc.). This chapter offers an overview of the barriers girls and women encounter in their sports participation in the United States. Although girls and women from other countries certainly face similar types of barriers and constraints, there may be important cultural, economic, and social dimensions that differentially shape those barriers and constraints.

Structural Barriers

Structural barriers to girls and women's participation in sports include but are not limited to unequal distribution of resources between girls'/women's and boys'/men's sports, differences in quality and quantity of equipment and uniforms, and overall economic support for sports participation. To comply with Title IX, athletics departments must provide equitable treatment of athletes. Such treatment includes the following: equipment, uniforms, and supplies; access to tutoring and academic support; medical training facilities and staff; support services; scheduling of games and practice times; assigned coaches; publicity; travel and daily per diem allowances; locker rooms, practice, and competitive facilities; and recruitment. Overall, evidence indicates universities devote fewer scholarship funds to women athletes, allocate fewer resources to women's sports, and manipulate rosters to appear to offer more opportunities to women than actually exist.[20] To be in compliance with Title IX, the Department of Education policy stipulates the distribution of athletic scholarships must be within plus or minus one percentage point of the distribution of athletes by gender.[21] In other words, if 45 percent of a university's athletes are women, the scholarship dollars distributed to women athletes should be between 44 and 46 percent of the total. Despite the policy, of the 107 Football Bowl Subdivision schools examined, only 32 met that criteria. According to *USA Today*'s analysis, "the schools that underfunded women would have needed to give them $23.7 million more in athletic scholarships in 2020–2021 alone to comply with the law—nearly a half-million per school."[22] In 2019–2020 only 30 percent of the overall recruiting dollars went to female athletes and male athletes received $252 million more in athletic scholarships.[23]

In addition to participation opportunities, scholarships, and other forms of funding, Title IX also applies to how high schools and universities publicize and promote their own athletic programs. Publicity covered under Title IX includes social media, school news coverage, marquee announcements, pictures on the school athletics website, and use of the cheerleaders and band. Unfortunately, there are very few studies that examine how athletic departments distribute resources to promote men's and women's collegiate sports programs, and the research at the high school level (on this topic among others) is nearly nonexistent. One of the few analyses of promotion of high school sports was conducted by the Povich-Howard Centers.[24] The findings indicate that at many high schools, gender inequities in promotion can be observed in terms of fewer social media posts on girls' sports and the lack of cheerleaders and the school band performing at girls' sporting events. The research that does exist on college athletics indicates disparities in the marketing and promotion of women's sports, specifically in terms of the quantity and quality of sports information and marketing personnel. Sports information and marketing roles continue to be male-dominated, and men's sports are assigned more resources, including personnel.

There are also indicators that publicity resources and investment in promotion is higher for men's sports and male athletes. There are disparities in quality and quantity of promotional devices such as social media content, campus newspapers, athletic department media guides, and other promotional materials and marketing efforts. As such, it seems that "female athletes continue to be underserved in terms of promotional efforts and that patterns within athletic departments appear to align with the larger pattern of limited coverage of women's sports."[25] Although Title IX does not apply to the editorial decisions of media outlets to broadcast and cover women's sports, the vast differences in the quantity and quality of coverage of women's sports (whether broadcast or news coverage, or social media content) indicates an ecosystem that creates and sustains interest and audiences for men's sports,[26] which subsequently translates into disparities in resources and opportunities for women's sports.

This ecosystem does not exist separate from the governing body of most collegiate sports in the United States: the NCAA. For example, during the 2021 NCAA Final Four basketball tournament, Sedona Prince, who played for the University of Oregon, posted several videos on social media depicting the stark inequality between the expansive weight room for the men in contrast to the small stack of hand-held weights in the corner of a small room available for the women.[27] Other inequities were noted, including food (prepackaged meals vs. full buffets), the differences in quality of gift or "swag" bags, et cetera. Prince's posts went viral and generated national news media coverage, which subsequently precipitated an external investigation of the NCAA. The external investigation into gender inequities in the NCAA revealed that the contract for the television rights fees for the NCAA Division I men's basketball tournament was negotiated as a single property with CBS Sports and Turner Network and worth $1 billion in revenue a year.[28] The contract for the television rights fees for NCAA Division I

Barriers to Girls' and Women's Sports

women's tournament was not a single property, and instead was bundled with twenty-nine other NCAA championships, worth $34 million per year. The external report assessed the value of the women's basketball tournament and determined it was undervalued based on this bundling of championships. In fact, the report estimated its worth at $84–$112 million if the NCAA were to negotiate it as a single property as it does with the men's tournament. According to the report, "The NCAA's broadcast agreements, corporate sponsorship contracts, distribution of revenue, organizational structure, and culture all prioritize Division I men's basketball over everything else in ways that create, normalize, and perpetuate gender inequities."[29]

The NCAA is not subject to Title IX from a legal perspective; however, given its own role in overseeing compliance in athletics, including gender equality, expectations for the NCAA to treat its women athletes and their athletic programs equitably to its men's is reasonable. Doing so would align with its mission as the governing body of collegiate sports in the United States. If the NCAA is perpetuating gender inequalities in how it negotiates media rights deals, this raises concerns regarding how member institutions might value the importance of gender equality and Title IX compliance in their own athletic programs.

The 2023 NCAA basketball tournament reflected some of the changes the NCAA has implemented to address the disparities identified in the external gender equity assessment. For example, the NCAA reduced the number of host cities for the tournament, which may have contributed to the 35 percent increase in attendance over the previous year as it reduced the number of cities by which fans were dispersed.[30] Other changes included expanding the number of teams in the women's tournament from sixty-four to sixty-eight, mirroring the men's tournament. The women's tournament is now able to use the "March Madness" label and logo in marketing and promotions. Prior to the external report, "March Madness" was the sole trademark for the men's tournament. The spending gap between the tournaments of $35 million was narrowed to only several million.[31]

The improvements and increased investment in marketing and promotion of the women's basketball tournament may have expanded the growing audience and increased viewership of women's basketball. Historically, the television audience for NCAA women's basketball is among its highest. The 2022–2023 season saw a 54 percent increase of viewers tuning into regular-season NCAA women's basketball. The 2023 tournament was the first time the championship game was televised on a major network, ABC. Previously, the championship games were broadcast on the cable network ESPN. Viewership for the NCAA championship was 9.9 million viewers, nearly double the viewership of the previous year and more than its previous record of 5.7 million for the 2002 tournament.[32] The record-breaking viewers continued through the 2023–2024 season, as more people tuned in to watch the women's NCAA basketball tournament than the men's (see chapter 7).

Cultural Barriers

In the United States, modern sports emerged from the late nineteenth to the early twentieth century, a time characterized by massive social changes to key structures, including the economy, work, family, and education, among others. These changes were precipitated by urbanization and industrialization, coupled with shifting gendered power relations.[33] There was also a decline in the centrality of physical prowess in the labor market and military. Despite these changes, the societal investment in gender differences between men and women persisted. As such, spectator sports, which symbolically illustrated the strength, virility, dominance, and power of the male body, rose in prominence to culturally reassert and reaffirm "natural" gender differences and men's dominance over women. Throughout the twentieth century, "sport was clearly one of the less contested, core institutions in which heterosexual men's embodied power was enabled and celebrated in ways that supported and naturalized patriarchal beliefs in male superiority and female inferiority and dependence."[34]

Understanding the historical development of sports in the United States provides a necessary context to understanding contemporary gendered dynamics, and specifically gender equality in sports. The linkage between cultural definitions of masculinity with those of sport sheds light into gender equality today. Cultural masculinity as it is embodied and represented in sports contexts often operates to explain, uphold, justify, and legitimate the differential treatment of girls and women. Women's participation in an institution that historically has been organized to establish, reaffirm, and reproduce hegemonic masculinity has the potential to challenge or disrupt dominant cultural definitions of femininity that link women with characteristics and qualities viewed as antithetical to sporting practices, such as cooperation, physical frailty, submission, and so on.[35] Feminist sports sociologists have argued, however, that much of the potential for such challenges or disruptions to lead to meaningful changes in gendered norms, meanings, expectations, or social institutions will be contained to primarily marginalized sporting spaces.[36] This is due to the way sports in the United States (and in many other countries) has been and continues to be a cultural site wherein hegemonic masculinity is displayed and celebrated, and is an institution dominated and controlled by men.

Political Barriers

Politics in the United States (and elsewhere) create new barriers or exacerbate existing ones to access opportunity in sports. According to National Public Radio (NPR), in 2021 and 2022 there were over three hundred bills introduced in state legislatures targeting LGBTQ+ populations; 86 percent focused specifically on trans youth.[37] These bills seek to prevent access to gender-affirming health

Barriers to Girls' and Women's Sports

care, require students to use the bathroom of the sex assigned at birth, and/or prohibit trans girls and transwomen from participating in girls and women's sports. Bills restricting participation in girls and women's sports to athletes who were identified as female at birth often cite the need to protect girls and/or to ensure a level playing field. Conversely, some critics cite a report from the Associated Press, which found that sponsors of these bills were unable to cite a single instance in their state or region where trans participation in sports was a problem.[38]

According to a Women's Sports Foundation report, assuming trans girls and transwomen will have an advantage over cisgender girls is problematic. First, it assumes generalized, categorical differences between boys and girls and conflates cisgender boys with trans girls. While there may be some boys who are stronger, taller, and faster than some girls, not all boys are stronger, taller, or faster than all girls. As the Women's Sports Foundation report notes, "When we tell cisgender girls that they are categorically disadvantaged relative to transgender girls, we unnecessarily reinforce sexist stereotypes that lead to girls' self-perception as athletically inferior, which in turn limits their athletic development."[39] A second problem with this assumption is that it ignores or discounts the other forms of diverse experiences or differences in athletic abilities among girls. Girls from more affluent communities may reasonably have more access to skill development programs than girls from underserved communities. This may result in competitive advantages for those girls. The Women's Sports Foundation report also notes the differences in athletic ability by age among girls. Girls in high school sports, for example, often compete with and against girls who are much older (seniors vs. freshman). This may also result in differences in athletic abilities resulting in competitive advantages. Rather than single out trans girls, the Women's Sports Foundation report suggests any concerns about safety or fairness can be addressed with gender-neutral policies that apply to all girls' athletic competitive events.

In addition to anti-trans bills prohibiting sports participation, the Supreme Court's decision to overturn of *Roe v. Wade*, which ended the constitutional right to abortion, serves as a barrier to access opportunities for women's sports participation. In September 2021, over five hundred women athletes filed an amicus (friend of the court) brief in support of *Roe v. Wade*.[40] The athletes included members of the Women's National Basketball Players Association, the National Women's Soccer League Players Association, as well as Olympic, Paralympic, and collegiate athletes. According to the Brief,

> All of the Amici have exercised, relied on the availability of, or support the constitutional right to abortion care in order to meet the demands of their sport and unleash their athletic potential. Amici are united in their deeply-held belief that women's athletics could not have reached its current level

of participation and success without the constitutional rights recognized in *Roe v. Wade*, 410 U.S. 113 (1973) and *Planned Parenthood of Southeastern Pennsylvania v. Casey*, 505 U.S. 833 (1992).[41]

Among other arguments, the Brief noted that the ability for athletes to control whether and when to get pregnant is "critical" for athletes, given the "limited window of time" athletes have to compete. As argued in the Brief,

> If forced to carry pregnancies to term, many women would have no choice but to sacrifice playing their sport—a sacrifice not required of their male counterparts, despite their equal role in engendering a pregnancy.[42]

Policy Barriers

Sports governing bodies write, implement, and enforce policies that serve as a barrier to participation in women's sports. For example, eligibility criteria to participate in women's events has historically relied on contested assumptions, including sex as a binary category, sports as a level playing field, and athletes who do not classify as "women" according to these policies as having an unfair advantage.[43] Critics of eligibility criteria policies for women's competitions note athletes from the Global South are more often subject to policies, given that the policies are informed and shaped by histories of colonialism and scientific racism.[44]

Media Coverage of Women's Sports

Media plays an important role in women's sports, in terms of promoting and building audiences for women's sports events, yet research on sports media consistently finds content and coverage centers primarily on men's sports, while ignoring or minimizing women's events and women athletes. The past four decades of sports media studies scholarship has found a lack of coverage of women's sports, particularly in legacy sports media.[45] When women athletes and women's sports are featured, historically they have been trivialized, marginalized, or objectified in sports media coverage. The implication of the hundreds of studies conducted on gender and sport media is that representation is an important indicator of not only gender equality (or inequality) in media coverage itself, but an indicator of gender in/equality in the larger sports context as well as in wider society.[46]

Sociologist Michael Messner and his colleagues (including the second author of this book, Cheryl) conducted a longitudinal study examining the quality and

Media Coverage of Women's Sports

quantity of coverage of men's and women's sports on local and national televised news and highlight shows.[47] The study found that over the thirty-year period studied (1989–2019), the coverage of women's sports did not exceed percentage double digits.[48] Moreover, the percentage of coverage of women's sports did not change from 1989 to 2019, with 5 percent of the coverage devoted to women's sports. The study also captured shifts in the media landscape (see chapter 7), and in the 2019 iteration, the researchers added an analysis of online and social media content. They found similar patterns in coverage on those platforms as well, with women's sports garnering just 5.4 percent of coverage online and 4.2 percent of coverage on Twitter.

Although the study found a continued dearth of coverage of women's sports, the ways in which women's sports were covered shifted over the thirty-year time frame. In 1989–1999 coverage of women's sports was characterized by humorous sexualization and trivialization of women and of women's sports. For example, in the coverage analyzed in the 1999 analysis, there were several lengthy stories on women's sports, including coverage of the 1999 US Women's World Cup Soccer win. The stories focused on a US player, Brandi Chastain, who removed her jersey after the match in a celebration of the team's win. Much of the coverage focused on the post-match celebration rather than the match itself, describing the moment as a "strip tease." In the 2004–2009 iterations of the study, there was a noted decline of overtly insulting framing of women and women athletes alongside an emergence of women and women athletes framed in stereotypical ways, as either mother, girlfriend, or wife. In the 2014–2019 iterations, there was almost no sexualization or trivialization of women and women athletes. The coverage of women's sports, however, was mostly dull and lackluster. The study noted that most of the women's stories were presented by commentators with far less verbal pop and excitement than had typically characterized stories on men's sports. Routinely delivered in a dull monotone, women's sports stories observed were usually presented as unexciting and uninspiring. The researchers referred to this type of coverage as *gender bland sexism*.[49]

A misperception is that sport media content reflects viewer fan interest and/or audience demand. The role sport media plays in building and sustaining audiences is often overlooked. Indeed, according to a survey conducted by Nielsen research, 84 percent of sports fans (over half of which were men) indicated interest in women's sports.[50] The perception that no one is interested in women's sports, and subsequently why the media does not cover or broadcast women's sports is not supported by the data. Social media may provide athletes with more agency and autonomy over their image and allow athletes more control over content,[51] yet engagement metrics may inadvertently produce similar imagery of women's athleticism as in the past.

Impact on Society of Girls' and Women's Sports Participation

Given the myriad benefits, which include improved health, social, psychological, academic, and career outcomes, investing in girls' and women's sports is critical for society as a whole. Research has found the following advantages of having opportunities for sports participation:

- Physical health: lower risk of obesity, lower blood pressure, higher levels of cardiovascular fitness, reduced risk of cardiovascular disease, reduced risk of breast cancer.
- Social/emotional well-being: improved psychological health, greater life satisfaction, stronger sense of belonging, improved self-esteem, reduced symptoms of anxiety, stress, and depression.
- Academic success: improved academic achievement, higher high school graduation rates, higher college attendance/retention, greater involvement in extracurricular activities, increased opportunities for leadership.

Sports also play a role in gender equality:[52]

- "Sport is one of the most powerful platforms for promoting gender equality and empowering women and girls, and sports coverage is very influential in shaping gender norms and stereotypes."

And a survey of female executives has linked sports to leadership skills:[53]

- 94 percent of women executives have a background in sports, over half at the university level.
- 80 percent of women Fortune 500 executives had played competitive sports.
- 74 percent of all the executives believed playing sports helps a woman progress faster.
- 61 percent of the women executives who responded believed playing sports contributed positively to their career success and advancement.

Conclusion

Since Title IX in the United States was passed fifty years ago there has been a dramatic increase in access and opportunities for girls and women in sports.

Conclusion

Yet, progress is not linear, and social change is often uneven and accompanied by stagnation or backlash. Indeed, as noted in the Women's Sports Foundation report, *50 Years of Title IX*, while there is much to celebrate in terms of the progress that has been made in advancing gender equality, there is still much work left to be done.

There are several emergent dynamics that signal shifts in the landscape of women's sports and potential to usher in further progress and change. Although Title IX specifically applies to educational institutions that receive federal funding in the United States, certainly the increased opportunities for girls and women to participate at the high school and college levels has translated to growth in opportunities to participate in professional leagues. Yet, similar to the disparities in high school and college sports noted previously, women athletes in the major American professional leagues (e.g., basketball, golf, tennis, soccer, and baseball/softball) earn significantly lower salaries than their male counterparts (see chapters 6 and 7). Taking into account revenues and collective bargaining agreements (CBAs) provides a more useful indicator of the pay gap.[54] Although leagues do not release specific revenue data, reports indicate the NBA generates over $8 billion USD in revenue. Conservative estimates place WNBA revenue at $60 million. Taking into account the collective bargaining agreements along with league revenues, a study found that the WNBA players were paid only 21 percent of league revenues whereas the CBA for the NBA guaranteed players 50 percent of league revenues. The analysis also took into account the different histories of the leagues. The NBA was formed in mid-1955–1956 while the WNBA was established in 1996. Some may speculate differences in revenue sharing to be based on where the leagues are in their historical development. Yet players in the early era of the NBA still earned 41.5 percent of league revenue, nearly double the 21 percent of what WNBA players earned in 2020, nearly twenty-five years after the league was formed. The analysis indicates, "clear evidence of a gendered hierarchy in sport."[55]

The US Women's National Soccer Team (USWNT) garnered national and international media attention in the mid- to late 2010s when they were the first athletes to file a wage discrimination suit against their employer, US Soccer, which is the governing body for soccer in the United States. According to the complaint, the USWNT was paid less than their male counterparts, despite having the same work requirements. While the specifics of the lawsuit are beyond the scope of this chapter, the US Women's National Soccer Team players reached a $24 million settlement with US Soccer in February of 2022.[56] US Soccer also agreed to pay the men and women at an equal rate moving forward. The agreement included $22 million for the twenty-eight players who filed the lawsuit and established a $2 million charitable fund for women's and girls' soccer, but it fell short of the $67 million they had asked for in their suit. US Soccer is the first federation to equalize FIFA World Cup prize money. The success of the USWNT in securing equal pay may influence other professional leagues and sports governing bodies to recognize the value of women athletes and compensate them accordingly.

At the collegiate level, changes in the next few years have the potential to open opportunities for women athletes and/or exacerbate existing forms of inequality. There have been dramatic shifts in collegiate athletics since 2021 when the NCAA's Name, Image and Likeness rule (NIL) was implemented (see chapter 8). NIL allows college athletes to be compensated for use of their name, image or likeness. Prior to the change, the NCAA rules on amateurism prohibited endorsements and compensation beyond that which was allowed under the NCAA's own policies. Scholarships, for example, were allowed as a form of compensation whereas athletes could not appear in advertisements, participate in promotional activities, sign autographs, run their own sports camps, or publish under their own names and be compensated. While the full implications of NIL have yet to be realized, initial evidence suggests gender disparities in NIL deals. According to data from H&R Block cited by the *Baltimore Sun*, only 23 percent of money generated from NIL deals goes to female athletes.[57]

There are a growing number of current and former women athletes advocating for and investing in women's sports, including equal pay advocacy discussed above, creating media platforms dedicated to women's sports (e.g., TOGETHXR), and investing in the business of women's sports (e.g., Sports Innovation Lab). There is also an increased recognition among industry leaders in the "business value" of women's sports. New and emerging sports news media platforms are devoted to covering women's sports such as *Just Women's Sports* and *The Gist*. There is also an increase in corporations addressing gender inequality in sports, for example in advertising campaigns and marketing/promotional events.[58] These efforts signal a shift among those in the sports industry to recognize the value of women's sports.[59]

The 2022 Women's Sports Foundation report, *50 Years of Title IX: We're Not Done Yet*, suggests the next fifty years will depend on the extent to which we invest in girls and women's sports and fully address the persisting forms of social inequality. The report offers targeted and detailed policy recommendations for stakeholders, for example, public policy makers, education administrators, sports governing bodies, coaches, students, parents, and researchers. Overall the Women's Sports Foundation recommends "stepping up enforcement of Title IX, increasing data transparency, providing specific policy guidance to enable the inclusion of transgender and nonbinary athletes, and addressing resource inequities with greater focus on those experienced by women of color, LGBTQ athletes, and athletes with disabilities." Readers are encouraged to access the report to learn more about targeted efforts based on their role and responsibility (e.g., policy maker, education administrator, athletic administrator, coach, athlete, parent, governing body administrator, researcher, etc.). These efforts will help ensure that in the next fifty years, full equality can be achieved for all girls and women athletes.

Notes

1. This chapter draws greatly on some of my other writing, including: C. Cooky and M. A. Messner, *No Slam Dunk: Gender, Sport and the Unevenness of Social Change* (New Brunswick, NJ: Rutgers University Press); Cheryl Cooky, "The Unevenness of Social Change in Women's Sports in the United States: Historical and Contemporary Perspectives," *Gatorade Sports Science Institute, Sports Science Exchange*, May 2023, https://www.gssiweb.org/en/sports-science-exchange/Article/the-unevenness-of-social-change-in-women-s-sports-in-the-united-states-historical-and-contemporary-perspectives.
2. In June 1972, President Nixon signed Title IX of the Education Amendments of 1972 into law. Title IX is a comprehensive federal law that has removed many barriers that once prevented people, on the basis of sex, from participating in educational opportunities and careers of their choice. It states that: No person in the United States shall, on the basis of sex, be excluded from participation in, be denied the benefits of, or be subjected to discrimination under any education program or activity receiving Federal financial assistance (Title IX Legal Manual, Department of Justice).
3. For a fascinating and illuminating discussion of the history of women's professional football leagues see: Britni (Frankie) De La Cretaz and Lyndsey D'Arcangelo, *Hail Mary: The Rise and Fall of the National Women's Football League* (New York: Bold Type Books, 2021).
4. "High School Participation Survey Archive," National Federation of State High School Associations, 2019, https://www.nfhs.org/ sports-resource-content/high-school-participation-survey- archive/.
5. *NCAA Sport Sponsorship and Participation Rates Report (1956–1957 through 2019–2020)*, 2020, National Collegiate Athletic Association, https://ncaaorg.s3.amazonaws.com/research/sportpart/2021RES_SportsSponsorshipParticipationRatesReport.pdf.
6. E. J. Staurowsky, C. L. Flowers, E. Busuvis, L. Darvin, and N. Welch, *50 Years of Title IX: We're Not Done Yet*, Women's Sports Foundation, 2022, https://www.womenssportsfoundation.org/articles_and_report/50-years-of-title-ix-were-not-done-yet/.
7. E. J. Staurowsky, N. Watanabe, J. Cooper, C. Cooky, N. Lough, A. Paule-Koba, J. Pharr, S. Williams, S. Cummings, K. Issokson-Silver, and M. Snyder, *Chasing Equity: The Triumphs, Challenges, and Opportunities in Sports for Girls and Women*, Women's Sports Foundation, 2020, https://www.womenssportsfoundation.org/articles_and_report/chasing-equity-the-triumphs-challenges-and-opportunities-in-sports-for-girls-and-women/.

8. R. Axon and L. Schnell, "50 Years after Title IX Passed, Most Top Colleges Deprive Female Athletes of Equal Opportunities," *USA Today*, December 15, 2022, https://www.usatoday.com/in-depth/news/investigations/2022/05/26/title-ix-falling-short-50-exposes-how-colleges-still-fail-women/9722521002/.
9. Staurowsky et al., *50 Years of Title IX*.
10. At the time of this writing, Senate Bill S. 3762 known as the "Fair Play for Women Act," had been introduced to the US Senate. One of the provisions of the bill would expand reporting requirements for K–12 athletics data to mirror the requirements for colleges, which would help identify gaps in opportunities and access in school-based sports.
11. Staurowsky et al., *Fifty Years of Title IX*.
12. K. Newhouse, "Federal Title IX Data on Sports Participation Is Unreliable," Povich Center and Howard Center, April 11, 2022, https://cnsmaryland.org/2022/04/11/title-ix-federal-sports-data/ (accessed June 6, 2023).
13. Staurowsky et al., *Fifty Years of Title IX*; R. Axon, "What Happens If a School Does Not Comply with Title IX? Not a Whole Lot," *USA Today*, December 22, 2022, https://www.usatoday.com/in-depth/news/investigations/2022/05/26/title-ix-falling-short-50-exposes-how-colleges-still-fail-women/9722521002/.
14. Axon, "What Happens If a School Does Not Comply?"
15. Axon.
16. Staurowsky et al., *Fifty Years of Title IX*.
17. D. Brake, *Getting in the Game: Title IX and the Women's Sports Revolution* (New York: New York University Press, 2010); Staurowsky et al., *Fifty Years of Title IX*.
18. D. Sabo and P. Veliz, *Go Out and Play: Youth Sports in America*, Women's Sports Foundation, 2008, https://www.womenssportsfoundation.org/articles_and_report/go-out-and-play/.
19. Staurowsky et al., *Fifty Years of Title IX*.
20. Axon, "What Happens If a School Does Not Comply?"; Staurowsky et al., *Fifty Years of Title IX*.
21. K. Jacoby, R. Axon, L. Schnell, and S. Berkowitz, "Female Athletes Stiffed on Scholarships at Some of the Biggest Colleges in the Country," *USA Today*, December 15, 2022, https://www.usatoday.com/in-depth/news/investigations/2022/05/26/title-ix-falling-short-50-exposes-how-colleges-still-fail-women/9722521002/.
22. Jacoby et al.
23. Staurowsky et al., *Fifty Years of Title IX*.
24. E. Riley, "Title IX Requires Girls to Get Equal Publicity. They Often Don't," Povich Center and Howard Center, April 11, 2022, https://cnsmaryland.org/2022/04/11/title-ix-publicity-pentucket-massachusetts/.
25. Staurowsky et al., *Fifty Years of Title IX*.
26. C. Cooky, L. D. Council, M. Mears, and M. A. Messner, "One and Done: The Long Eclipse of Women's Televised Sports, 1989–2019," *Communication & Sport* 9, no. 3 (2021): 347–71.

Notes

27 A. Nierenberg, "The Video That Changed the NCAA," *New York Times*, March 16, 2022, https://www.nytimes.com/2022/03/16/us/the-video-that-changed-the-ncaa.html.

28 Kaplan Hecker & Fink, LLP, "NCAA External Gender Equity Review," 2021, https://ncaagenderequityreview.com/.

29 Kaplan Hecker & Fink, LLP.

30 B. Witz, "As Women's Basketball Grows, Equity Is Trying to Catch Up," *New York Times*, March 29, 2023, https://www.nytimes.com/2023/03/29/sports/ncaabasketball/womens-basketball-equity.html.

31 Witz.

32 R. Tumin, "NCAA Women's Tournament Shatters Ratings Record in Final," *New York Times*, April 3, 2023, https://www.nytimes.com/2023/04/03/sports/ncaabasketball/lsu-iowa-womens-tournament-ratings-record.html.

33 S. Cahn, *Coming On Strong: Gender and Sexuality in Twentieth-Century Women's Sport* (New York: Free Press, 1994); C. Cooky, "Sport, Femininities, and Heteronormativity," in *Oxford Handbook on Sport and Society*, ed. L. Wenner (Oxford: Oxford University Press, 2022), 907–23; M. A. Messner, "Sports and Male Domination: The Female Athlete as Contested Ideological Terrain," *Sociology of Sport Journal* 5 (1988): 197–211.

34 Messner, "Sports and Male Domination."

35 L. Heywood and S. Dworkin, *Built to Win: The Female Athlete as Cultural Icon* (Minneapolis: University of Minnesota Press, 2003).

36 M. A. Messner, *Taking the Field: Women, Men, and Sports* (Minneapolis: University of Minnesota Press, 2002).

37 K. Nakajima and Jin C. Hanzhang, "Bills Targeting Trans Youth Are Growing More Common—and Radically Shaping Lives," National Public Radio, November 28, 2022, https://www.npr.org/2022/11/28/1138396067/transgender-youth-bills-trans-sports.

38 D. Crary and L. Whitehurst, "Lawmakers Can't Cite Examples of Trans Girls in Sports," Associated Press, March 3, 2021, https://apnews.com/article/lawmakers-unable-to-cite-local-trans-girls-sports-914a982545e943ecc1e265e8c41042e7.

39 Staurowsky et al., *50 Years of Title IX*.

40 *Dobbs v. Jackson Women's Health Organization*, "Brief for Amicus Curiae of Over 500 Women Athletes, September 21, 2022. https://www.supremecourt.gov/DocketPDF/19/19-1392/193017/20210920155533026_19-1392%20Amici%20Curiae.pdf.

41 *Dobbs v. Jackson Women's Health Organization*.

42 *Dobbs v. Jackson Women's Health Organization*.

43 C. Cooky and S. L. Dworkin, "Policing the Boundaries of Sex: A Critical Examination of Gender Verification and the Caster Semenya Controversy," *J. Sex Res.* 50 (2013): 103111; K. Henne, "The 'Science' of Fair Play in Sport: Gender and the Politics of Testing," *Signs* 39 (2014): 787–812; M. Pape, "Ignorance and the Gender Binary: Resisting Complex Epistemologies of Sex and Testosterone," in *Sports, Society, and Technology*, ed. J. Sterling and M. McDonald (Singapore:

Palgrave Macmillan, 2020) 219–45, https://doi.org/10.1007/978-981-32-9127-0_10; L. Pieper, *Sex Testing: Gender Policing in Women's Sports* (Urbana: University of Illinois Press; 2016).

44 K. Karkazis and R. Jordan-Young, "The Powers of Testosterone: Obscuring Race and Regional Bias in the Regulation of Women Athletes," *Feminist Formations* 30 (2018): 1–39; N. Hoad, "'Run, Caster Semenya, Run!': Nativism and the Translations of Gender Variance," *Safundi: J. South Afr. Amer. Studies* 11 (2010): 398–405; T. Nyong'o, "The Unforgivable Transgression of Being Caster Semenya," *Women & Performance: A Journal of Feminist Theory* 20 (2010): 95–100.

45 Cooky et al., *One and Done*; T. Bruce, "New Rules for New Times: Sportswomen and Media Representation in the Third Wave," *Sex Roles* 74 (2016): 361–76; K. Crouse, "Why Female Athletes Remain on Sports' Periphery," *Communication & Sport* 1 (2013): 237–40.

46 C. Cooky and D. Antunovic, *Serving Equality: Feminism, Media and Women's Sports* (New York: Peter Lang Publishers; 2022).

47 As I write this chapter, my colleague (Michela Musto) and I along with Purdue and Brown University student research assistants are collecting the data for the 2024 iteration of the study. We expect to publish the results of the study some time in 2025.

48 Cooky et al., *One and Done*.

49 M. A Musto, C. Cooky, and M. A. Messner, "From Fizzle to Sizzle: Televised Sports News and the Production of Gender-Bland Sexism," *Gender & Society* 31 (2017): 573–96.

50 L. Douglas, *The Rise of Women's Sports: Identifying and Maximizing the Opportunity*, Nielsen, 2018, https://www.nielsen.com/wp-content/uploads/sites/3/2019/04/the-rise-of-womens-sports.pdf.

51 "Women's Sports Gets Down to Business: On Track for Rising Monetization," Deloitte Insights, 2021, https://www2.deloitte.com/cn/en/pages/technology-media-and-telecommunications/articles/tmt-predictions-2021-womens-sports-revenue.html.

52 *Gender Equality and Inclusion Report 2021*, International Olympic Committee, https://stillmed.olympics.com/media/Documents/Beyond-the-Games/Gender-Equality-in-Sport/2021-IOC-Gender-Equality-Inclusion-Report.pdf.

53 "Why Female Athletes Make Winning Entrepreneurs," Ernst & Young, ESPNW, 2018, https://assets.ey.com/content/dam/ey-sites/ey-com/en_gl/topics/entrepreneurship/ey-why-female-athletes-make-winning-entrepreneurs.pdf.

54 N. Agha and D. Berri, "Gender Differences in the Pay of Professional Basketball Players," in *The Professionalisation of Women's Sport*, ed. A. Bowes and A. Culvin (Bingley, UK: Emerald, 2021), 53–70.

55 Agha and Berri.

56 B. Strauss, "U.S. Soccer Announces Historic CBA Agreement, Equal Pay Between USMNT, USWNT," *Sports Illustrated*, May 18, 2022, https://www.si.com/soccer/2022/05/18/us-soccer-cba-equal-pay-uswnt-usmnt-world-cup-prize-money.

Notes

57 E. Lee, "Citing Gender Gap in NIL Money, Two Baltimore Area College Athletes Join Fight to Level Playing Field," *Baltimore Sun*, April 5, 2023, https://www.baltimoresun.com/sports/college/bs-sp-mia-ewell-olivia-rothfeld-nil-disparity-20230405-gkwdfxyx4fbxviwxemsfa2igjq-story.html.

58 "Women's Sports Gets Down to Business."

59 K. Balasaygun, "For Women's Sports, the Media Buys Are Becoming a Big Deal," CNBC, March 4, 2023, https://www.cnbc.com/2023/03/04/for-womens-sports-the-media-buys-are-becoming-a-big-deal.html.

4
SPORT IS HEALTHY, SPORT IS DESTRUCTIVE

The exercise required of sports participants is good for them. It promotes coordination, stamina, strength, strong bones, joint flexibility, and heart and lung capacity. Exercise diminishes the ill effects of diseases such as diabetes. It reduces hypertension (high blood pressure), lowers bad cholesterol, and raises good cholesterol. Physical activity is an important part of maintaining a healthy body. Without exercise, bones become brittle, muscles atrophy (including the heart muscle), the efficiency of blood circulation diminishes, plaque in the arteries builds up rapidly, and the aging process accelerates. The positive effects of physical exercise cannot be denied. The health benefits of exercise are the motive for requiring physical education and sports programs in schools, youth sports, community adult recreation, and corporation-sponsored sports teams.

Yet sports often are organized in ways that encourage unhealthy behaviors to gain competitive advantage.

Sports and Girls' and Women's Health

As an example of the health benefits of sport, let's examine the consequences of participation for girls and women. During the late nineteenth and early twentieth centuries when modern sports were developing in the United States and in other Global North countries, the commonly held assumption was that certain types of sports participation were harmful to the health of girls and women. Physical exertion and the encouragement of aggressive behavior were seen as the main culprits. As a result, women (and specifically white women from affluent backgrounds) were excluded from physically demanding sports. This exclusion was not wholesale, nor does the historical development of women's sports follow a linear timeline, one progressing from exclusion to inclusion. It is important to note that women have been included or excluded in various sports at various times over the course of history.[1] Girls and women played basketball when the game was first invented in the late 1890s. Yet, over the course of the sport's historical development various rules constrained and contained girls' and women's physicality. This was particularly the case for educated affluent girls and women. For example, girls' basketball teams were divided into offensive and defensive players, who played one end of the court only and were limited to no more than two dribbles at a time to minimize physical effort. The beliefs about female frailty didn't apply to all women equally. Medical concerns centered on the reproductive capacities of white women and were rooted in racist fears regarding the perpetuation of the (white) race. At the time, many in the scientific community adhered to a "fixed energy" theory which meant any expenditures on physical exertion would detract from women's energy toward reproduction. Young girls (mostly white, affluent, educated) were channeled into sports that emphasized graceful movement (diving, gymnastics, and ice-skating) and limited physical contact with opponents. The most popular women's sports often separated the athletes by a net (tennis, badminton, volleyball). The first Winter Olympics was held in 1924. Then, the women were limited to only one sport—figure skating.[2] According to sociologist Nancy Theberge, "Women have been discouraged or prevented from participating in sport by a complementary set of exclusionary practices and cultural ideals that viewed them as fragile and unsuited to strenuous physical activity."[3] Women from minoritized backgrounds were subject to racial discrimination and racial exclusion. Even when white women were gaining access and opportunity, they were subject to segregation and limited to participating in segregated sports spaces such as "Negro leagues" or at historically Black colleges and universities (HBCUs).

Since the 1970s, these barriers to participation in all types of sports have weakened (in part due to the passage of Title IX in 1972; see chapter 3 for a discussion). The numbers of girls and women participants in high school sports, college sports, and adult running and fitness activities rose dramatically. Prior to Title IX, one out of every twenty-seven girls participated in high school sports. Today, one out of every 2.5 girls participate in sports. As we discussed in chapter 3 and as documented in the Women's Sports Foundation's 2022 report, along with this dramatic increase in sports participation have come important academic, psychological, physical, and mental health benefits for girls and women.[4]

- Physical/health: lower risk of obesity, lower blood pressure, higher levels of cardiovascular fitness, reduced risk of cardiovascular disease, reduced risk of breast cancer.
- Social/emotional: improved psychological well-being, greater life satisfaction, stronger sense of belonging, improved self-esteem, reduced symptoms of anxiety, stress, and depression.
- Academic/leadership: improved academic achievement, higher high school grad rates, higher college attendance/retention, greater involvement in extracurricular activities, increased opportunities for leadership.

The *Thriving Through Sport* report from the Women's Sports Foundation found that when compared to nonathletes, girls who play sports "in high quality environments have decreased levels of depression and anxiety and stronger peer relationships and greater levels of meaning and purpose."[5] The report also found that girls who play multiple sports for five years or more have five times lower the rate of mental health disorders compared to girls who do not play sports.

Sports participation for girls has also been shown to have a "protective" effect against the negative impacts of the COVID-19 pandemic on mental health and academic outcomes. In another report by the Women's Sports Foundation, researchers found that during the pandemic there was a decline in self-esteem and social support an increase in depression, and a decline in the belief they would attend a four-year college among twelfth-grade high school girls. Girls who played sports during the first year of the pandemic experienced more positive outcomes. According to the study's findings, girls who played sports were more physically active; had higher levels of self-esteem, self-efficacy, and social support; had more positive perceptions of their academic achievement and goals; and lower levels of loneliness and depression.[6]

The Destructive Aspects of Sport

Running, jumping, lifting, throwing, swimming, skiing, skating, cycling, rowing, and calisthenics enhance the physical, mental, and emotional health of participants. But athletes can also be injured during sporting activities. Behind the popular myth that sport is a healthy activity is the reality that many aspects of sport are unhealthy—physical injuries, mental abuse from coaches or parents, drug use and abuse, "the female athlete triad"—what is now referred to as relative energy deficiency in sports (RED-S), overtraining, and even the sexual abuse of athletes by authority figures. These latent tragedies of sport are its dark side, often hidden from view. Because they usually do not make the headlines of the sports section, they are emphasized here.

Physical Injuries to Children and Youth from Sport

Prior to the COVID-19 pandemic, nearly three million emergency room visits were the result of injuries sustained during youth sports participation.[7] For boys, the sports causing the most injuries were basketball and football, and for girls, gymnastics and cheerleading. Among children between the ages of five and nine, playground injuries were the most common type of injury. These statistics understate the actual number of sports-related injuries because many children when injured will not go to an emergency room but rather to an urgent care center, their regular doctor, or a sports medicine clinic. Also, these statistics do not necessarily include overuse injuries, which account for nearly 50 percent of all sports injuries among middle and high school students.[8]

Overuse injuries result from overdoing a certain action without giving the body sufficient time to recover. Swimmer's shoulder, for example, is caused by a repetition of shoulder strokes that can reach 400,000 for a typical male athlete over a ten-month training season, and 660,000 for a female athlete. Overuse injuries like swimmer's shoulder, Little League elbow, tennis elbow, gymnast's back, tendinitis, bursitis, ligament tears, shin splints, and stress fractures pose special dangers to young bodies that are undergoing growth and development. Dr. Lyle Micheli, youth sports medicine pioneer, estimates that 75 percent of the young patients he sees are victims of overuse injuries. In the early 1990s, the figure was about 20 percent.[9]

Athletes of any age who train seriously every day, year-round, engage in what sport sociologists call "positive deviance." This concept refers to

> cases of conformity that are so intense, extensive, or extreme that they go beyond the conventional boundaries of behavior. They are cases of over-

conformity rather than counter-conformity, but they are considered "deviant" or nonnormative because of their extreme nature. "Positive deviants" in sport take the sport ethic to the extreme—subordinating other interests for the sake of sport, including being dedicated to becoming a highly ranked or top competitor, accepting risk and playing through pain, and believing that there are no limits for someone who is dedicated enough.[10]

At greatest risk are young people striving for elite sport status. Their ambition leads to accelerated training regimens that can include more than one workout a day, cumulative daily workouts of six hours a day, six days a week, year-round.

Some sports involve higher risks of serious injury than others, and the relative risk of injury varies by age, gender, and other factors. Much of the recent focus on sports injury among the public has centered on concussions in football. The overall higher rates of concussions among boys and young men are due in part to their higher rates of participation in football, a sport for which girls have not had full access. Yet the increased growth of girls' participation in tackle football[11] in the late 2010s and early 2020s raises concern.[12] This is particularly so given that girls have a risk of concussion 1.5 times higher than boys when playing comparable sports. Athletes with a prior concussion had 3–5 times greater risk of sustaining a concussion, and wrestling and martial arts had the highest relative risk of a concussion, followed by cheerleading, football, and track and field.[13]

The relatively high rate of concussions in youth football has serious implications. Most experts agree that while preadolescence is a critical time, brain development continues well into one's twenties and even through the thirties. This raises questions as to when it is "safer" to play the sport. Research indicates that after a concussion, high school students perform worse on neuropsychological tests and require longer periods of time to regain neurocognitive function than college and professional athletes.[14] Research also demonstrates beyond the dangers of concussive hits, sub-concussive hits can be just as damaging.[15] In the case of some athletes, sub-concussive hits (hits to the head that do not cause acute concussion symptoms) can lead to chronic traumatic encephalopathy (CTE), "a progressive degeneration of the brain that leads to mood instability and problems with memory, focus and thinking."[16] A 2023 study conducted by Dr. Ann McKee and her colleagues at the Boston University CTE center, one of the leading research centers and the first to link CTE to the brains of football players, found that *of the* 40 percent of donors below the age of thirty *who* had CTE based on the established criteria, three-quarters of those donors had played football.[17]

Violent sports are, by definition, dangerous, which is why most experts agree the one way to be truly "safe" from the risks associated with sports is not to play, an unrealistic goal given sports' popularity and an undesirable one, given the positive benefits associated with sports participation discussed earlier in the chapter.

Research by sociologists has found that Black football players come from communities that are more socioeconomically disadvantaged than the national average, whereas white football players are less socioeconomically disadvantaged. According to the researchers, the findings suggest that

> A lack of opportunities in these areas, combined with persistent racial bias and discrimination, may make certain sports, such as football, seem like the most likely pathway to upward mobility for some black men. . . . By implication, if black NFL players are disproportionately from poor and working class families and disadvantaged hometowns, the financial necessity of participation in the NFL is higher for black than white players.[18]

This raises important questions regarding which families and which boys may be incentivized to make the choice to put their bodies at risk in the hopes of financial security for themselves and their families. Similarly, a recent *Washington Post* report found that while participation rates in high school tackle football are declining overall, "boys in the most conservative, poorest states continue to play high school tackle football at higher rates than those in wealthier and more politically liberal areas."[19] The report also found that at the college level, the proportion of white athletes in football is declining and that of Black players is rising and doing so at faster rates than overall national demographic trends.

Although football garners headlines when it comes to risks associated with the sport, one of the most dangerous organized sports is bull riding, where riders are ten times more likely than football players to be seriously injured.[20] Bull riders start young. At the age of three or four, boys ride sheep ("mutton busting"); at six, they ride calves; by nine or ten, they get on their first steers; and then by twelve or so, they ride or attempt to ride bulls. In rodeo country (most generally, the American Southwest), bull riding is viewed as a rite of passage to manhood, with young riders admired for their courage and grit. This argument is also made for other violent sports such as football and hockey. Sport scholar Richard Crepeau wonders about this association with violent sports turning boys into men.

> Invariably reports on head trauma in football lead to comments on football as a means to turn boys into men, or to prepare young boys for the real world. What is meant by these comments? What does it mean "to be a man"? Does it mean a willingness to inflict pain on a fellow human being? Does it mean being willing to accept pain from fellow human beings? Does it mean physically intimidating others by aggressive or violent actions?[21]

Sports Injuries: The Case of Men's Professional Football

Football is the most popular sport in the United States. According to USA Football, 2.5 million youth play football, and the Aspen Institute's State of Play report indicates 677,000 children between the ages of six and twelve years participate in tackle football. Just over one million boys played high school football in 2022–2023; 46,482 participated at the college level; and about 1,700 men play in the NFL. While injuries, some serious, occur at all levels of sports as we have discussed, in the following section we focus specifically on the findings for professional football in part because of the popularity of football in the United States, the ongoing public discussion regarding the "concussion crisis" in the NFL and the sport more generally, and because football players have a cumulative effect from many years of playing football.

Gridiron (i.e., tackle) football is a collision sport. The result is a high injury rate. A statistic called "Adjusted Games Lost" indicates that during the 2023 NFL season, the average team's starters lost 68.9 games due to injury (up from 38.1 in 2006, yet down from 79.3 in 2022).[22] Some of these are short-term injuries such as strains and sprains, but there are long-term injuries of a higher magnitude. Broken bones take time to heal. Torn muscles in the knee take a year or so to be fixed and rehabilitated. More serious than knees, however, are long-term injuries to the brain. In a survey of over 3,500 NFL players, one in eight experienced serious cognitive issue, such as memory loss.[23] And a study commissioned by the NFL in 2009 found NFL players experienced higher rates of Alzheimer's and similar memory-related diseases relative to the national population of men aged thirty to forty-nine. Chronic traumatic encephalopathy (CTE) is connected to football-related concussions. The symptoms of CTE include memory loss, confusion, aggression, and rage, and it can lead to suicidal behavior. There is a 61 percent increased risk of developing Parkinson's disease for those who have a history of playing football.[24] A 2019 study comparing NFL players to MLB players who had played at least five seasons between 1959–1988, found "the death rate from heart disease was 2.4 times higher for NFL players than that of former MLB players; for brain disease, it was three times as high."[25] The study also found the average age of death for the former NFL players was 59.6 compared to 66.7 for the MLB players. As journalist Selena Roberts notes, "The math is cruel. Studies estimate that an NFL player will lose an average of one to three years of life expectancy for every year he spends in the League."[26]

Repetitive concussions are certainly a problem, but the bigger problem is with repetitive sub-concussive trauma. That is, it's not just a few big hits that matter but the cumulative effect of lots of little hits, too. Concussion specialist, Robert Cantu explains,

> That's why so many of the ex-players who have been given a diagnosis of CTE were linemen: line play lends itself to lots of little hits. The hits data suggest that, in an average football season, a lineman could get struck in the head a thousand times, which means that a ten-year NFL veteran, when you bring in his college and high school playing days, could well have been hit in the head eighteen thousand times: that's thousands of jarring blows that shake the brain from front to back and side to side, stretching and weakening and tearing the connections among nerve cells, and making the brain increasingly vulnerable to long-term damage.[27]

For years, the NFL ignored evidence that playing professional football may cause traumatic brain injury. The resistance of the league to address the risks associated with the sport was compellingly documented in a PBS "Frontline" episode, "League of Denial."[28] In effect, the NFL denied any connection between repeated concussions from football and subsequent lasting brain damage, despite scientific evidence (and the NFL's own admission in the early 1990s) of a connection. After decades of denial, more than five thousand former players filed a class action lawsuit against the NFL. The courts sided with the players. The settlement reached required the NFL to establish a pool of $765 million for players who develop compensable injuries. Most significantly, the NFL reversed its long-standing position and agreed that nearly a third of retired players are expected to develop long-term cognitive problems and that the conditions likely to emerge will occur at notably younger ages than in the general population, and further, the gap between the players and the general population grows wider with increasing age.[29]

There are other injuries that have lasting physical problems for football players. Surely that will be the case of former Denver Bronco guard Mark Schlereth, who has had twenty-nine surgeries, including a combined twenty on his knees. "Routine actions become mission impossible. Schlereth cannot bend down to line up a putt. He cannot bend down to catch when his son, Daniel, tries to pitch to him. He cannot sleep through a night without waking up as many as a dozen times because his knee hurts, his back aches, or his body throbs."[30]

Team doctors and trainers may compound the injury problem. Prescribing painkillers that allow players to participate before they are physically ready can lead to a greater likelihood of permanent damage. Yet athletes may insist on this because they (1) are socialized to accept pain and injury as part of the game and to "play hurt"; (2) fear losing a starting position or even a place on the team; (3) want to keep their careers going as long as possible; (4) feel the pressure of teammates or coaches to play; or (5) want to sacrifice themselves for the good of the team. Team doctors may also inject painkillers such as Novocaine, cortisone, Vicodin, and Toradol or anti-inflammatories because their primary task is to keep players on the field, not in the training room.[31] These doctors and trainers are in a bind between doing what is medically appropriate for a player and doing what benefits their employer. Hall of Fame linebacker Dick Butkus was given cortisone and other drugs by the Chicago Bears' team doctor during the last two years of his career to deaden the pain in his knees. Butkus argued that the doctor had put the short-term needs of the team over his long-term health. He sued for $1.6 million and received $600,000 in an out-of-court settlement.

Football players continue to get bigger, stronger, and faster and as a result, serious injuries remain a concern. In "one of the gravest N.F.L. medical crises in decades,"[32] on January 2, 2023, Buffalo Bills safety Damar Hamlin suffered cardiac arrest after a routine tackle to the chest during a Monday Night Football game against the Cincinnati Bengals. Emergency medical personnel rushed to the field and performed lifesaving procedures for over thirty minutes all while thousands in the stands and millions at home watched until Hamlin was able to be placed in an ambulance and rushed to the nearby trauma medical center. The game was eventually suspended. Hamlin was later diagnosed with commotio cordis, "an extremely rare, serious medical condition that can happen after a sudden, blunt impact to the chest," as defined by the American Heart Association (AHA).[33] Hamlin eventually recovered and returned to play for the Buffalo Bills in the 2024 season. According to media reports, within a week after Hamlin's collapse, the manufacturers of automated external defibrillators were sold out in the United States, many purchased for use on high school football fields. The NFL also bolstered its emergency protocols and procedures.

The increase in injuries and increased severity of injuries is in part because football players are getting bigger without sacrificing speed. In 1970, there was one three-hundred-pound player in the NFL. In 1980s there were three. By 1990 the number jumped to 94, followed by subsequent increases: 301 players over 300 pounds in 2000, 360 in 2014, and 427 in 2020. The Green Bay Packers were the heaviest team in 2023 with the average weight of the team's roster hovering at nearly 250 pounds. The New York Giants had fifteen players that weighed 300 pounds or more in 2023. Many of these players 'train' to weigh this much, eating as much as five thousand calories a day, well above dietary guidelines and recommendations.

When players put on more weight than their frames were meant to hold, it puts extra stress on ligaments and joints, leading to more sprains, strains, and ligament tears. The additional bulk without loss of speed makes collisions even more violent, leading to an increase in the number and severity of injuries of both the player and their opponents. The added weight also places additional strain on the heart during exertion, especially when the weather is hot. There are long-term health consequences with weight increases, including heart problems and diabetes. One study found that for every ten pounds gained by football players, heart disease risk rose 14 percent compared to players who saw little weight increase.[34] Another study of 3,850 NFL players found that the heaviest athletes were twice as likely to die before age fifty than their lighter teammates.[35]

Excessive size of football players begins in middle school and high school. Young players (and their parents), with dreams of playing Division I football and professional football, see that their odds are greater of making it to the next level if they have the desired size. Scouts for big-time college football programs are looking for offensive linemen who weigh at least 280 pounds in high school.[36] No matter what the high school player's weight, the odds are slim that he will play at the next level, as we will see in chapter 8, but as a preview, according to NCAA statistics, about 7 percent of high school seniors will play football in college, and less than 2 percent of college football players will play a single game in the NFL. So to increase the odds players are encouraged by their coaches to increase their weight; they lift weights, perhaps with the guidance of a personal trainer, consume excessive calories, and take supplements (e.g., protein shakes and muscle-building creatine). For the rare athlete who makes it into a big-time college program, many are asked (required) to put on considerable additional weight. In an in-depth interview with *Cronkite News*[37] Kyle Murphy, a former offensive lineman at Arizona State University recalls the constant struggle to gain and maintain weight during his time in college. During high school, his parents were able to support the economic costs of football-required weight gain, spending $1,200 every two weeks on groceries. Once Murphy entered college, finding enough time and money to spend on food became challenging. As Murphy explains,

> So trying to get that many calories in was hard because of the amount of money you had to spend. I was on scholarship, I took loans out—more than I should have. A lot of that was just so I could go to the movies or hang out, or go out to eat, and really replenish my refrigerator because we would just eat so much food.

On a typical day for breakfast, Murphy recounts he would go to a local campus restaurant and eat three eggs, half a plate of home fries, four pieces of bacon, two pieces of toast and a drink. Murphy continues, "I would then go to class, which was usually about three hours. I'd come back and have a foot-long (sandwich), bowl of potato salad, bowl of macaroni salad, a bag of chips and a cookie and 32-ounce soda." Followed by practice and another high-calorie meal.

Injuries in Other Sports

Sports injuries are common in other contact sports, most notably boxing. Chronic Traumatic Encephalopathy (CTE), relatively common to football players, also comes with the elevated risk of concussions among boxers. Like the heads of football players, the heads of boxers are vulnerable to thousands of hits, which result in cognitive and emotional issues. "It's no secret that even the greatest fighters tended to end up in bad shape, demented or enfeebled from the punishment of their trade—[Joe] Louis, [Sugar Ray] Robinson, [Muhammad] Ali, and so many others."[38] Although girls and women historically have not participated in football or boxing to the same extent they have in other sports, girls and women athletes are also at risk for head/brain trauma injuries. Although much of the media attention and research on traumatic brain injury has focused on male athletes, it is important to acknowledge the research indicating that athletes in women's sports may be at a greater risk of concussions than male athletes in most sports.[39]

Injuries are not limited to head trauma in combat sports, however. Another common injury in sports, particularly in sports (or positions) that require rapid changes in movement, sudden starts and stops, and jumping, is Anterior Cruciate Ligament (ACL) injuries. Research indicates that female athletes are at a higher risk of ACL injury, and in particular women soccer players have a higher risk of ACL tears, although there is a high prevalence of ACL tears in male football players.

Athletes of all types of sports (and at all competitive levels) often follow the sports ethic without question, to the point of risking their own safety and well-being. This may lead to self-injurious overtraining, rigid training schedules, uncritical commitment to playing through pain and injury (what sports scholars call the "pain principle"), "relative energy deficiency in sports" (RED-S), and problems with family relationships and challenges balancing school and work responsibilities with the demands of training.

Relative Energy Deficiency in Sports (RED-S)

Intensive sports training has detrimental effects for athletes regardless of gender. The International Olympic Committee's (IOC) 2023 Consensus statement on RED-S offers an overview of the 170+ research studies published since the IOC's first consensus statement in 2014. This research demonstrates two important developments in our understanding of what had previous been described as "eating disorders/disordered eating" or the "female athlete triad." The first is a more expansive understanding of energy deficiency and its impacts on athletes' overall health. RED-S is defined in the consensus statement as

> a syndrome of impaired physiological and/or psychological functioning experienced by female and male athletes that is caused by exposure to

problematic (prolonged and/or severe) low energy availability. The detrimental outcomes include, but are not limited to, decreases in energy metabolism, reproductive function, musculoskeletal health, immunity, glycogen synthesis and cardiovascular and haematological health, which can all individually and synergistically lead to impaired well-being, increased injury risk and decreased sports performance.[40]

Second, the research on RED-S demonstrates that any athlete, regardless of gender, sport, or competitive level, can develop the syndrome. Both male and female athletes experience physiological and psychological effects of limited energy. The research also expands our understanding of low energy beyond "eating disorders" or the "female athlete triad" to include the vast array of health-impacts. It is important to note that athletes in sports that require either the expenditure of significant energy (i.e., endurance sports) or incentivize athletes to minimize their weight to enhance/improve performance, or sports organized by weight classes are at risk of RED-S. For example, bodybuilding, boxing, mixed martial arts, wrestling, gymnastics, horseracing, diving, figure skating, dance, track and field, running, and swimming often impose a great deal of pressure for an athlete to meet weight requirement, to adhere to stereotypical body type, or have a specific muscle/fat ratio to enhance performance. According to Professor Margo Mountjoy, the lead author of the IOC's Consensus Statement,

> REDs is common in both male and female athletes in many sports, and although we understand a lot more about its causes, awareness of the syndrome, and its consequences for health and performance, is still low among athletes, their medical and performance support teams, and the general public.

Drug Use

Athletes use restorative drugs, such as painkillers, anti-inflammatories, and muscle relaxants, to help them overcome injuries. Used properly, with adequate time to restore health before vigorous exercise, these drugs are helpful. They may, however, be used to return athletes to play before their bodies are healthy, leading to long-term health problems. Athletes may use other drugs, such as alcohol, marijuana, and cocaine, to mask pain or to help them deal with anxiety and stress. There are dangers in using these drugs, among them drug dependency. Also, since some drugs have been defined as illegal, use or possession can lead to problems with the criminal justice system, jail time, and a criminal record.

A more important drug issue is athletes' use of additive drugs—that is, drugs that improve performance. Some examples are beta blockers (used by golfers, archers, and those in the shooting sports), which slow down the heart, steady the nerves, and calm performance anxiety, and so-called brake drugs, such as cyproterone acetate, that delay puberty (used by female gymnasts and ice skaters). Human growth hormones increase strength and size (weightlifters, football linemen); amphetamines get players fired up and keep them stimulated and aggressive (football and rugby players). Prescription drugs are also misused. Approximately 10 percent of the population has some degree of asthma, but 60 percent of Olympic athletes use a prescription drug for asthma, presumably not because they have asthma but because it increases the lung capacity for endurance athletes. Similarly, athletes in baseball, football, hockey, and NASCAR have used controlled substances such as Ritalin and Adderall; some were suspended from play while others received "therapeutic exemptions" that would allow them to take them legally. These drugs are stimulants that help with reaction time, increase focus, and mask pain.[41]

The hormone erythropoietin (EPO) is chosen by endurance athletes, such as distance runners and cyclists, because it stimulates the production of red blood cells, thereby increasing the oxygen-carrying capacity of the blood. Anabolic steroids, along with human growth hormone, constitute the most commonly abused performance-enhancing drugs used by athletes.

There are also dangerous practices that increase athletic performance. Wrestlers and boxers use diuretics for weight loss to compete at lower-weight classes, and drug-using athletes often use diuretics to minimize detection of other drugs by diluting the urine. Blood doping (removing a pint of blood, allowing the blood volume to return to normal, and then transfusing the blood back into the blood supply in order to enhance the body's oxygen-carrying capacity) is thought to increase fitness by as much as 20 percent. In a fit, elite athlete blood doping appears to add 1 to 3 percent, which translates into running a 1,500-meter race three seconds faster than would be possible without the extra oxygen-carrying blood.[42]

When it comes to high school-age athletes, many doctors, nutritionists, coaches, and some players themselves wonder whether taking sports supplements now will haunt them later, perhaps in the form of damaged kidneys or malfunctioning livers. They worry that the products could mess up an adolescent's development. They fear that gung-ho young bodybuilders will assume that if one daily dose is good, five are even better. The most common illegal drugs used to enhance sports performance are anabolic steroids, a group of compounds that are related to the hormone testosterone. The adjective "anabolic" refers to protein building, since the steroids promote dramatic increases in muscle bulk, strength, and power. The use of anabolic steroids has serious health consequences. Prolonged use can damage the liver. It increases total cholesterol and decreases good forms of cholesterol, thus increasing the risk of coronary heart disease. It causes the body to retain sodium, potassium, and water, which increases the chances of congestive heart failure. Like other muscles, the heart often becomes enlarged, raising the risk of sudden heart attacks and blood clots. The tendons, which connect muscle to bone, become less resilient as bigger muscles put more pressure on them. Anabolic steroids cause testicular atrophy and breast enlargement in males, and menstrual-cycle difficulties, deepening of the voice, and increased body hair growth in women. Acne is common in both sexes. Mood swings and an increase in aggressive behavior are also byproducts of steroid use.

Synthetic steroids were first developed in 1935, and weightlifters began using them in the early 1950s. The practice spread rapidly among athletes whose performance was improved by increased size and strength. An unofficial poll taken by a US athlete at the 1972 Munich Olympics revealed that over two-thirds of the track and field athletes used some form of steroids in preparing for the games.[43] Some governments, as a matter of public policy, used performance-enhancing drugs as building blocks to international sports success (indirectly demonstrating the superiority of their culture). After the breakup of the Soviet Empire and the fall of East Germany, documents were found showing that one thousand to fifteen hundred scientists, physicians, and trainers ran controlled experiments on East German athletes in an effort to boost athletic performance while avoiding detection. This was confirmed by twenty former East German coaches who admitted that anabolic steroids had been used for over two decades as East German women dominated international swimming.[44] Illegal drug use and doping continues to plague the sports world. The World Anti-Doping Agency (WADA), an international governing body that ensures athletes are not engaged in illegal drug use or performance enhancing drugs, found twenty-three Chinese swimmers had tested positive for "banned substances" before the 2021 Tokyo Olympics, yet the athletes competed in events that summer due to pressures by the Chinese government to cover up the positive tests. WADA only recently acknowledged the positive results.[45] Drug violations are not limited to communist countries. Many individuals from the West have been disqualified for drug violations in international competitions in various sports, for example, skiing, speedskating, hockey, snowboarding, swimming, canoeing, cycling, weightlifting, track (mostly sprinters), and field (throwing weights—shot, discus, hammer).

US athletes take these drugs by choice, not as a matter of state policy. They want to be bigger, stronger, and faster, which may lead to a college scholarship, all-star status, a professional career, or success in international sports. Elite athletes in weightlifting, bodybuilding, and weight throwing are almost required to take steroids if they are to compete successfully internationally. Competitive cycling has a history of illicit drug usage, with winners being disqualified

The Destructive Aspects of Sport

after failing a drug test and there are rumors of those who pass these tests, having superior techniques to mask their usage. One of the most egregious examples is Lance Armstrong, seven-time winner of the Tour de France, who denied accusations for many years that he used performance-enhancing drugs but finally was exposed, stripped of his medals, and given a lifetime ban from competitive cycling.[46] Armstrong came into the sport during a time when there were a number of high-profile doping scandals including the ban of the French team, Festina, in 1998, and several of Armstrong's competitors, including Italian cyclist Marco Pantani and German cyclist Jan Ulrich, were caught doping. Armstrong's downfall was precipitated by the sworn testimony of almost a dozen of Armstrong's former teammates, who had also taken part in blood doping and the use of performance enhancing drugs. As George Hincapie, American cyclist and teammate of Armstrong, testified,

> Early in my professional career, it became clear to me that, given the widespread use of performance enhancing drugs by cyclists at the top of the profession, it was not possible to compete at the highest level without them.[47]

And yet, while much of the focus on drug use or "doping" in sports focuses on the athletes themselves and the individual choices athletes make to use drugs that have been banned from sports competition, sports leagues, governing bodies, corporate sponsors, media entities, and the sport itself benefits when athletes are able to push the limits of the capacities and capabilities of the human body. In an ironic example, the pharmaceutical company Amgen, which developed and markets the synthetic version of Erythropoietin (EPO), prescribed for cancer patients and those with amenia and also used by endurance athletes as a performance enhancing drug, was the title sponsor of the Tour de California, a major professional cycling race. This is the same drug that the French newspaper *L'Equipe* reported in 2005 that six of Armstrong's urine samples from his victorious 1999 Tour de France (when an EPO test was not yet available) later tested positive in an EPO research study by a French lab.[48]

And there are other questions for us to ponder. As Stan has written elsewhere:

> Athletes have long used artificial means to enhance performance. These practices raise many questions: Is it fair to have competitions where some athletes compete against those who have used artificial means to improve upon their natural abilities? If you feel that is unfair, then where do you draw the line? Should any athlete who uses a stimulant be disqualified? Then what about the caffeine in coffee? Should athletes who sleep in parabolic chambers to simulate the conditions of high altitude be disqualified but not those endurance athletes who train at high altitudes? What about vitamins?

Bee pollen? Is it all right for wrestlers and boxers to use over-the-counter diuretics to lose weight in order to compete at lower-weight classes? Should access to the wonders of the pharmaceutical world trump training, hard work, and strategy? Or is it cheating?[49]

Mental Health and Sports

Physical activity and sports participation are associated with a number of benefits to psychological health, including moderating stress levels, improvements in mood, and help with depression, and they may improve symptoms of other more serious mental health issues. At the same time, many elite-level athletes struggle with mental health issues, due in part to the demands of highly competitive sports and public spotlight placed upon them. Recently, a number of professional and elite level athletes have publicly disclosed their struggles with mental health. American Olympic swimmer and twenty-three-time gold medalist Michael Phelps has openly discussed his struggles with depression and anxiety and has indicated at a low point he had considered suicide. He credits therapy for his improved mental health and encourages men to seek therapy if they too are experiencing depression.[50]

After refusing to participate in a press conference during the 2021 French Open, professional tennis player, Naomi Osaka withdrew from the event and announced on social media that she would take some time off from the sport. A few weeks later, Osaka wrote an article for *Time* magazine titled, "It's OK to Not Be OK," where she explained why she did not attend the obligatory post-match press conference,

> I communicated that I wanted to skip press conferences at Roland Garros to exercise self-care and preservation of my mental health. I stand by that. Athletes are humans. Tennis is our privileged profession, and of course there are commitments off the court that coincide. But I can't imagine another profession where a consistent attendance record (I have missed one press conference in my seven years on tour) would be so harshly scrutinized. In any other line of work, you would be forgiven for taking a personal day here and there, so long as it's not habitual. You wouldn't have to divulge your most personal symptoms to your employer; there would likely be HR measures protecting at least some level of privacy. In my case, I felt under a great amount of pressure to disclose my symptoms—frankly because the press and the tournament did not believe me. I do not wish that on anyone and hope that we can enact measures to protect athletes, especially the fragile ones. I also do not want to have to engage in a scrutiny of my personal

medical history ever again. So I ask the press for some level of privacy and empathy next time we meet. Perhaps we should give athletes the right to take a mental break from media scrutiny on a rare occasion without being subject to strict sanctions.[51]

A few months later, gymnast and four-time Olympic gold medal winner, Simone Biles developed a condition referred to as the "twisties" in the opening days of the 2021 Tokyo Olympics. She withdrew from the team competition to "focus on her mental health."[52] In many of these cases, athletes were essentially forced to disclose their mental health issues by the sports news media.[53] Unfortunately, the 24-7 news cycle and constant demand by both the sports media and fans to have full access to super star athletes often denies those athletes the same protections and treatment we would expect to receive in our workplaces. We often see athletes as entertainers rather than as human beings with a complex set of diverse emotions. For athletes of color, mental health issues can result from or be exacerbated by racist abuse from either fans or the media.[54]

Even for college-level athletes, mental health issues are of concern. A 2022 survey of over 9,800 college athletes conducted by the NCAA found that although 69 percent of women athletes and 63 percent of men athletes agreed or strongly agreed they knew how to access mental health services on campus, less than half or 48 percent of women and 46 percent of men athletes said they agreed or strongly agreed they would feel comfortable with accessing those services. Mental health issues were most cited as reasons why athletes request a transfer.[55] This may be explained by an athlete's reluctance to share mental health concerns with a coach for fear of losing playing time or a scholarship, particularly if the coach does not signal an openness to addressing mental health with their players. To address the barrier to accessing services, Dr. Emmitt L. Gill Jr., a licensed clinical social worker, founded AthleteTalk, a smartphone application which provides content to address mental health. He also developed training and certification for social workers who provide targeted services to college athletes. Although athletes may have similar incidence and prevalence of mental health issues as the general college population, they do have a unique set of circumstances as an athlete that may require specialized forms of support.

Sexual Abuse of Athletes

Athletes, male and female, are sometimes targets for sexual abuse by persons in authority, usually coaches. Researchers estimate anywhere between 2 to 20 percent of young athletes experience sexual harassment or abuse in sports. If we consider the number of athletes who participate in sports, this translates to anywhere between seven hundred thousand and seven million athletes who are subject to sexual abuse.[56] The social conditions that make female athletes vulnerable to sexual harassment and abuse are just as real for male athletes. These factors include unequal power dynamics between athletes and coaches[57] that subsequently contribute to authoritarian interpersonal dynamics and blurred or ambiguous roles in the coach-athlete relationship.[58]

In elite youth and high school sports, harassment by the coach might be tolerated more easily than in other social spheres, since the athletes accept the coach as an authority figure who gives orders that extend into the private sphere of their lives. This includes control over medical treatment, nutrition, injuries, social activities, the use of alcohol and tobacco, and sexual behavior. Individual rights in athletes often take a backseat to the notion of "winning" and the "good of the team." Given societal gendered dynamics and male dominance in coaching, there is a particular risk for abuse among girls and young women. As Helen Lenskyj explains, "Even the most assertive and independent women rarely question the coach's authority, nor do they challenge psychologically manipulative or abusive behavior on the part of coaches."[59] In some sports, there is a lot of hands-on instruction, for example, in gymnastics and wrestling. Close physical contact between the coach and the athlete occurs during practice and is part of the sporting experience. However, this also creates possibilities for inappropriate touching, harassment, and abuse. This potential is intensified by the physical, technical, and social power that coaches have over athletes.[60]

Coaches, most of whom are men, have enormous power over athletes. The coaches decide who makes the team, who gets to play, who gets scholarships, and who gets to remain on the team. To say no to this all-powerful person places the athlete's career in jeopardy. Athletes have been socialized to obey their coaches, even if they disagree with their demands. Author Joan Ryan says that "the very traits that make young girls good gymnasts or figure skaters—obedience, reticence, pliability, naïveté—also make them prime targets for sexual abuse."[61]

The perceived and actual separation from "normal" life inside sport increases the reliance on support systems, especially coaches. Athletes spend most of their time with other athletes and coaches, practicing, eating, and playing. Athletes do not have time to build relationships outside the sports sphere. Many athletes, some as young as ten, are separated from their parents, removing the parents as protectors and confidants. Their team becomes their surrogate family. A survivor of sexual abuse by a coach called his actions incest. "I consider it incest—that's what this is all about. Because of time spent, the demands, the friendship, the opportunity . . . they are giving you something no-one else can. They're brother, uncle, father . . . the child feels safe and will do anything. That's why it's incest."[62]

Another factor increasing the likelihood of sexual abuse (in this case, the abuse of young athletes) is that they are under a coach's control when they begin to mature sexually. The onset of puberty is a crucial time for a young athlete. Referring to boys and young men, sociologist Mike Messner says that "the athlete's relationship with his coach takes place during boyhood and young adulthood, when the young male's masculine identity is being formed, when he is most insecure about his public status, about his relationships, his sexuality, his manhood."[63] Girls in swimming, ice-skating, and gymnastics can be world-class at fourteen, whereas boys typically do not achieve elite status in these (and other sports) until their late teens or early twenties. This means that young girl athletes, more so than young boys, are going to live away from home and be coached by someone with a top-notch reputation, making them vulnerable to sexual and other forms of abuse.

A final variable leading to a higher risk of sexual abuse is an athlete's level of performance, the highest risk occurring when the athlete has the most at stake. Celia Brackenridge and Sandra Kirby's research reveals that athletes who have reached a high standard of performance but are just below the elite level (the "stage of imminent achievement," SIA) are most vulnerable.[64] Novices can drop out or change coaches rather easily because they have invested less time, effort, money, and family sacrifice. Elite athletes have a proven record of success and may be less dependent on their coaches for continued achievement. These established athletes are also more likely to have high self-esteem and personal confidence, which provides them with the personal resources to operate independently of coaches. Athletes on the verge of stardom, however, are more likely than novices or elite athletes to be dependent on a coach. Brackenridge and Kirby claim that athletes whose SIA coincides with or precedes their age of sexual maturity are at greatest risk of sexual abuse in sport.

Sports and the #MeToo Movement

On August 4, 2016, the *Indianapolis Star* published a disturbing investigative report[65] regarding USA Gymnastics, the governing body overseeing the sport in the United States, which had ignored or failed to investigate allegations of sexual abuse of gymnasts by coaches for decades. Several weeks later, former gymnast Rachel Denhollander filed criminal charges with Michigan State University's police against MSU team doctor, Larry Nassar, who had abused her when she received medical treatment following a lower back injury. In September of 2016, a former

Olympic medalist would file a civil suit against Nassar, who had also served as the team doctor for the Olympic gymnastics teams, for sexual abuse dating as far back as 1994. Both athletes would go public with their cases, which led to a series of allegations and charges brought forward by other athletes who had been victims of Nassar's abuse. In October 2017, several athletes of the "Fierce Five" Olympic gold-medal-winning team, including McKayla Maroney, Ali Raisman, and Gabby Douglas all came forward publicly with their stories of abuse at the hands of Nassar. Nassar faced multiple criminal and civil cases and was given a 60-year prison sentence for child pornography charges. He also received a 40- to 175-year sentence for sexual assault. During the sentencing portion of the trial in January 2018, 156 girls and women gave victim-impact statements.[66] The sentencing of Nassar coincided with the height of the #MeToo movement, a social movement that gave voice to sexual harassment and assault victims/survivors, helped to dispel myths about sexual abuse, and served as a platform to publicly out perpetrators and harassers, which in many cases helped end years, if not decades, of abuse as was illustrated in the Larry Nassar case. The victim-impact statements were powerful and, in many ways, unprecedented given that the statements directly challenged the typical silencing of victims of abuse, the protection perpetrators receive from institutions and organizational bodies, and the overall reticence in our society to believe victims of sexual abuse, especially young girls and women.

Unfortunately, the Larry Nassar sexual abuse case is not the only high-profile case of sexual abuse in American sports. In the early 2010s, Jerry Sandusky, who was on the Penn State football coaching staff under Joe Paterno, was found guilty of abusing ten boys over the course of several decades. Like Larry Nassar's victims, many would come forward with allegations of abuse only to be ignored or dismissed by the individuals and institutions that were responsible for ensuring their safety. A US Justice Department investigation found evidence that a swim and diving coach at the University of Maryland, Baltimore County, had sexually abused and harassed male athletes between 2015–2020 and that the university failed to respond to the allegations. In the early 2020s, hundreds of former Ohio State University college male athletes, mostly wrestlers, came forward with their experiences of sexual abuse and assault against an OSU team doctor.[67] Their experiences of abuse dated as far back as the 1970s and continued through the late 1990s. And in a similar pattern in other sexual abuse cases, the athletes' claims of abuse were ignored or dismissed by coaches and the institution for decades. It was not until 2018 that Ohio State University would investigate; an "institutional failure," according to Michael Drake, OSU president at the time when the investigative report was publicly released.[68] Over two hundred athletes filed a federal case against Ohio State University. The case is set to go to trial some time in 2025.[69]

Conclusion

Sport encapsulates a fundamental duality—it is healthy yet unhealthy. Some sports are inherently dangerous. In others, overtraining may lead to injury. The nature of sport is such that to be good requires commitment and dedication. Sometimes this dedication leads to ethical distortions such as taking dangerous drugs, engaging in unsafe practices such as taking diuretics, perhaps even trying to hurt an opponent to gain a competitive advantage. Should sports organizations and schools not be guided by the principle that the ends do not justify the means? Putting this principle into practice requires sponsoring organizations to monitor coaches for abusive behaviors or other demands with unhealthy consequences for their athletes. To maximize the health of the athletes, one operating principle should prevail—the outcome of the athlete (physically and emotionally) is infinitely more important than the outcome of the game.

Notes

1. Collette Dowling, *The Frailty Myth: Redefining the Physical Potential of Women and Girls* (New York: Random House, 2001).
2. Maura Grogan, "Female Athletes Lack Parity in Olympics," *USA Today*, January 3, 2014, 11A.
3. Nancy Theberge, "Women's Athletics and the Myth of Female Frailty," in *Women: A Feminist Perspective*, ed. Jo Freeman, 4th ed. (Mountain View, CA: Mayfield, 1989), 507.
4. E. J. Staurowsky, C. L. Flowers, E. Busuvis, L. Darvin, and N. Welch, *50 Years of Title IX: We're Not Done Yet*, Women's Sports Foundation, 2022.
5. W. V. Massey, P. T. Veliz, N. Zarrett, and A. Farello, *Thriving Through Sport: The Transformative Impact on Girls' Mental Health*, Women's Sport Foundation, 2024.
6. N. Zarrett and P. T. Veliz, *The Healing Power of Sport: COVID-19 and Girls' Participation, Health, and Achievement*, Women's Sports Foundation, 2023.
7. Katelyn Newman, "Sports Cause Nearly 3 Million ER Visits Each Year," *US News and World Report*, November 15, 2019, https://www.usnews.com/news/healthiest-communities/articles/2019-11-15/sports-cause-nearly-3-million-er-visits-each-year-study.
8. "Overuse Injury Prevention in Youth Sports," University of California, Davis Health, https://health.ucdavis.edu/sports-medicine/resources/youth-injury-prevention.
9. Micheli cited in Mark Hyman, "The Kids Aren't Alright," *Sports Illustrated*, April 13, 2009, 14–15.
10. Robert Hughes and Jay Coakley, "Positive Deviance among Athletes: The Implications of Overconformity to the Sport Ethic," *Sociology of Sport Journal* 8, no. 4 (1991). See also Jay Coakley, *Sport in Society: Issues and Controversies*, 9th ed. (New York: McGraw-Hill, 2007), 157–69.

11 "More Girls Are Playing Tackle Football," National Football League, January 9, 2020, https://operations.nfl.com/gameday/analytics/stats-articles/more-girls-are-playing-tackle-football/.

12 Frankie de la Cretaz, "The Complicated Case for Gender Equality in Football," *In These Times*, May 1, 2023, https://inthesetimes.com/article/wfa-nfl-womens-football-gender-equality.

13 W. T. Tsushima, A. M. Siu, H. J. Ahn, B. L. Chang, and N. M. Murata, "Incidence and Risk of Concussions in Youth Athletes: Comparisons of Age, Sex, Concussion History, Sport, and Football Position," *Arch Clin Neuropsychol*. 34, no. 1 (2019): 60–69.

14 B. D. Semple, S. Lee, R. Sadjadi, N. Fritz, J. Carlson, C. Griep, V. Ho, P. Jang, A. Lamb, B. Popolizio, S. Saini, J. J. Bazarian, M. L. Prins, D. M. Ferriero, D. M. Basso, and L. J. Noble-Haeusslein, "Repetitive Concussions in Adolescent Athletes—Translating Clinical and Experimental Research into Perspectives on Rehabilitation Strategies," *Front Neurol*. 6 (April 2, 2015): 69.

15 M. Ntikas, F. Binkofski, N. J. Shah, and M. Ietswaart, "Repeated Sub-Concussive Impacts and the Negative Effects of Contact Sports on Cognition and Brain Integrity," *Int J Environ Res Public Health* 19, no. 12 (2022): 7098.

16 Nina Kraus, Danielle Colegrove, Rembrandt Otto-Meyer, Silvia Bonacina, Trent Nicol, Jenna Cunningham, and Jennifer Krizman, "Subconcussion Revealed by Sound Processing in the Brain," *Exercise, Sport, and Movement* 1, no. 3 (Summer 2023): 1–4.

17 Brian Doctrow, "Chronic Traumatic Encephalopathy in Young Athletes," *NIH Research Matters*, September 12, 2023, https://www.nih.gov/news-events/nih-research-matters/chronic-traumatic-encephalopathy-young-athletes.

18 Rachel Allison, "Assessing the Patterns: Race, Class, and Opportunities in American Football," *Engaging Sports*, January 11, 2018, https://thesocietypages.org/engagingsports/2018/01/11/assessing-the-patterns-race-class-and-opportunities-in-american-football/.

19 Dave Sheinin and Emily Giambalvo, "The Changing Face of America's Favorite Sport," *Washington Post*, December 18, 2023, https://www.washingtonpost.com/sports/interactive/2023/football-participation-decline-politics-demographics/?_pml=1.

20 Burkhard Bilger, "The Ride of Their Lives," *New Yorker*, December 8, 2014, 48–63.

21 Richard Crepeau, "Manhood and Football," Sport and Society for Arete, University of Central Florida, January 17, 2014.

22 Aaron Schatz, "Texans Lead 2023 AGL Numbers with OL Injury Record," FTN Fantasy, March 5, 2024, https://ftnfantasy.com/nfl/texans-lead-2023-agl-numbers-with-ol-injury-record.

23 Karen Hensel, "One in Eight NFL Players Develop Serious Cognitive Problems," NBC Boston, August 30, 2019, https://www.nbcboston.com/news/local/study-1-in-8-nfl-players-develop-serious-cognitive-problems/88366/.

24 Katherine Lang, "Does Playing American Football Increase the Risk of Parkinson's Disease?," *Medical News Today*, August 17, 2023, https://www.medicalnewstoday.com/articles/does-playing-american-football-increase-the-risk-of-parkinsons-disease.

Notes

25 Meredith Wadman, "Former Football Pros Die at a Faster Rate Than Baseball Veterans—and the Reasons Are Surprising," *Science*, May 24, 2019, https://www.science.org/content/article/former-football-pros-die-faster-rate-baseball-veterans-and-reasons-are-surprising.

26 Selena Roberts, "The NFL's Growing Pains," *Sports Illustrated*, September 6, 2010, 164. See also, Nate Jackson, "The NFL's Concussion Culture," *Nation*, August 15, 2011, 22–23.

27 Quoted in Malcolm Gladwell, "Offensive Play," *New Yorker*, October 19, 2009, 57.

28 "League of Denial," *Frontline*, National Public Radio, October 8, 2013. This documentary was based on the expose by Mark Fainaru-Wada and Steve Fainaru, *League of Denial: The NFL, Concussions, and the Battle for Truth* (New York: Crown Publishing, 2013).

29 Ken Belson, "Brain Trauma to Affect One in Three Players, NFL Agrees," *New York Times*, September 12, 2014, A1.

30 Adam Schefter, "World of Hurt," *Denver Post*, November 12, 2000, 1K. See also Adam Schefter, "Working through Pain," *Denver Post*, December 7, 2003, 1J, 6J.

31 Greg Easterbrook, *The King of Sports: Football's Impact on America* (New York: St. Martin's, 2013), 189–98.

32 Alan Blinder, "What the N.F.L. Says, and What It Doesn't, about Injuries," *New York Times*, January 3, 2023, https://www.nytimes.com/2023/01/03/sports/football/nfl-injuries-statistics.html.

33 Alaina Getzenberg, "How Damar Hamlin's Cardiac Arrest Affected the Sports World," ESPN, November 4, 2024, https://www.espn.co.uk/nfl/story/_/id/38802749/buffalo-bills-damar-hamlin-cardiac-arrest.

34 Logan Stanley, "Pancake Blocks to Pancake Stacks: Eating 'a Chore' for Offensive Linemen in Complex Relationship with Football, Food," *Cronkite News*, November 7, 2023, https://cronkitenews.azpbs.org/2023/11/07/offensive-linemen-detail-their-complex-relationship-with-food-for-weight-gain/.

35 Thomas Hargrove, "Heavy NFL Players Twice as Likely to Die before 50," Scripps Howard News Service, January 31, 2006, http://sports.espn.go.com/nfl/news/story?id=2313476.

36 "Football Recruiting 101," Go Big Recruiting, https://www.gobigrecruiting.com/recruiting101/football/positions_guidelines/offensive_line.

37 Stanley, "Pancake Blocks to Pancake Stacks."

38 Bob Herbert, "The Sport Needs to Change," *New York Times*, March 14, 2011, http://www.nytimes.com/2011/03/15/opinion/15herbertt.html?_r=1&re.

39 T. Covassin, R. Moran, and R. J. Elbin, "Sex Differences in Reported Concussion Injury Rates and Time Loss from Participation: An Update of the National Collegiate Athletic Association Injury Surveillance Program from 2004–2005 through 2008–2009," *Journal of Athletic Training*, 51, no. 3 (2016): 189–94.

40 M. Mountjoy, K. E. Ackerman, D. M. Bailey, et al., "International Olympic Committee's (IOC) Consensus Statement on Relative Energy Deficiency in Sport (REDs)," *British Journal of Sports Medicine* 57 (2023): 1073–98.

41 A. J. Perez, "Adderall: NFL's New, Trendy PED," *Foxsports*, June 2, 2014, http://www.foxsports.com/nfl/story/adderall-fls-newptrendy-ped-drug-steroids-112912.

42 For a detailed account of blood doping and EPO in cycling, see Reed Albergotti and Vanessa O'Connell, *Wheelmen: Lance Armstrong, the Tour de France, and the Greatest Sports Conspiracy Ever* (New York: Gotham Books, 2013).

43 Terry Todd, "Anabolic Steroids: The Gremlins of Sport," in *Sport in America: From Wicked Amusement to National Obsession*, ed. David K. Wiggins (Champaign, IL: Human Kinetics, 1994), 285–300.

44 Steven Ungerleider, *Faust's Gold: Inside the German Doping Machine* (New York: St. Martin's, 2002).

45 Leana S. Wen, "The Chinese Doping Scandal Demands a Dramatic U.S. Response," *Washington Post*, June 4, 2024, https://www.washingtonpost.com/opinions/2024/06/04/biden-doping-china-wada-olympics/.

46 Albergotti and O'Connell, *Wheelmen*.

47 "From Former Teammates, Words Tinged with Regret," *New York Times*, October 10, 2012, https://www.nytimes.com/2012/10/11/sports/cycling/from-former-teammates-words-tinged-with-regret.html.

48 Mark Zeigler, "Amgen, Cycling Tour Make an Odd Couple," *San Diego Union-Tribune*, February 20, 2009, https://www.sandiegouniontribune.com/sdut-1s20amgen223514-amgen-cycling-tour-make-odd-couple-2009feb20-htmlstory.html.

49 D. Stanley Eitzen, "Introduction to Problems of Excess: Performance-Enhancing Drugs in Sports," in *Sport in Contemporary Society*, ed. D. Stanley Eitzen, 9th ed. (Boulder, CO: Paradigm, 2012), 147.

50 Drew Weisholtz, "Michael Phelps Reflects on His Depression and the 'Great Change' That Came from It," *Today*, May 10, 2024, https://www.today.com/health/michael-phelps-shares-great-change-came-experience-depression-rcna151620.

51 Naomi Osaka, "It's OK to Not Be OK," *Time*, July 8, 2021.

52 Torrey Hart, "Simone Biles Opens Up about 'Twisties' Timeline, Pressure in Tokyo," *NBC Sports*, August 4, 2021, https://www.nbcolympics.com/news/simone-biles-opens-about-twisties-timeline-pressure-tokyo.

53 Andrew C. Billings and Scott Parrott, *Head Game: Mental Health in Sports Media*, 2022 (New York: Peter Lang).

54 Leah Asmelash, "Why Mental Health Matters for Athletes—Even as They Give Their All to Win," CNN, July 26, 2022, https://www.cnn.com/2022/07/22/us/athlete-mental-health-united-shades-wellness-cec/index.html.

55 Greg Johnson, "Mental Health Issues Remain on the Minds of Student-Athletes," NCAA, May 24, 2022, https://www.ncaa.org/news/2022/5/24/media-center-mental-health-issues-remain-on-minds-of-student-athletes.aspx.

56 "Preventing Sexual Abuse in Sports," Global Sports Development, https://globalsportsdevelopment.org/sexual-abuse-sport-prevention/.

57 The following is taken primarily from Celia H. Brackenridge, "Fair Play or Fair Game? Child Sexual Abuse in Sports Organizations," *International Review for the Sociology of Sport* 29 (1994): 287–99; Celia H. Brackenridge, "He Owned Me Basically: Women's Experience of Sexual Abuse in Sport," *International Review for the Sociology of Sport* 32 (June 1997): 115–30; and Celia Brackenridge and Sandra

Notes

Kirby, "Playing Safe: Assessing the Risk of Sexual Abuse to Elite Child Athletes," *International Review for the Sociology of Sport* 32 (December 1997): 407–18.

58 Sonja Gaedicke, Alina Schäfer, Brit Hoffmann, Jeannine Ohlert, Marc Allroggen, Ilse Hartmann-Tews, and Bettina Rulofs, "Sexual Violence and the Coach–Athlete Relationship—a Scoping Review from Sport Sociological and Sport Psychological Perspectives," *Frontiers in Sports and Active Living* 3 (2021), https://doi.org/10.3389/fspor.2021.643707.

59 Helen Lenskyj, "Unsafe at Home Base: Women's Experience of Sexual Harassment in University Sport and Physical Education," *Women in Sport and Physical Activity Journal* 1 (1992): 19–33.

60 Karen A. E. Volkwein et al., "Sexual Harassment in Sport: Perceptions and Experiences of American Female Student-Athletes," *International Review for the Sociology of Sport* 32 (September 1997): 285.

61 Joan Ryan, *Little Girls in Pretty Boxes: The Making and Breaking of Elite Gymnasts and Figure Skaters* (New York: Warner Books, 1995), 168–69.

62 Brackenridge, "He Owned Me," 118.

63 Michael A. Messer, *Power at Play: Sports and the Problem of Masculinity* (Boston: Beacon, 1992), 105.

64 Brackenridge and Kirby, "Playing Safe," 413–14.

65 Marisa Kwiatkowski, Mark Alesia, and Tim Evans, "A Blind Eye to Sex Abuse: How USA Gymnastics Failed to Report Cases," *Indianapolis Star*, August 4, 2016, https://www.indystar.com/story/news/investigations/2016/08/04/usa-gymnastics-sex-abuse-protected-coaches/85829732/.

66 "Read Rachael Denhollander's Full Victim Impact Statement about Larry Nassar," CNN, January 30, 2018, https://www.cnn.com/2018/01/24/us/rachael-denhollander-full-statement/index.html; "Larry Nassar's Survivors Speak, and Finally the World Listens—and Believes," *Believed*, Season 1, Episode 8, National Public Radio, December 10, 2018, https://www.npr.org/2018/12/07/674525176/larry-nassars-survivors-speak-and-finally-the-world-listens-and-believes; "'I Thought I Was Going to Die': Read McKayla Maroney's Full Victim Impact Statement in Larry Nassar Trial," *Time*, January 18, 2018, https://time.com/5109011/mckayla-maroney-larry-nassar-victim-impact-statement/.

67 "Supreme Court Won't Hear Cases over Ohio State Doctor's Sexual Abuse, Allowing Lawsuits to Proceed," *PBS News Hour*, June 26, 2023, https://www.pbs.org/newshour/nation/supreme-court-wont-hear-cases-over-ohio-state-doctors-sexual-abuse-allowing-lawsuits-to-proceed.

68 "Former Ohio State Team Doctor Abused at Least 177 Students, Report Says," *PBS News Hour*, May 17, 2019, https://www.pbs.org/newshour/nation/former-ohio-state-team-doctor-abused-at-least-177-students-report-says.

69 Samana Sheikh, "Strauss Sex Abuse Victims Say They Could Be Headed to Trial Against OSU," *Spectrum News 1*, March 1, 2024, https://spectrumnews1.com/oh/cleveland/politics/2024/02/29/news--sports--court--case.

5

THE ORGANIZATION OF YOUTH SPORT: ISSUES AND CONSEQUENCES

Two Fundamentally Different Forms of Play for Young Children

Stan's Story: When I was growing up in Southern California in the 1940s, I did not play in an adult-organized game until I was eligible for high school sports. Before high school, my sports activities were limited to playground games in grade school and middle school, and most frequently to games after school with friends in vacant lots, backyards, driveways, streets, and parks.

Cheryl's Story: When I was growing up in the near-west suburbs of Chicago, Illinois in the 1980s, like Stan, I too played with friends on the playground, backyards, streets, and driveways. I rode my bike for hours in the summer and organized games in the vacant lot down the street. Before high school, I played on a Little League softball team, took swim lessons at the local recreation center, and participated on my school's volleyball team. This was in the immediate aftermath of Title IX's passage, and although there were opportunities to participate in organized sports, they were few. And they certainly were not equal to the opportunities boys had, in terms of quality and resources. The community and peer support for girls' participation was also minimal, yet more than when my mother was of that age.

Over the course of the twentieth century, the informal play Stan experienced as a youth transitioned to the growth of recreation and school-based sports alongside the informal play that I (Cheryl) experienced, and in the past several decades these have been superseded by adult-organized sport for youth that is often "pay to play," highly competitive, and highly structured.[1] Sociologist Michael A. Messner provides four interrelated reasons for this shift toward adult-organized competitive youth sports.[2] First, there is the concern that began in the 1960s with the physical fitness of children, which transitioned into contemporary fears surrounding the "obesity epidemic." Second, a range of fears over children's safety because of perceived threats from bullying, gangs, and predators who might abuse or kidnap children has led to the "need" for more adult supervision. Third, changes in family structure, with more dual-income families mean that children do not have a parent at home during the day, giving rise to unsupervised children after school. This concern leads to the more controlled scheduling of children's educational, cultural, artistic, and athletic experiences. Related to this is the urge by parents to give their children advantages such as in sports with private coaches and trainers and specialized sports camps. The fourth reason for the surge in organized youth sports is the feminist-inspired growth in girl's and women's sports. As Messner puts it: "As youth sports grew, much of that growth reflected changing cultural attitudes and values about the value of sports for girls."[3]

According to the State of Play 2023 report from the Aspen Institute,[4] in 2022, 63 percent of youth ages six to twelve played sports at least once a day, although there has been a decline in participation since 2019. Despite the mass movement of girls into organized sports over the past five decades, boys had higher participation rates than girls (40 percent vs. 35 percent). This may change in the near future as the percentage of boys participating in sports is declining while for girls it is increasing, according to the State of Play report. Another change is in the percentage of children from the lowest-income households participating in sports, which has increased since 2019, while participation has declined among the highest-income youth. The State of Play report attributes this particular shift to the number of programs targeting low-income youth and to the "declining quality of experiences among kids with the greatest opportunities to play." Moreover, children who have a disability "are two times more likely to have zero days with sixty minutes of physical activity than their peers." Only fourteen states offered adapted high school sports. For trans and nonbinary youth, opportunities to participate in school-based sports is limited in the twenty-three states (at the time of this writing) that have passed legislation requiring students to participate in the sport of the sex of which they were assigned at birth. This requirement is untenable for most trans and nonbinary students as it forces them to deny fundamental parts of their self, identity, and humanity. When considering participation rates and opportunities, it is important to consider how opportunities and access differ by these key demographics.

Overall, children still engage in unorganized peer-group sports activities, but adult-organized sports, and in particular highly expensive travel teams and other privatized sports teams are now the dominant sports forms. The differences between these two forms of children's sports are profound. In the following sections, we discuss these two forms of sports, recognizing that these are generalizations and there may be some important distinctions depending on the key demographic differences noted above.

Organization

In adult-organized sports for children, games are modeled after professional sports (teams typically have names and logos of professional teams), with uniforms, standard practice and game facilities, practice and game schedules, tournaments, referees, rules, and coaches who teach strategy and skills to players who listen passively. Players are assigned to teams either by neighborhood or by tryouts followed by a draft in which coaches select players. Decisions are made by ruling bodies, referees, and coaches rather than the participants. The emphasis in this organized setting is on the development of sport skills and winning. Games are played with spectators (most commonly, parents) present.

Conversely, peer play is player controlled. The players gather and teams are selected, rules are decided, and the playing field demarcated by consensus. The children vary the rules during play to suit the situation. Adults are missing in these settings. They neither make the rules nor watch these games.

Journalist Daniel Sanger describes the differences between these two types of play, using hockey in Canada as the sport. He begins with a description of a minor hockey league for teenagers:

> Inside an arena, inside cumbersome equipment, most of the players sit on the bench most of the time, behind which a pacing, anxious coach barks out orders, behind whom one or more idiot fans or parents take it way, way too seriously. The players are said to be *playing* hockey, but judging by the limited laughter and smiling, there is little play involved. Rather, organized hockey is about following instructions, executing set plays, confronting opponents, scoring, and winning. Open-air pickup hockey on the other hand, is a game of endless variety, spontaneity, adaptation, and unspoken rituals. With no coaches telling players what to do and no prescribed way to play, it lends itself to an often beautiful creativity. With no referees and few hard-and-fast rules, it insists on self-regulation and, in so doing, encourages accommodation and tolerance. Pickup hockey is always unpredictable and almost always instructive, even edifying, in a life-lessons kind of way. . . . [These players are] engaged in a pleasurable pursuit together. [They are] playing.[5]

Although this article was written almost twenty years ago, it still resonates in its description of the stark differences between adult-organized and peer-organized play.

Process

In peer-group sport, the games begin quickly without warm-ups. Players must negotiate rule interpretations or when a player is "safe" or "out." A consensus often occurs, but when it doesn't, the decision may be to play it over. Kids want action. Instead of a situation common in adult-centered baseball, for example, where the action is mainly with a pitcher either striking out or walking batter after batter, in peer-group sports, a dominant player may not be allowed to pitch, or they may shout "let him hit it." The emphasis is on action, not winning.

Kids prefer close scores, not blowouts. As such, they divide the talent more or less equally, and sometimes place constraints on more skilled or experienced players, such as requiring a right-handed player to bat with their left hand. Less skilled players are granted "do-overs" and "interference" calls to compensate for deficiencies or mistakes, minimizing the embarrassment that could cause them to walk off—and leave the game short on players. Abuse of such special exemptions is regulated by teasing. Rules go ignored if doing so doesn't interrupt the flow of the action. In baseball, called strikes are forbidden to ensure everyone gets a chance to hit (and there are more balls to field). In football, every kid is eligible to receive a pass on any play.[6]

In contrast, the process in adult-organized youth sports emphasizes order, punctuality, respect for authority, obedience to adult directions, and a strict division of labor. Practices start and end by a coach's decision. Coaches may interrupt practice to discuss mistakes, demonstrate the proper skill, or punish misbehavior. The players become so accustomed to following orders in an organized sport setting that they frequently cease playing altogether if the coach is absent or not directly supervising.[7]

Typically, winning is the overriding goal of organized youth-sports programs. Games can be very lopsided. A team in a league may be dominant, but the adults make no effort to equalize the teams. Moreover, "By striving for league standings, by awarding championships, by choosing all-star teams, such programs send the not-so-subtle message to youngsters that the most important goal of sports is winning."[8]

Impetus

The impetus for peer play comes entirely from the players. They begin and terminate a game based on player interest. They participate to have fun. Conversely, the play in organized sports programs is initiated by the coaches. Practices are scheduled by coaches and games by a league authority to be played in a very rigid time frame. Instead of having fun, players do repetitive drills. They are expected to work hard. Indeed, practice is work.

Although everyone wants to win, victory seems to be most important for coaches and parents. While winning is preferable to losing—and many children will try hard to win, even crying when they come up short—they don't linger on the result. Ten minutes after the final whistle, they've moved on. Coaches and parents are the ones who keep talking about the game long after it is over. Adults exist in an adult world that dispenses rewards based on the bottom line, where the destination matters more than the journey.[9]

Analysis of Differences

Informal sports are action centered, while organized sports are rule centered. In the former, youngsters are involved, developing decision-making skills. Sociologist Jay Coakley says:

> Children must be creative to organize games and keep them going. They encounter dozens of unanticipated challenges, requiring on-the-spot decisions

and interpersonal abilities. They learn to organize games, form teams, cooperate with peers, develop rules, and take responsibility for following and enforcing rules. These are important lessons, many of which are not learned in adult-controlled organized sports.[10]

Unfortunately, opportunities for young people to engage in peer-organized play are declining. Children spend their leisure time on screens—social media, gaming, and texting (smartphone)—and on homework more than previous generations and less time on play and sports. Many schools, in an effort to meet state or federal curriculum guidelines have cut or eliminated unstructured play, for example recess after lunch.

While adult-organized sports encourage passivity by the participants and overemphasize winning, there are some benefits. Again, turning to Coakley:

> Organized sports help children learn to manage relationships with adult authority figures. Children also learn the rules and strategies used in activities that are defined as important in the culture, and through their participation, they often gain status that carries over to other parts of their lives. When they play organized sports, they learn about formal structures, rule-governed teamwork, and adult models of work and achievement.[11]

An interesting difference involves adherence to rules (or what in the past has been referred to as unsportsmanlike conduct). In peer-centered games, violating rules and other unethical behavior is not tolerated. Peer pressure demands good behavior, but if violations occur, the offender is banished from the game by his or her peers. In adult-organized sports, while dominated by fair play and playing within the rules, the pressure to win sometimes encourages unethical behavior by coaches, players, and parents. This may involve trash talking, intimidating opponents, taunting or ridiculing opponents, and deliberately violating the rules of sport to gain a competitive advantage in order to win the sporting event. As the economic incentives increase, including the potential to earn a college scholarship or to secure lucrative Name-Image-Likeness sponsorship deals, more youth athletes, coaches, and parents may become inclined to gain any competitive advantage to excel in sports at any cost.

The Dark Side of Adult-Centered Play

The following section focuses on the "dark side" of organized children's sports. It is important to note that there are also a number of benefits to adult-centered youth sports. Exercise in moderation and with overall well-being as a priority can confer physical and mental health benefits. Young athletes learn sports skills and have access to proper equipment for safety when playing under adult supervision, which helps children avoid dangerous situations. Individual sports foster self-reliance, while in team sports children can learn lessons on cooperation and gain acceptance from their peers for their accomplishments and contributions to the team.

There are also important benefits for girls who participate in sports. The Women's Sports Foundation, a nonprofit advocacy group founded by tennis great Billie Jean King and dedicated to gender equality in sports, notes the key benefits to girls' participation, which include physical and health benefits (e.g., reduced risk of cardiovascular disease, higher levels of cardiovascular fitness, lower risk of breast cancer), psychological benefits (e.g., improved psychological well-being, improved self-esteem, lower levels of anxiety/stress) and improved academic outcomes (e.g., higher graduation rates, higher college attendance). In addition to positive outcomes for cis-gender youth, sports participation also has positive benefits for trans youth, including an increased sense of belonging at school, lower levels of suicide and suicide ideation, and improved mental health. A former athlete, current coach, Emet who identifies as a transman explains the importance of trans participation in sports,

> It's a dangerous thing to mess with, to force someone into a position where they either hide themselves to be able to have this outlet and this community, or they lose that if they can't participate in sports and live as their authentic selves. Sport is more than just recreation. It impacts mental health and physical health. It's a huge piece of a person's life and provides community. And the physical exercise is really important. It's an outlet for so many people. And then when you take away sports as an outlet, and that support system, that's wreaking havoc and honestly, taking people's lives away, either metaphorically or parts of their identity.[12]

But accompanying these benefits are problems, sometimes serious problems.

Beginning Too Early

When is it too early for a child to be in adult-organized sports? There is no definitive answer, but surely there is an age when it is inappropriate for the physical and psychosocial development of the child. Consider preadolescent athletes as racecar drivers or becoming professional athletes in skateboarding and hiring professional coaches and personal trainers to improve performance. Youth baseball players may play over seventy-five games a year. Girls as young as four years old compete at the AAU Junior Olympics. Parents enroll infants in swimming lessons and buy their two-year-olds custom-made golf clubs.[13]

Or how about children as young as six, with the blessing of their parents, participating in ultimate fighting? One father defended this sport for his sons: "As a parent, I'd much rather have my kids here learning how to defend themselves and getting positive reinforcement than out on the streets."[14]

At what age do you "draw the line"? When should a child begin a hard-core strength regime? When should a child begin running marathons? Is it appropriate to have a child undergo genetic testing to determine their likelihood at success in certain sports?

Specialization

Kids used to play year-round alternating the sport with the season. That's not the case anymore as parents let unrealistic dreams shoehorn their children into one-sport misery. The day of the three-sport high school athlete is rapidly disappearing as coaches tell even ten-year-olds who show some promise in a particular sport to stick to that sport year-round.[15]

Youth with special talent now play on travel teams or club teams. They have two- or three-hour practices three or four times a week and play in single-day or in weekend tournaments with similarly skilled teams, sometimes at great distances. Such specialization and intense training run counter to recommendations by the National Athletic Trainers Association, which urges parents to delay specialization for as long as possible, and to ensure kids have at least two days off a week to rest, and do not play one sport more than eight months out of the year. Former NFL Super Bowl-winning quarterback Drew Brees played multiple sports in high school, and before that played recreational tennis with his family on weekends.

The Costs—Familial and Financial—of Youth Sports

The commitment of parents to develop their children into elite athletes is costly, both in a financial sense and in interruptions to family activities. Sport sociologist George Sage characterizes this phenomenon:

> For both the young athletes and their families the commitment to traveling teams is almost total. The young athletes must abandon other organized sports to concentrate on the travel team. They must commit to specializing in one sport, and often must compete with their team year-round. Family lives must be re-centered around the sports world of the traveling teams. The new breed of sports parents are road warriors who drive thousands of miles every

The Dark Side of Adult-Centered Play   111

season and spend weekends and evenings watching their kid's practice and play. And they write lots of checks because it is very expensive to support a traveling or club team athlete.[16]

The Aspen Institute Report discussed earlier in the chapter found families spend between $30 billion and $40 billion on children's youth sports activities. The costs are much greater—perhaps ten times as much—if the child goes to year-round training at a sports boarding school/academy (typically for gymnasts, figure skaters, tennis players, and golfers).[17] These high costs, of course, limit access only to those who can afford them or to those families willing to go into debt to develop their child's sports prowess. Indeed, according to the Aspen Institute, only 24 percent of children from low-income families participate on travel teams. Thus, those on the economic margins are shut out, moving to community-based sports where the financial obligation may not be as great. Community-based and school-based sports tend to be less competitive; players often have fewer skills as a result of the lack of "specialization" required of those competing on travel teams. Moreover, according to a *Washington Post* article, girls' basketball recently dropped to the fourth-most-popular school sport, given the shift to travel and club teams.[18]

Families suffer when the sport schedule trumps the family calendar. Traditional family time such as sit-down suppers, Saturdays, Sundays, and the month of August are violated by travel, games, tournaments, practices, and meetings.[19] Family interaction patterns are disrupted, vacations delayed or abandoned, and sibling rivalries intensified if family activities are centered disproportionately on one child. Then there are the potential scars for young children separated from the families in a sports-related boarding school.

Out-of-Control Parental Behavior

There are many instances of abusive behavior by parents at their child's games. This includes berating officials; mocking opponents; and using abusive language toward their own child, their child's teammates and coaches, and/or the opponents. Sometimes this verbal abuse spills over into physical assaults.[20] In October 2023, a St. Louis youth sport football coach for nine- and ten-year-old boys was shot four times by a parent who, according to news media reports, was upset with his son's playing time.[21] Fortunately the coach survived the assault. Although an extreme example, concerns regarding safety of officials are widespread. According to a survey of thirty-six thousand sports officials, 50 percent reported feeling unsafe while officiating sports events, and nearly 70 percent indicated that "sportsmanship" at games was declining, with parents as the "biggest offenders" and 50 percent surveyed indicated sportsmanship in youth sports was far worse than other competitive levels.[22] As Ron Nocetti, executive director of the California Interscholastic Federation (CIF) explains,

> Just the fact that there's even a threat of physical violence is completely uncalled for. This is a game, and I think that's what people are forgetting here. When we're talking about education-based athletics, we're supposed to be teaching life lessons to students about how to deal with adversity, how to learn from mistakes, how to appreciate the fact that no one is perfect. Your child's gonna make mistakes during games. The coaches are gonna make mistakes and the officials are gonna make mistakes, and if we can't see that in education-based athletics, then we're really lost.[23]

Untrained Coaches

Many coaches of children are excellent and enlightened leaders, teachers, and role models. However, over half of youth and school coaches in the United States are volunteers and many volunteer coaches lack the skills or training to provide meaningful instruction. The 2023 Aspen Institute report documents that "less than one-third of youth coaches in 2022 were trained in the previous year in concussion management, general safety, physical conditioning, sports skills and tactics, and effective motivational techniques."[24] Untrained coaches are likely unaware of the social, psychological, and physical development of children; they are likely to focus their coaching methods on winning rather than on skill development or other learning outcomes.[25] This increases the likelihood of physical and emotional injuries to the players. The Aspen Institute, the National Alliance for Youth Sports, and the National Committee for Accreditation of Coaching Education work to promote the following values: "youth sport should be about having fun while learning to work hard for a common goal, to prioritize developing skills over winning, to persist in the face of adversity, to be a good sport and to be competitive."[26] Yet children in youth sports often drop out because of coaches who fail to adhere to those values.

Intrusion of Organizations on Children's Sport

The actions by various organizations have enticed many parents to push their children toward athletic greatness. Some examples:

- Children's sports and the feats of elite child athletes have been glamorized in the media. Major legacy media outlets feature youth sports, including the national ranking of high school teams and high school players. ESPN and ABC-TV (not so incidentally, both are owned by the Walt Disney Company) televises the Little League World Series.

- Corporations such as Nike and McDonald's sponsor basketball tournaments for teenagers, which are frequented by college coaches who are scouting for talent. The McDonald's all-star game is nationally televised.
- Talent evaluators such as The *HoopScoop Online* rank basketball prospects as young as the fourth grade. Another, *Middle School Elite*, ranks junior high school players.[27]

All of this adds to the pressures and distractions of teenage athletes.[28]

Excessive Parental Demands

Some parents and coaches are too demanding, making sport work instead of fun—something to be dreaded rather than enjoyed. Kids are pressured by parents who live vicariously through their children's accomplishments (the "achievement-by-proxy" syndrome). This may manifest itself in starting the children in sport too soon, narrowing the choice of sports by specialization, forcing them to train or play when injured, and being too critical of their performances. At the extreme, it can result in programming a child to become a star athlete.

The emergence of social media and short form videos in the past decade have created opportunities for youth sport parents to promote their child's athletic accomplishments online in hopes of attracting not only followers but also the attention of recruiters, corporate sponsorships, and NIL deals. In an extreme case, one father has created a 'brand' strategy for his second-grade twin boys. As the *Washington Post* reports,

> Jolly has taught his boys that everything they do is part of their brand—from the way they play to their shoulder-length brown braids, which their father has made clear must be allowed by any middle school or high school coach recruiting them. He curates their social media feeds, spends hours editing their YouTube highlight videos and sometimes wears a T-shirt he made with the logos of seven youth basketball rankings websites, all of which have rated his sons the top second-graders in the country. "That's part of my strategy: Build their name up, build the expectations up, build their skills up, build their bodies up, so that by the time they get to high school, these companies are going to pay them to play," Jolly said. "We want to do it as early as possible. I believe we're going to be the pioneers."[29]

The potential for Name-Image-Likeness deals in college is trickling down to high school and youth sports. Youth sport families and parents may feel increased pressure to not only get their child involved in sports but to cultivate a social media presence and corresponding brand identity to ensure future opportunities.

This pressure is not "new" nor is it the result of the emergence of social media; however, it certainly has shifted pressures youth sports athletes face.

Conclusion

For many children, adult-organized sport is a positive experience, but for many it is not. Some children are pushed into sports too early. Adult-organized sports are often highly pressurized by overzealous parents and coaches. Play is transformed into work. Participation rates in adult-organized sports peak at age nine but before they become teenagers seven in ten will quit. They walk away for a number of reasons including the realization that they do not have the skills to compete or because of an injury. But more likely they disengage because the activity is not fun. They fear failing on the field and disappointing their parents who have invested so much in their success. The fault lies in the way sports for children have become organized: too adult centered, and with the focus on a redefinition of fun in terms of the outcome (winning and becoming a better athlete), rather than on the process. Society, parents, and children would be better served if the children's sports were recentered—focusing on the interest of the children rather than the interests of adults.

Notes

1 This first section and various parts of this chapter depend greatly on George H. Sage and D. Stanley Eitzen, *Sociology of North American Sport*, 10th ed. (Boulder, CO: Paradigm, 2016), chap. 4. Other sources used in this section are: Jay J. Coakley, *Sport in Society: Issues and Controversies*, 7th ed. (New York: McGraw-Hill, 2001), 118–24, and Melissa Fay Greene, "Sandlot Summer: Hyperscheduled, Overachieving Children Learn How to Play," *New York Times Magazine*, November 28, 2004, 40–44. For some ideas on how to fix children's sports, see Peter Cary, "Fixing Kids' Sports," *US News & World Report*, June 7, 2004, 44–53; and Peter Applebome, "What's to Come, Soccer Tryouts in the Cradle?" *New York Times*, October 17, 2004, 28YT.
2 Michael A. Messner, *It's All for the Kids: Gender, Families, and Youth Sports* (Berkeley: University of California Press, 2009), 9–13.
3 Messner, *It's All for the Kids*, 17.
4 "State of Play 2023: Participation Trends," Project Play, Aspen Institute, https://projectplay.org/state-of-play-2023/participation.

Notes

5   Daniel Sanger, "5, 6, Pickup Sticks," *The Walrus* (December/January 2007): 64.
6   Tom Farrey, *Game On: The All-American Race to Make Champions of Our Children* (New York: ESPN Books, 2008), 115.
7   Bob Bigelow and Tom Moroney, *Just Let the Kids Play: How to Stop Other Adults from Ruining Your Child's Fun and Success in Sports* (Deerfield Beach, FL: HCI, 2001); Patricia A. Adler and Peter Adler, *Peer Power: Preadolescent Culture and Identity* (New Brunswick, NJ: Rutgers University Press, 1998).
8   Eitzen and Sage, *Sociology of North American Sport*.
9   Farrey, *Game On*, 122.
10 Coakley, *Sports in Society*, 136–37.
11 Coakley, 137. See also Adler and Adler, *Peer Power*.
12 Shoshana K. Goldberg, "Fair Play: The Importance of Sports Participation for Transgender Youth," Center for American Progress, February 8, 2021, https://www.americanprogress.org/article/fair-play/.
13 Farrey, *Game On*, 13.
14 Quoted in Marcus Kabel, "Small Fists, Big Brawls," *Chicago Tribune*, March 28, 2008, Section 1, 2.
15 Tim Wendel, "When Smiles Leave the Game," *USA Today*, August 23, 2005, 13A. See also Patrick Welsh, "One-Sport Athletes: A Losing Proposition for Kids," *USA Today*, August 23, 2004, 11A.
16 Sage and Eitzen, *Sociology of North American Sport*, chap. 4.
17 Mark Hyman, *The Most Expensive Game in Town: The Rising Cost of Youth Sports and the Toll on Today's Families* (Boston: Beacon Press, 2012).
18 Roman Stubbs, "In Youth Sports, Talent Helps but Money Rules," *Washington Post*, December 12, 2022, https://www.washingtonpost.com/sports/2022/12/12/youth-sports-rising-costs/.
19 K. J. Kell'Antonia, "When Sports and Family Time Conflict, Speak Up," *New York Times*, August 15, 2014, http://parenting.blogs.nytimes.com/2014/08/15/when-sports-and-family-time-conflict-speak-up/.
20 For example, see Christine Brennan, "'Rec Rage' Is Unfit for Youth Sports," *USA Today*, May 17, 2012, 3C.
21 S. Borelli, "Sports Parents Are Out of Control and Officials Don't Feel Safe. Here's What's at Risk," *USA Today*, October 15, 2023, https://www.usatoday.com/story/sports/2023/10/15/parent-behavior-in-youth-sports-is-abusive-officials-dont-feel-safe/71194511007/.
22 Borelli.
23 Borelli.
24 Nancy Justis, "Why It's Getting Harder to Find Youth Sports Coaches," January 26, 2024, *The Gazette*, https://www.thegazette.com/iowa-prep-sports/why-its-getting-harder-to-find-youth-sports-coaches/.
25 Jennifer L. Etnier, "Your Kids' Coach Is Probably Doing It Wrong," March 11, 2020, *New York Times*, https://www.nytimes.com/2020/03/11/opinion/youth-sports-coaches.html.

26 Etnier.

27 Will Leitch, "Million Dollar Babies," *Bloomberg Businessweek*, October 25, 2010, 113–15.

28 Jim Halley, "Prep TV Has Pros and Cons," *USA Today*, August 22, 2013, C1–C2; and Christine Brennan, "Prep FB Best as Local Fare," *USA Today*, August 22, 2013, C3.

29 Roman Stubbs, "They're Top Ranked Basketball Players and Ready to Cash In. Up Next: Third Grade," *Washington Post*, https://www.washingtonpost.com/sports/2022/08/11/basketball-nil-second-grade/.

PART TWO
SPORTS AS A MICROCOSM OF SOCIETY

6
ARE SPORTS PLAYED ON A LEVEL PLAYING FIELD? ISSUES OF RACE, CLASS, AND GENDER

A widely held belief is that sport is perhaps the only societal institution that is fair. That is, physical ability, skill, strategy, and energy (and occasionally luck) determine the winners rather than arbitrary notions based on race, gender, social class, or other ascribed characteristics that are barriers that marginalize so many in other areas of social life. Indeed, sport policies including anti-doping policies, criteria for eligibility in women's competition (sometimes referred to as "sex testing" or gender verification policies), anti-trans inclusion policies, as well as rules and regulations on clothing and uniforms, and equipment are all designed to limit or prevent "unfair advantages" in sport. Under these conditions, athletes and teams are winners because of their achievements, not who they are and where they come from. And, of course, sport does work this way some of the time. But historically and in contemporary sport, exploring the three hierarchies of social stratification—race, class, and gender—exposes how this belief that sport is fair is a myth.

Although the following sections discuss each type of stratification independently of one another, Black feminist scholars offer important theoretical contributions to understanding forms of social stratification or social inequality as "interlocking" or "intersectional" forms of oppression. Feminist legal scholar, Kimberlé Crenshaw noted the ways in which the legal system conceptualizes discrimination as occurring based on one identity, or one axis of oppression (to use the language of scholars), which ignores how individuals often encounter discrimination based on the intersection of multiple identities.[1] As Crenshaw explains,

> [Intersectionality is] basically a lens, a prism, for seeing the way in which various forms of inequality often operate together and exacerbate each other. We tend to talk about race inequality as separate from inequality based on gender, class, sexuality or immigrant status. What's often missing is how some people are subject to all of these, and the experience is not just the sum of its parts.[2]

In other words, Black women do not confront discrimination based solely on their race or solely by their gender. Instead, they encounter racialized sexism, sexualized racism—what is now termed misogynoir.[3] While much of these conceptual frameworks are based in Black feminist thought,[4] scholars have found utility in the concepts to explain how systems of inequality operate.

Racial Inequities

When Barack Obama was elected in 2008, many believed the first Black president in US history signified the country was now in a new era, a "color-blind" society where race no longer mattered in determining what one could become or achieve. Indeed, the election had important implications for representation. Being able to see oneself reflected in the most powerful position in the world is certainly inspiring and meaningful change for not just Black Americans, but for everyone. As then-First Lady Michelle Obama said in a Democratic Convention speech, "I wake up every morning in a house that was built by slaves."[5] Obama's presidency signified racial progress, a product of social change in American society. Certainly, beyond representation, Obama's electoral win was indicative of the successes of the 1960s civil rights movement, which culminated in the end of Jim Crow legal segregation and the enfranchisement of non-white voters with the passage of the 1965 Voting Rights Act. The civil rights movement expanded opportunities for People of Color in education, politics, and the workforce by establishing the legal rights to those institutions, paving the way for the election of the nation's first Black president.

Despite the significance of President Obama's electoral victory, and the gains achieved by minoritized racial groups since the civil rights movement began in the 1950s, racial division and discrimination continues. Some would suggest the election of Donald J. Trump in 2016, over Hillary Clinton (the country's first woman president, had she succeeded), was an outcome of a "'backlash" to the Obama presidency and what the historic 2008 and 2012 elections represented for many Americans. During his term, Trump appointed three new justices to the Supreme Court, creating what has been called, "the most conservative-leaning [court] in modern US history."[6] The U.S. Supreme Court has decided, with its now-established six-to-three conservative majority, on several major challenges to key pieces of civil rights legislation, including affirmative action in higher education, which was overturned in June of 2023,[7] the Voting Rights Act of 1965,[8] wherein the Court's decisions have diluted the power of Black voters by, for example, preventing states from taking race into account when determining voting districts. Also, in June of 2023 the Court overturned *Roe v. Wade*, ending five decades of a pregnant person's constitutional right to abortion. The Court's decision activated so-called "trigger laws" in thirteen states, immediately banning abortion. As of June of 2024, fourteen states had complete bans, with no exception for cases of rape, incest, or protecting the health of the mother. Many pregnant people must either travel out of state (often cost- and time-prohibitive), carry an unwanted pregnancy to term, or (for now) rely on medical abortions. During the summer 2024 session, the Court will decide whether to impose restrictions on the pill mifepristone. Mifepristone is a "drug that blocks a hormone called progesterone that is needed for a pregnancy to continue."[9] The drug has been approved by ninety different countries, including in by the US Federal Drug Administration in 2000, and used for decades (since 1987 in France). The United States is the only country considering rescinding its use.[10] Barriers on access to higher education, on determining who one's representatives will be in local, state, and federal governments, and on making decisions regarding one's reproductive health all have concerning implications on one's life chances and opportunities, particularly for members of minoritized communities. Disparate economic advantages continue to accrue disproportionately to the white majority, and this is even before the effects of these laws have been realized. Consider some examples from the most recent data supplied by the US Census Bureau:[11]

- The median household income in 2022 was $108,700 for Asian Americans, $81,060 for white Americans, $62,800 for Latino Americans, and $52,860 for Black Americans.
- The official poverty rate in 2022 overall was 12 percent, yet it was 19 percent for Hispanic people and 17 percent for Black people. This was the largest one-year increase in the overall poverty rate ever reported in the United States, due in part to the elimination of many governmental programs for the poor as well as rising inflation and increased cost of living.[12]
- The median net worth of white households in 2021 was ten times greater than that of Black households. Black householders were more likely than white householders to have zero or negative wealth, and more likely to have unsecured debt, such as student loans or medical debt.[13]

Moreover, the unemployment rate for Black people is consistently twice that for their white counterparts.[14] As of the first quarter in 2024, the unemployment rate of white Americans was 3.1 percent, 6.0 percent for Black Americans, and 4.7 percent for Latino Americans. Asian American and Asian Pacific Islanders had unemployment rates similar to their white counterparts, 3.2 percent.

Historically, those from minoritized communities, particularly economically disadvantaged communities, do not believe the US criminal justice system to be just. The #BlackLivesMatter movement began first on social media in 2013 by three Black organizers, Alicia Garza, Patrisse Cullors, and Opal Tometi, in response to the acquittal of George Zimmerman (a white man who brutally murdered sixteen-year-old Trayvon Martin). The movement went from social media to nationwide street protests during the summer of 2020 after the murders of Breonna Taylor, a Black medical worker who was killed in her home during a botched police raid, and, a few weeks later, of George Floyd, a former collegiate football player who was detained and murdered by Minneapolis police officers. Video of the murder went viral on social media and depicted Floyd begging then-officer Derek Chauvin for his life, proclaiming he couldn't breathe, while Chauvin pinned him to the ground with his knee on Floyd's neck.

In addition to police brutality, bias against minoritized communities is reflected in differentials in incarceration rate, length of sentence, and application of the death penalty, even when white and Black people are accused of similar crimes. According to the National Association for the Advancement of Colored Peoples (NAACP), "one out of every three Black boys born today can expect to be sentenced to prison, compared 1 out 6 Latino boys or one out of 17 white boys."[15] Even skin color among Black people makes a difference. A study of twelve thousand inmates in North Carolina found that darker-skinned Black women were sentenced to nearly 12 percent more prison time than lighter-skinned Black women.[16] Racial and ethnic discrimination also occurs in hiring, firing, and selection to leadership positions in various occupations.

Our questions to consider: Is sport an exception? Is the playing field level for athletes from minoritized identities? Does race restrict opportunities in sports, or are sports color-blind? If sport indeed offers social mobility for minorities, one expects it to distribute opportunities so that members of minoritized communities are found throughout the social structure, not disproportionately at the bottom of the hierarchy. The answers to these questions, however, are not clear-cut since a case can be made for both sides. Let's review both by focusing on Black athletes in our discussion.

The case for the affirmative begins with history. There are opportunities now for Black athletes today in sport that were not always present throughout the development of modern sports in the United States. In the first half of the twentieth century, segregation kept most Black athletes, with few exceptions, from intercollegiate and professional sports. Instead, the majority of opportunities existed in what are now in "historically Black colleges and universities" (HBCUs) or in the Negro leagues. Major League Baseball integrated in 1947, and the National Football League officially desegregated in 1946. Yet the NFL's Washington Commanders (at the time the team had a racist name and logo) did not hire a Black player until 1962. The last major college conference to integrate was the Southeastern Conference (SEC) in 1966, and it was the last conference to have a Black head football coach (hired in 2004).

The year 1966 is significant in this history because of a watershed event—an all-Black starting lineup for Texas Western (now the University of Texas–El Paso) upset the all-white University of Kentucky team for the NCAA men's basketball championship. Fast forward to 2001 at the SEC tournament championship basketball game, where Kentucky faced Mississippi. Both head coaches, all three officials, and most of the players in that game were Black.

And it was not until 2024 that Major League Baseball (MLB) integrated statistics from the Negro league with MLB. This shifted many records held by white players to Black players like John Gibson, known as the "Black Babe Ruth," whose lifetime batting average of .372 beats MLB's all-time highest held by Ty Cobb (.367).[17] Although Major League Baseball is integrating its statistics, a move that is seen as either a much-needed remedy to past discrimination or indicative of the MLB becoming "woke," during the 2024 season only 5.7 percent of MLB players were Black (Latino athletes made up 30 percent of baseball players, the largest racial group in the league). David

Justice, a former all-star and World Series champion with the Atlanta Braves explains some of the barriers to participation:

> There's this thing called [youth] travel ball and it costs a lot of money. A [proper] baseball bat costs $400. And if you don't have the family, you don't have the money. But I can go out here and grab that basketball, and we can go hoop all day.[18]

In other major professional leagues, there are a disproportionate number of Black athletes, which some consider a sign of progress from the days when leagues were segregated. According to the Pew Research Center, in 2022 just over 14 percent of the US population identified as Black. Yet 70.4 percent of the players in the NBA and 53 percent of NFL players are Black. In Division I college men's basketball, 57 percent of the athletes were Black. In the Power 5 conference, 46 percent of athletes were Black. For all NCAA sports, Black players constituted 16 percent of the athletes in 2022.[19]

Once sports racially integrated, there was more diversity particularly in the sports most popular in the United States like football and basketball. When considering these sports in the United States, racial inclusion has shifted significantly over the past century.

Another argument for sport as a level playing field is the incredible incomes that many racial minority athletes make. In a 2024 *Forbes* list of the top fourteen "world's celebrity billionaires," a number of athletes made the list, all of whom are Black male athletes, including current and former Los Angeles Lakers' stars Magic Johnson ($1.2 billion) and Lebron James ($1.2 billion), professional golfer Tiger Woods ($1.3 billion), and Chicago Bulls' (and, according to Cheryl, the greatest men's basketball player of all time) Michael Jordan ($3.2 billion).[20] A list of the highest paid NBA players for the 2024–2025 season revealed that nine of the top ten salaries went to Black athletes (Nikola Jokic was the exception), with salaries ranging from over $48 million for Jimmy Butler (number 10) to over $55 million for top-paid NBA player, Steph Curry.[21]

But that is only part of the story. There are still limits placed on Black athletes and athletes of color. Athletes from minoritized communities are rarely found in certain sports in the United States (golf, tennis, bowling, skiing, ice-skating, swimming, polo, auto racing) where barriers exist in terms of access and opportunity. Before 1990, for example, the US Golf Association (USGA) and the Professional Golf Association (PGA) regularly played their golf tournaments at country clubs that only allowed white members. When the various governing bodies in golf adopted antidiscrimination guidelines for their host clubs, eleven country clubs that hosted tournaments refused to racially integrate. Moreover, many of those that integrated did so by admitting a "token" Black golfer, an attempt to silence the protesters and do the bare minimum to adhere to those guidelines. In 2021, over thirty years since the antidiscrimination guidelines were passed, only two Black male golfers were in the top one hundred rankings, and only one Black female golfer was in the top three hundred rankings. And as much as fans believe Tiger Woods changed the sport of golf, there are fewer golfers from Black communities than when he entered the PGA in 1996.[22]

In the major US team sports, athletes from minoritized communities are underrepresented in central leadership and tactical positions and overrepresented in decentralized and physical positions. This form of discrimination, known as "stacking," is one of the most-documented forms of discrimination in both US college (e.g., men's football and women's volleyball) and professional ranks (football, baseball) and in other countries as well (e.g., Canadian football, British soccer, German soccer, and Australian rugby).[23] In a study on the racial composition of players in the National Football League from 1960 to 2020, researchers found white athletes are much more likely to play on the offensive line (67.5 percent) than defensive line (35.7 percent); and if on offense they are disproportionately at quarterback (87 percent) and kicker/punter (91.3 percent). Black athletes are found disproportionately on defense, at wide receiver (79.5 percent), running back (77.7 percent) and defensive back (82.3 percent).[24] The researchers also note that over the history of the NFL, defensive positions desegregated and are now dominated by Black players, while central positions like quarterback and kicker/punter remained white-dominated throughout the history of the league. Are these differences in racial composition by position accidental or based on actual performance criteria, or are the decisions made by athletes, coaches, scouts, and general managers based on racial stereotypes?

Athletes of color do not have the same opportunities as white athletes when their playing careers are finished. This is reflected in media positions, where Black and Latino athletes are rarely found in radio and television broadcasting, even less so as play-by-play announcers, and very infrequently as sportswriters or officials. And white men tend to dominate in positions of authority in sport—head coaches, athletic directors, general managers, and owners.

In the major professional and collegiate sports where they are overrepresented as athletes, Black players are conversely underrepresented among coaches and then they tend to be assigned to roles with fewer opportunities for upward mobility. In football, Black assistant coaches are typically assigned to coach receivers, running backs, and defensive backs, positions dominated by Black athletes. Most offensive or defensive coordinators, the most important coaching positions after head coach and ones that eventually lead to head coaching jobs, are white. Indeed, a study commissioned by the NFL in 2019 found that Black coaches were less likely to receive second chances (no Black coach has coached for three or more teams in the league, while a number of white coaches get "second" or "third" chances on other teams). In 2022, Brian Flores, head coach of the Miami Dolphins, sued the NFL for racial discrimination.

In 2024, there were nine Black head coaches in the NFL. Prior to 2024, in the last five seasons only three head coaches were Black. Some see this as significant progress, while others question how long the change will last, particularly when the NFL hired no Black offensive coordinators for the 2024 season.[25] In major league baseball, those from minoritized communities overwhelmingly coach first base, where the responsibilities are much less important than at third base. This is significant because the third-base coach is the most important on-field coach. When managing jobs open, third-base coaches have the best experience for moving to the top job.

College and university programs lag behind the professional leagues in hiring Black head coaches. The Institute for Diversity and Equity in Sport (TIDES) reports that in 2020–2021, Black head coaches held 9.9 percent, 6.7 percent, and 6.3 percent of the men's head coaching positions in Divisions I, II, and III, respectively, and held 10.2 percent, 6.4 percent, and 6.3 percent of the women's head coaching positions in Divisions I, II, and III, respectively.[26] Among Football Bowl Subdivision (FBS) schools, 89 percent of football coaches were white in 2023, and similar to their counterparts in the NFL, Black coaches seldom get "second chances" or hired by another university after they are fired. In men's Division I basketball almost 25 percent of coaches were Black, compared to 43 percent of the coaches in the NBA. This pattern holds for Black coaches of women's sports. In the 2024 season, there were only three Black head coaches in the WNBA (or 25 percent), which was down from six the previous season. In Division I women's basketball only 18.5 percent of the head coaches were Black.

Dr. Jeff O'Brien, the CEO of the Institute for Sport and Social Justice, had this to say about the findings from the TIDES study,

> In the aftermath of the so-called 2020 racial reckoning, we were told that change was inevitable regarding the leveling of the playing field for coaches and AD's in college athletics. The data in this Racial and Gender Report Card make clear that this change has not occurred. The abysmal percentages of women and people of color in head coach and athletic director roles provide us with the tip of the iceberg. The real story lies beneath the surface, in the darkness, where systemic racism and sexism thrive and ensure the status quo is maintained. But, bemoaning this dynamic or promising to do better in the future are not adequate. A true reckoning, with clear expectations and consequences, is required if we intend to manifest an equitable tomorrow.[27]

The dearth of members from minoritized communities in positions of leadership (coaches and administrators) in professional and college sports could be the result of two forms of discrimination. Overt discrimination occurs when owners ignore competent candidates because of their own prejudices or because they fear the negative reaction of fans to non-white leaders. The other type of discrimination is covert. It takes two forms. First, non-white candidates may not be considered for coaching positions because they did not (due to stacking) play at high interactive positions requiring leadership and decision-making. We know that major league managers, for example, tend to have played as catchers or infielders. Black athletes because of stacking practices have been typically in the outfield and therefore do not possess the requisite infield experience that has traditionally provided a pipeline to a manager position. The situation is similar in football, where research has shown that most coaches played at the central positions of quarterback, offensive center, guard, or linebacker during their playing days. Since Black athletes rarely play these positions, they are more likely to be excluded from head coaching responsibilities. The second form of discrimination addresses the question: Who is doing the hiring? The people who select head coaches are overwhelmingly white. According to the 2022 Racial and Gender Equity Report Card, 78.6 percent of chancellors and presidents, 78.6 percent of athletic directors, 83.6 percent of faculty athletic representatives, and 80.0 percent of conference commissioners were white. Important to note, 60.3 percent of chancellors and presidents, 67.9 percent of athletic directors, 50.0 percent of faculty athletic representatives, and 70.0 percent of conference commissioners were white men. The report also notes white people held 321 of the 402 leadership positions on colleges campuses in 2022.[28] These data suggest, says Dr. Richard Lapchick, founder of The Institute for Diversity and Ethics in Sport (TIDES) at the University of Central Florida, that the "old boys" network continues to operate in sport:

> The people tasked with leadership positions should be a reflection of those who they lead. Unfortunately, in college sports, specifically at the FBS institutions, the overrepresentation of white men represents most of the leadership resulting in a lack of opportunities for women and people of color. While women and people of color serving in leadership positions at FBS institutions is improving, it should be noted that the numbers are not a reflection of the student-athlete body. To provide the best experience and services for student-athletes, individuals in leadership positions need to be able to relate to the student-athlete body. I challenge the leadership at all colleges and universities to mirror the diversity of their students and student-athletes in a way that is more equitable for all leadership positions.[29]

Class Inequities

In the United States, one's social class location is based on income, wealth, and the related variables of occupation, education, and social connections.[30] The lines dividing the social classes in the United States are quite blurred, except for those that delineate the very rich and the very poor. Money separates. Economic resources or the lack thereof are hugely consequential in determining the possibility of one's life chances. The question we will consider in the following section is: Does sport break down these economic and social barriers or does it uphold and reinforce them?

Despite the "rags to riches" narrative prevalent in sports journalism and film, the opportunity for upward social mobility is limited. As discussed in chapter 5, children from families with fewer economic resources tend to participate in sports that do not require expensive equipment and are publicly funded, such as community youth programs and school-based sports. Given the relatively small budgets for publicly funded youth sports, participants' opportunities to excel are often limited to sports that are inexpensive and do not require special facilities, such as football, basketball, baseball, track, and boxing. Children from affluent families with greater economic resources, on the other hand, have access to a wider range of sports and are more likely to live in communities with golf courses, tennis courts, ice-skating rinks, private gymnasiums, and swimming pools. They also have access to coaching in those sports, through private country clubs, neighborhood associations, and parental subsidies. Moreover, some sports such as gymnastics and ice-skating require considerable money for coaching, access, equipment, and travel. Young elite ice-skaters, for example, sometimes spend in the six figures annually on costumes, coaching, ice time, and travel. Children from affluent families can also attend expensive year-round sports academies for specialized training and coaching in their sport, most notably gymnastics, tennis, and golf. Often beyond the means of those who are from economically disadvantaged communities are opportunities to participate in traveling club leagues, hire personal trainers and private coaches, and attend sports camps. Regarding the latter, just in football there are hundreds of specialized camps run by entrepreneurs that focus exclusively on the quarterback position.[31]

Economically privileged children are also advantaged in sport over their economically under-privileged peers by the schools that they attend. They are more likely to attend private schools or public schools in wealthy school districts. Economically advantaged school districts are able to provide more sports opportunities, more coaches, and better facilities and equipment than economically disadvantaged school districts. In sharp contrast, schools in economically disadvantaged communities often must cut back or eliminate sports programs due to budget cuts or funding constraints. The first to go are freshman and sophomore sports and girls' sports. Less likely to experience cuts are the so-called revenue sports of football and basketball. An alternative to slashing sports is to charge participation fees, which average approximately $160 per high school sport, which can be a burden for families from economically disadvantaged communities. For example, a study of school districts in Michigan found a $100 fee reduced sports participation by 10 percent, and the reduction in participation doubled when the fee was $200.[32]

Gender Inequities

There have been significant gains in the United States since the 1960s in women's (particularly white, affluent women's) access and opportunities to institutions from which they had previously been excluded or marginalized, such as higher education, medicine, law, politics, and certain segments of the workforce. Despite these gains, achieved largely by the feminist social movements of the 1960s and 1970s, women in the 2020s continue to encounter institutional barriers and occupy secondary status to men. Consider the following statistics on the gender gap in leadership in 2023:[33]

- Within the US government, while a woman of color was elected as Vice President for the first time in 2020 (and the first time any woman was elected as Vice President), women held only 25 percent of seats in the US Senate, 28.5 percent of seats in the US House of Representatives, and just under 33 percent of seats in state legislatures. Only 24 percent of governors were women. The percentage of women appointed to presidential cabinets varies greatly by administration and fluctuates over the course of a presidential term, particularly if the president serves a second term. When Trump was sworn into office in 2017 only 26.1 percent of the cabinet positions were held by women, compared to 48 percent appointed at the beginning of Biden's term in 2021.
- In 2021 women comprised 47.4 percent of the American workforce yet held just 42.1 percent of all managerial positions and 37.1 percent of top executive positions.[34] In 2023, only 10 percent of CEOs of US Fortune 500 companies were women and approximately 30 percent of Fortune 500 board members were women.

We consider the following question: Does the world of sport reinforce this gender imbalance, or does it work to challenge gender inequality? As with race- and class-based issues, a case can be made for both.

Until the 1970s, high school, college, and professional sports in the United States were, with few exceptions, male dominated. The barriers were breached finally by court cases (for example, a legal decision to open Little League baseball to girls) and by federal legislation (Title IX in 1972). With these changes, sports opportunities for girls and women have increased greatly (see chapters 3 and 5).

Yet prejudice and discrimination are not altered by the courts or legislation, and culturally informed responses to gender ideologies are ubiquitous and often resistant to social change. Therefore, laws may force institutions into compliance with equality of opportunity for women athletes, but other forms of inequities continue, albeit in more subtle and insidious forms, as we discussed in the previous section on race and racism.[35]

The passage and eventual (partial) implementation of Title IX has closed the gap between men and women in sport (see chapter 3). Participation by girls and women in sports increased dramatically in high schools and colleges over the five decades Title IX has been the law. For example, according to an NCAA report, in 2020 women's collegiate participation rate was just under 44 percent, compared to just under 28 percent in 1982 when the NCAA became the governing body for women's collegiate athletics.[36] Yet, given that approximately 58 percent of all college students are women, most schools are not providing equitable opportunities. And as we will see, advantages accrue to athletes in men's sports despite Title IX.

At the professional level, women historically have had fewer opportunities than men although this is beginning to shift with the success of the National Women's Soccer League, the emergence of the Professional Women's Hockey League (which had its first season in 2023–2024), and in the early 2020s Athletes Unlimited launched women's professional leagues for softball, volleyball, basketball, and lacrosse. Despite this recent growth in professional opportunities, pay equity continues to be an issue and women receive less compensation and sponsorship dollars than their counterparts; although there are recent efforts by leagues to address athletes' concerns with gender pay equity, in part due to the USWNT lawsuit against the US Soccer federation. Moreover, the pay is highly skewed in many professional organizations that have men's and women's leagues. The top NBA players receive in excess of $30 million a year, while the mandated highest salary in the WNBA in 2023 was $234,936 (in 2022 it was $117,500). The prize money for PGA tournaments (for men professional golfers) in 2023 was $460 million compared to $101.4 million for women professionals playing in the LPGA. A 2023 study by researchers from Aldephi University[37] found that, on average, professional athletes in the major men's sports make considerably more than professional athletes in the major women's sports. Consider the following: the average salary in the NBA is over $10 million, the WNBA is just over $113,000; the average salary in the PGA is just over $1 million, the LPGA is just over $346,000; the average salary in the MLS is just over $471,000 and for the NWSL its $54,000; and in professional tennis, despite the successful efforts of Billie Jean King and Venus and Serena Williams to have equal prize money in the Grand Slam tournaments, the average salary in the ATP is close to $1.6 million, and in the WTA it is slightly over $1 million.

Gender Inequities

The above statistics are based on average salaries. A limitation in interpreting averages is that outliers (a very high or a very low data point) can skew the average one way or another. Examining the gender salary gap from another measure, however, offers similar trends. The Aldelphi study also compared the top paid athletes in men's sports and in women's sports. Drawing from data compiled by *Forbes*, which included salary, prize money, and endorsements, the top paid athletes in 2022 in men's sports were: Lionel Messi (soccer), $130 million, LeBron James (basketball), $121.2 million, Cristiano Ronaldo (soccer), $115 million, Neymar (soccer), $95 million, and Stephen Curry (basketball), $92.8 million. In comparison, the top-paid athletes in 2022 in women's sports were Naomi Osaka (tennis), $51.1 million, Serena Williams (tennis), $41.3 million, Eileen Gu (freestyle skier), $20.1 million, Emma Raducanu (tennis), $18.7 million, and Iga Świątek (tennis), $14.9 million. Most significantly, while men have the chance for careers as relatively well-paid professional athletes in many sports, including baseball and gridiron tackle football both of which are among the most popular sports in the United States, women do not yet have an equivalent league.

There are indicators some of these inequities might change. Since the COVID-19 global pandemic officially ended, women's sports in the United States have experienced an unprecedented amount of (visible[38]) fan interest, individual and corporate investment, and media attention, particularly in women's collegiate and professional basketball. This so-called "rise" in women's sports is complex and multifaceted as we discussed in chapter 3. Even with the growth in women's sports, elite-level, professional women athletes are still trailing behind the resources, investment, salaries, and opportunities afforded to men athletes.

Sport continues to perpetuate male dominance in society. After Title IX brought greater public attention and wider participation in women's sports, control over women's collegiate athletics shifted dramatically to men. Before Title IX in 1972, over 90 percent of collegiate women's teams had a woman head coach; in 2021–2022, the percentage was 41 percent.[39] Women coaches overall are paid less than men coaches. According to a Knight-Newhouse College Athletics study, between 2014 and 2021, average Power 5 men's coaching salaries increased by 55 percent, while women's only increased 33 percent;[40] thus, the gender gap in pay has only increased in the past decade. Moreover, prior to Title IX's passage, more than 90 percent of women's intercollegiate programs were administered by a woman, but only 25 percent were in 2023, and 15 percent among Division I programs.[41] The pattern seems to be: the higher the level of competition and the better paying the positions, the more likely men will be head coaches and top administrators of women's teams and programs. For ancillary positions in sports, women again have many fewer opportunities than men. For example, in the NCAA 14.9 percent of team physicians were women during the

2022–2023 season. As we noted above in our discussion of the TIDES reports, the majority of sports media is overwhelmingly white and male.

Women from minoritized communities encounter intersectional forms of oppression (as was discussed earlier in the chapter), racialized sexism, and gendered racism. Thus, women from minoritized backgrounds experience fewer job opportunities in sports than white women or Black men. For example, a study by the Global Sport Institute at Arizona State University examined the percentage of people of color and women hired as athletic directors between 2010 and 2019 and found that no Asian-American women or Latina women were hired in seven of the ten years studied.[42]

Major inequities remain for athletes of women's sports, despite the progress achieved since the passage of Title IX. For example, women comprise 58 percent of college student populations, yet they received only 44 percent of participation opportunities and athletic scholarships. Women who play sports in Division I-FBS schools receive only about 18 percent of the total money spent on athletics, 29 percent of recruiting dollars, and 41 percent of athletic scholarship dollars. In addition, at the typical FBS school, for every dollar spent on women's sports, about two and a half dollars are spent on men's sports.[43]

Sport also perpetuates male dominance through the media (see chapter 7). For example, my colleague Michael Messner and I have documented the coverage of women's and men's sports on televised news and highlight shows, as well as online newsletters and social media accounts of major legacy sports media outlets and found nearly 90–95 percent of the coverage and content was devoted to men's sports.[44]

Male dominance is maintained when communities build very expensive stadiums and arenas to keep their professional teams or to entice other teams to move there (see chapter 9). These stadiums, costing hundreds of millions of dollars in tax revenue, are for men. They are for male owners, male athletes, male coaches, male trainers, male media, male-controlled corporations, and mostly male fans. The symbolic message is clear: men count for much more than women.

Men's dominance in sports is also promoted when the focus is on celebrating beautiful and sexy women athletes, thereby de-athleticizing them. Women are often used as entertainers at men's professional and collegiate sports events. Men's sports events (and some women's college sports) feature majorettes, cheerleaders, and dancers dressed in revealing uniforms intended to appeal to a stereotypical cisgender, white, heterosexual, young male fanbase. Historically, the media coverage of sports has focused more on the appearance and hetero-sexy appeal of women athletes (and in particular white women athletes) than the on-the-court performance and athleticism, although there are indications of a shift in certain segments of the sports media landscape. For example, a common exercise professors had for students in sociology of sport courses was for students to look up "top female athletes" in an online search engine. For many years, the results were overwhelmingly websites featuring "top hottest female athletes" or the "sexiest female athletes in sports." The results now (which are in part dependent upon algorithms drawing from a user's search history and other data points) might bring up articles about the "highest-paid female athletes," "top female athletes on social media," "the world's greatest female athletes," and other topics not devoted to how "sexy" or "hot" a female athlete is. This is not to say that an athlete's appearance or adherence to hetero-femininity is no longer a factor in how American society evaluates women athletes, and in particular white women athletes; rather, it has become decentered from the narratives, representation, and content surrounding women athletes and women's sports.

Despite some of the recent shifts we've seen in women's sports in the past few years (see chapter 3), overall, the data continue to illustrate the ways in which women in sport are second-class citizens. Women have fewer sports participation and career opportunities, fewer resources devoted to their programs, and they receive less coverage in legacy sports media. Black women athletes are often the target of gendered racism and racialized sexism (or what is referred to as misogynoir) in the legacy media coverage. One example of this type of coverage was evidenced in the media narratives surrounding the 2024 WNBA's rookie class and the so-called rivalry between the Indiana Fever's Caitlin Clark and the Chicago Sky's Angel Reese.

Conclusion

We have made the case in this chapter that sport is sometimes structured to be unfair—that sport does not always take place on a level playing field. In each of these illustrations (racial, class, and gender inequities), structural changes could correct the imbalances. The entrenched benefactors of the status quo, however, are reluctant to give up their advantages and level the playing field, calling into question the notion that success is based solely on performance.

Notes

[1] Kimberlé Crenshaw, "Demarginalizing the Intersection of Race and Sex: A Black Feminist Critique of Antidiscrimination Doctrine, Feminist Theory and Antiracist Politics," *University of Chicago Legal Forum* 1989, no. 1: Article 8, 139–67.

2. Katie Steinmetz, "She Coined the Term 'Intersectionality' Over 30 Years Ago: Here's What It Means to Her Today," February 20, 2020, *Time*, https://time.com/5786710/kimberle-crenshaw-intersectionality/.

3. Moya Bailey, *Misogynoir Transformed: Black Women's Digital Resistance* (New York: New York University Press).

4. Patricia Hill Collins, *Black Feminist Thought, 30th Anniversary Edition: Knowledge, Consciousness, and the Politics of Empowerment* (New York: Routledge, 2022).

5. Julie Hirschfeld Davis, "Yes, Slaves Did Help Build the White House," *New York Times*, July 26, 2016, https://www.nytimes.com/2016/07/27/us/politics/michelle-obama-white-house-slavery.html.

6. "Who Are the Justices on the Supreme Court?," *BBC News*, February 8, 2024, https://www.bbc.com/news/magazine-33103973.

7. Nina Totenberg, "Supreme Court Guts Affirmative Action, Effectively Ending Race-Conscious Admissions," National Public Radio, June 29, 2023, https://www.npr.org/2023/06/29/1181138066/affirmative-action-supreme-court-decision.

8. Joan Kiskupic, "Voting Rights Act Ruling Latest Attempt by Trump-Nominated Judges to Overturn Supreme Court Precedent," CNN, November 20, 2023, https://www.cnn.com/2023/11/20/politics/voting-rights-act-supreme-court-thomas-gorsuch/index.html.

9. "Questions and Answers on Mifepristone for Medical Termination of Pregnancy Through Ten Weeks Gestation," US Food and Drug Administration, September 1, 2023, https://www.fda.gov/drugs/postmarket-drug-safety-information-patients-and-providers/questions-and-answers-mifepristone-medical-termination-pregnancy-through-ten-weeks-gestation.

10. Miriam Berger and Mikhail Kilmentov, "Abortion Pill at Heart of Supreme Court Ruling Is Approved in Over 90 Countries," *Washington Post*, March 26, 2024, https://www.washingtonpost.com/world/2023/04/19/abortion-pill-mifepristone-global-approved/.

11. Gloria Guzman and Melissa Kollar, "Income in the United States: 2022," US Census Bureau, September 12, 2023, https://www.census.gov/library/publications/2023/demo/p60-279.html, and Jeremy Ney, "The Surprising Poverty Levels Across the U.S.," *Time*, October 4, 2023.

12. Ney, "The Surprising Poverty Levels."

13. Briana Sullivan, Donald Hays, and Neil Bennett, "Households with a White, Non-Hispanic Householder Were Ten Times Wealthier Than Those with a Black Householder in 2021," US Census Bureau, April 23, 2024, https://www.census.gov/library/stories/2024/04/wealth-by-race.

14. Max Zahn, "The Black Unemployment Rate Is Consistently Twice That of White Workers: Here's Why," *ABC News*, February 3, 2024, https://abcnews.go.com/Business/black-unemployment-rate-consistently-white-workers/story?id=106910140.

15. "Criminal Justice Fact Sheet," NAACP, https://naacp.org/resources/criminal-justice-fact-sheet.

16. Jill Viglione, Lance Hannon, and Robert DeFina, "The Impact of Light Skin on Prison Time for Black Female Offenders," *Social Science Journal* 48 (July 2010): 250–58.

Notes

17 Steve Buckley, "MLB's Integration of Negro League Stats Invites Us to Explore Baseball as Never Before," *The Athletic*, May 31, 2024, https://www.nytimes.com/athletic/5531132/2024/05/31/negro-leagues-statistics-mlb-satchel-paige/.

18 Andrew Lawrence, "MLB Has Integrated Negro Leagues Stats. Is It Too Little, Too Late?," *Guardian*, June 20, 2024, https://www.theguardian.com/sport/article/2024/jun/20/negro-baseball-leagues-mlb-stats-integration.

19 Solomon Siskind, "What Black History Month Means to Those in Athletics," NCAA, February 17, 2023, https://www.ncaa.org/news/2023/2/17/media-center-what-black-history-month-means-to-those-in-athletics.aspx.

20 Devin Sean Martin, "The World's Celebrity Billionaires," *Forbes*, April 3, 2024, https://www.forbes.com/sites/devinseanmartin/2024/04/02/the-worlds-celebrity-billionaires-2024-taylor-swift-kim-kardashian-oprah/.

21 "NBA Player Salaries, 2024–25," ESPN, https://www.espn.com/nba/salaries/_/seasontype/3.

22 Lex Pryor, "Golf's Historic Problems with Race Aren't Getting Any Better," *The Ringer*, April 7, 2021, https://www.theringer.com/2021/4/7/22370057/golf-diversity-issues-history-pga-lpga-the-masters.

23 For a survey of the research, see George H. Sage and D. Stanley Eitzen, *Sociology of North American Sport*, 10th ed. (New York: Oxford University Press, 2016): see also, Kyle Siler, "Pipelines on the Gridiron: Player Backgrounds, Opportunity Structures and Racial Stratification in American College Football," *Sociology of Sport Journal* 36, no. 1 (2019); Tina Nobis and Felicia Lazaridou, "Racist Stacking in Professional Soccer in Germany," *International Review for the Sociology of Sport* 58, no. 1 (2023): 1–20.

24 G. Marquez-Velarde, R. Grashow, C. Glass, A. M. Blaschke, G. Gillette, H. A. Taylor, and A. J. Whittington, "The Paradox of Integration: Racial Composition of NFL Positions from 1960 to 2020," *Sociology of Race and Ethnicity* 9, no. 4 (2023): 451–69.

25 Tashan Reed, "The Number of Black NFL Head Coaches Doubled This Offseason, Is It a Sign of Lasting Change?," *New York Times*, June 13, 2024, https://www.nytimes.com/athletic/5293988/2024/06/13/nfl-black-coaches-hiring-insider-diversity/.

26 Richard Lapchick, "College Sports' Racial, Gender Hiring Practices Getting Worse Instead of Improving," ESPN, March 22, 2023, https://www.espn.com/college-sports/story/_/id/35918942/college-sports-racial-gender-hiring-practices-getting-worse-improving.

27 Lapchick.

28 "2022 College Sport Racial and Gender Report Card (NCAA)," The Institute for Diversity and Equity in Sport (TIDES), https://www.tidesport.org/college.

29 Richard Lapchick, "College Sports Leadership Again Earns Poor Grades for Racial, Gender Hiring Practices," ESPN, February 23, 2023. https://www.espn.com/college-sports/story/_/id/35719577/college-sports-leadership-again-earns-poor-grades-racial-gender-hiring-practices.

30 D. Stanley Eitzen, Maxine Baca Zinn, and Kelly Eitzen Smith, *In Conflict and Order: Understanding Society*, 13th ed. (Boston: Allyn and Bacon, 2013), 227.

31 Paul Wachter, "Just Win, Baby," *Bloomberg BusinessWeek*, August 1, 2011, 82–83.

32 J. Zdroik and P. Veliz, "The Influence of Pay-to-Play Fees on Participation in Interscholastic Sports: A School-Level Analysis of Michigan's Public Schools," *J Phys Activ Health* 13, no. 12 (2016): 1317–24.

33 Katherine Schaeffer, "Fact Sheet: The Data on Women Leaders," *Pew Research Center*, September 27, 2023, https://www.pewresearch.org/social-trends/fact-sheet/the-data-on-women-leaders/.

34 Chris Gilligan, "States with the Highest Percentage of Female Top Executives," *US News and World Report*, March 6, 2023, https://www.usnews.com/news/best-states/articles/2023-03-06/states-with-the-highest-percentage-of-women-in-business-leadership-roles.

35 Sage and Eitzen, *Sociology of North American Sport*, 310.

36 Sarah Weissman, "Growing Participation, Widening Funding Gap," *Inside Higher Ed*, June 27, 2022, https://www.insidehighered.com/news/2022/06/28/gap-widens-spending-ncaa-mens-and-womens-teams.

37 "Male vs Female Professional Sports Salary Comparison," Aldelphi University, October 23, 2023, https://online.adelphi.edu/articles/male-female-sports-salary/.

38 We indicate "visible" here as interest in women's sports has existed for quite some time. In part due to the emergence of social media, fan interest is "measurable" now and as such is more visible to leagues, corporations, and media entities.

39 Corbin McQuire, "WeCOACH Continuing Mission to 'Move the Numbers' and Serve Women in Coaching," NCAA, February 2, 2023, https://www.ncaa.org/news/2023/2/3/media-center-wecoach-continuing-mission-to-move-the-numbers-and-serve-women-in-coaching.aspx.

40 Amanda Christovich, "The Growing Gender Disparity in Power 5 Coaching Salaries," May 30, 2024, *Front Office Sports*, https://frontofficesports.com/the-growing-gender-disparity-in-power-5-coaching-salaries/.

41 Christina Gouch, "NCAA Athletic Departments Directors in 2023, by Gender," Statista, February 27, 2024, https://www.statista.com/statistics/1120375/ncaa-athletic-director-gender/.

42 Patrick Hruby, "Lonely at the Top: Few College Athletic Directors Are Women and People of Color," *Global Sports Matters*, https://globalsportmatters.com/business/2021/05/07/few-college-athletic-directors-minorities-ncaa/.

43 "The Battle for Gender Equity in Athletics in Colleges and Universities," National Women's Law Center, June 21, 2022, https://nwlc.org/resource/the-battle-for-gender-equity-in-athletics-in-colleges-and-universities/.

44 Cheryl Cooky and Michael Messner, "Gender in Televised Sports," https://dornsife.usc.edu/cfr/gender-in-televised-sports/.

7
MEDIA AND SPORT: CHANGING SPORTS, CHANGING MEDIA

The media provide information and entertainment. More subtly, they provide a collective experience for members of society, contributing to their socialization and serving to integrate persons into that culture. Significantly, sports media "are on the forefront of reporting social change, while also contributing to it."[1] Indeed, it might be difficult to see the significant influence the media has had on sports and sports has had on the media. One might argue sport in the twenty-first century is nearly indistinguishable from the media. Outside of athletes, coaches, and those employed by sports organizations, much of the way we experience, understand, and consume sport is through the media. Whether watching a game on ESPN, the B1G Ten Network, or Fox Sports; streaming sports content, reality programming, documentary films, and limited series on Fubu, Hulu, or Netflix; following our favorite athletes and teams on social media such as Instagram or TikTok; reading about sports on online news platforms like *Front Office Sports*, *Bleacher Report*, or *SB Nation*; getting updates and staying current on scores, trades, and other sports news via online newsletters like *The Athletic* or *The Gist* that are sent directly to our email inboxes; following our favorite sports journalists, commentators and bloggers on X (formerly known as Twitter); or listening to "in depth" interviews and conversations with our favorite athletes (current and former) on podcasts, there is a plethora of ways and a diversity of sites to fill the needs of sports fans.

Moreover, since the 2010s, the number of "niche" media outlets has exploded. Where once most media content focused on the "big three" sports, men's professional and collegiate football, baseball, and basketball, there are myriad opportunities to watch and follow sports that used to be eclipsed by the dominance of men's sports in the media landscape. Indeed, sports coverage and content are no longer confined to the "sports pages" or to media outlets specifically or solely focused on sports. Important changes in the media landscape have blurred the line between "sports" and "news," such that many outlets now cover social, political, and cultural issues, as well as the meanings for and implications of sports and society. It is not uncommon to see articles on sport published outside the "sports pages" of mainstream news outlets, in fashion and entertainment magazines, for example. This has created opportunities for audiences beyond the stereotypical sports fan to learn about sport, as it plays out both on and off the field. There have been shifts in the narratives or stories we tell about sports, who gets to tell those stories, and what stories get told. The questions for this chapter are whether these shifts in the media landscape have changed how sports are played and how sports are understood.

Shifts in the Media Landscape

Over the past few decades there have been significant shifts in how we produce and consume media content. Researchers have used various terms such as "old" versus "new" media, "legacy" versus "emergent" to describe the media before and after this shift. Some mark this shift with the emergence of the internet and digital forms of communication. "Old" media thus includes print media, such as newspapers and magazines, and electronic media, such as radio and television. Conversely, "new" media includes digital media such as online websites and blogs (the "new" version of print media), podcasts (the "new" version of radio), as well as streaming (the "new" version of television) and social media platforms. In this chapter, we use the term *legacy media* to refer to old media and *emergent media* to refer to new media.

There are several distinguishing features of the shift in the media landscape that we should consider, especially in terms of the ways sports are produced, represented, and consumed. The first is related to media production, and specifically who is responsible for the production of media content. With most legacy media produced in the late twentieth century and the turn of the twenty-first century, corporations owned the means to produce media content. As late as 2011, 90 percent of US media was controlled by six corporations (GE/Comcast, News Corp, Disney, Viacom, CBS, and Time/Warner). Owners of those corporate entities had enormous power to dictate what would be covered and how; what television programs, films, and music would be produced and sold; what stories would be told and by whom; what news would be covered and how; and what sports would be broadcast and televised and in what ways.

When considering legacy sport media, men (and specifically white men) have historically dominated the sport media industry, representing well over 80–90 percent of key positions as editors, associate editors, and writers.[2] A 2023 Pew Research Center survey of journalists (this includes those who report, edit, or create news stories and have the job titles of reporter, columnist, writer, correspondent, photojournalist, video journalist, data visualization journalist, host, anchor, commentator, or bogger) found 51 percent of reporting journalists were men and 46 percent were women. Yet 83 percent of journalists covering sports were men and only 15 percent were women. Thus, while there is relative gender parity in the journalism profession, men were significantly more likely to report on sports than women. According to the survey, sports journalism was also overwhelmingly white—82 percent.[3]

Historically, newspapers, magazines, radio, and the internet have been important media for sports, with television as the dominant medium. Even with the advent of emergent media at the turn of the twenty-first century, most sports fans tune in to television broadcasts to watch and follow sports. According to a 2022 YouGov survey,[4] 64 percent of sports fans watch sports on live TV and 30 percent watch sports highlights on television. Conversely 30 percent watch sports on social media and 26 percent watch sports live via online streaming platforms. The survey allowed respondents to indicate more than one response, and so some fans might be watching live sports on both television and streaming online depending on where the game is broadcast. While previously leagues had media rights contracts with one or possibly two networks, increasingly leagues are breaking up their product and selling specific games to different media outlets, combining not only different channels but also different platforms. For example, during the 1970s and 1980s, NFL games were broadcast on either

CBS or NBC, with the exception of Monday Night Football, which up until 2005 was broadcast on ABC. This consistency of when and where games will be televised makes it easier for fans to find and watch the game. In comparison, for the 2024 season, an NFL fan can watch games on a number of different television and cable channels like FOX, ESPN, ABC, and CBS. Some NFL games are broadcast on streaming platforms, like Amazon Prime, Peacock, and ESPN+. For the avid NFL fan, there are subscriptions to the NFL Network and to NFL+, the streaming platform of the league, where fans can watch out-of-market games. Other leagues like the WNBA, NBA, and MLB also have "season pass" subscription-based streaming platforms that provide viewing options for out-of-market games. Although this system may make it challenging for an NFL fan to find games and/or require additional subscriptions to multiple streaming platforms, it also has the effect of expanding viewing options, not just for fans of the NFL but for other sports. Streaming platforms are not limited by time the way television and cable networks are. Put simply, there is no limit on how much content can appear on a streaming platform, whereas ABC can only broadcast one televised program in any given timeslot. And the number of timeslots is limited by the number of hours in a day.

Many consumers have "cut the cord" and no longer have cable TV subscriptions; less than 50 percent of households have a subscription to cable TV although the number of televisions in households has increased over the past two decades. The use of television has not declined and in fact the number of households with a television has steadily increased over the past several decades. Rather than cable, households are subscribing to digital streaming platforms like YouTubeTV or Hulu Live for linear television content. Moreover, the legacy networks CBS, NBC, and ABC have streaming platforms Paramount+, Peacock, and ESPN+/Disney+ respectively where sports content may migrate. Amazon and Apple each have streaming platforms where sports are streamed live (Amazon Prime and Apple+). All of this has both expanded the sports media landscape, creating opportunities for viewers to watch sports that otherwise would not have space in a limited broadcast lineup (and especially sports outside of the "big three"), and made it more challenging for sports fans to find their favorite teams or know whether a game would be broadcast online or on linear television and what channel or platform would have the broadcast. To a certain extent, sports news media and social media platforms provide viewers information about the game schedule, however this also requires a certain level of knowledge and "know-how"—fans must now know what sites to visit, what smart phone apps to download or log in to, to find out where a game is being broadcast (assuming they know the game will be on)!

Because of the continued influence of network television in the sports world, we will focus on the impact of sports-related broadcast television [linear and streaming] on audiences and society.

Televised Sports as a Window on Reality or a Social Construction?

On the surface, a televised sports event appears to be an objective window through which we observe the reality of sports events. If anything, television's use of slow motion and instant replay enhances the reality of watching these contests. So, too, television's framing, camera angles, and sportscaster commentary typically appear as neutral conduits for presenting "the facts" of the event.[5] This apparent "reality show" is enhanced further by "lifting the veil" from what consumers of sport do not normally witness. Coaches and athletes are sometimes miked during games, allowing viewers to listen to pregame pep talks and their halftime and postgame comments, as well as game-time decisions.[6] But is what we watch reality or the illusion of reality? Are consumers of sports television watching images and hearing narratives that distort our view of sport through television's "window"?

Rather than observing a televised event through a clear window, we see and hear that event through a smudged and distorted glass. In short, television presents a heavily edited version of what takes place on the field. Certain images are chosen, while others are not. Commentary is added that emphasizes certain things, while ignoring others. In this way, what we are seeing is a social construction by the media (another way of saying this is that televised sport is a mediated event). There are several ways we can understand televised sports as social construction: in the influence on coverage/content and representation of that coverage/content as shaped by commercial interests.

Commercial Interests

Television networks are commercial ventures. They pay large sums of money for the rights to televise sports contests[7] (through contracts with, for example, the NFL, NCAA, B1G Ten conference, International Olympic Committee). The networks sell advertising time to corporations based on the size of the audience and the demographics of those in that audience. So, television does all it can to increase the size of the audience, which, in turn, increases profits. To do this, as sociologist Jay Coakley notes,

> television commentaries and images highlight action, competition, aggression, hard work, individual heroism and achievement, playing with pain, teamwork, and competitive outcomes. . . . Sports rivalries are hyped as a basis for serializing stories through and even across seasons; conflict and chaos are highlighted in connection with an ever-changing cast of "good guys," "bad

guys," and "redemption" or "comeback" stories designed to reproduce ideologies favored by upper-middle-class media consumers—the ones that corporate sponsors want to reach.[8]

The themes highlighted by the commentaries and images accomplish three goals of the television networks. The first is entertainment. The presentation of a sports event covers the pageantry, which is appealing to a wide swath of fans. In violent sports such as football and hockey, when a player collides with another player with an extra hard hit, the commentators can celebrate it, condemn it, or treat it matter-of-factly. Typically, the networks have chosen to highlight these acts during the game, showing them in slow motion and from different angles and later replayed on *Sports Center*. Similarly, when an athlete cheats (e.g., faking being fouled, which is common in football, basketball, and soccer), the commentators have a choice: to glorify it, ignore it, or justify it. A typical comment is to say, with an implied wink, "it isn't cheating unless you are caught" or otherwise indicating how clever the perpetrator was. This may be especially popular with young adult males, an important demographic category for advertisers.

The second theme promoted in sports telecasts is the reinforcement of American values, such as patriotism, the myth that anyone can make it if they try hard enough, working together for the common goal, the idea that no sacrifice is too great for the team, the emphasis on winning, and the importance of inspired leadership (hero worship of highly successful coaches and heroic athletes).

The third theme involves raising controversial issues. ESPN, for example, occasionally engages in critical reporting of problematic issues such as sports injuries to youth, domestic violence by players, or player use of performance-enhancing drugs on programs such as *Outside the Lines* and *30 for 30*. But there is a conflict of interest. Broadcast corporations do not want to offend their sponsors. Hence, there is a tendency to play it safe in programming and commentary. When television is critical of sports, it points the finger at bad people rather than a faulty system, bad people such as Lance Armstrong or Jerry Sandusky. In the latter instance, when the Sandusky criminal case went public, the answer was to put the perpetrator in jail and to dishonor those who covered up the sexual abuse for thirteen years (e.g., Coach Joe Paterno and certain Penn State administrators).[9] But what about the role of football at Penn State? Why did its power trump humanitarian concerns? Dave Zirin raises the important questions that direct our attention to the system:

> Did Joe Paterno, and the campus leadership, care more about their brand than anything that resembled human morality? Was a football program that had become the economic, social, and cultural center of an entire region,

Commercial Interests

more important than all other concerns? Had abused children become, in the view of Penn State's leadership, an unfortunate collateral damage necessary to keeping the cash registers ringing?[10]

This critique was written by a sports journalist and activist. Television networks (and the legacy sports media landscape), on the other hand, did not ask these types of questions but focused, rather, on the individuals who facilitated, ignored, or silenced the abuse.

Legacy print news media are much more likely than sports television networks to engage in critical coverage of the dark side of sports because they are not tied contractually to what they are programming. A prime example is the series of articles on Black athletes in *Sports Illustrated* in 1968 by journalist Jack Olsen that hammered the athletic establishment, showing how Black athletes faced discrimination in professional and college sports.[11] Other pioneering efforts from the print media critical of sport are: the *Sports Illustrated* article in 1973 on how sport was unfair to women;[12] exposés of the exploitation of college athletes in the *Atlantic*;[13] books that exposed the NFL for its suppression of evidence in dealing with player head injuries and their consequences;[14] and the corruption in the International Olympics Committee and FIFA (the ruling organization in soccer).[15] It was investigative reporting by the *Indianapolis Star* in 2016 that exposed Larry Nassar's sexual abuse of athletes and USA Gymnastics' role in ignoring or dismissing the abuse.[16] Nassar was sentenced to 175 years in prison, as the case against Nassar expanded to include 156 women who reported accounts of abuse. An important shift in today's media environment is in the proliferation of journalists and online and digital media outlets that are dedicated to covering sports in all its complexity and contradiction, focusing on how social issues and social problems are often perpetrated by sports organizations and sports cultures. This is in stark contrast to earlier eras of sports journalism, when it was viewed as "the toy department" in many news media outlets.

The networks, unlike the print media, have a conflict of interest because they cover sport journalistically while at the same time paying the entities that it covers billions for the rights to broadcast their games. Thus, it has difficulty being critical of the NFL or the NCAA. For instance, ESPN, at the urging of the NFL, bowed out of its collaboration with the Public Broadcasting System in a documentary that was critical of the NFL's suppression of head and brain damage to players, connecting concussions to football and brain damage.[17] Similarly, ESPN had a scripted drama series *Playmakers*, which dealt with the dark side of pro football players' lives. Although successful, the show was canceled by ESPN because the NFL was unhappy with the image that it portrayed of NFL athletes.[18]

Each of these themes is manifest in the media's decisions on what to emphasize and what to ignore or whitewash. In doing so, the perceptions of the audience are affected. Clearly, the media do not present a clear window through which we observe sports. Rather the image is an edited version that distorts that reality.

Sport as a Male Preserve

Researchers who study the media note the "agenda setting" function of legacy media. *Agenda setting* refers to the ways in which media entities can draw attention to particular issues and topics, and thus publicize those issues thereby shaping public perceptions and understandings. Television producers and editors select and neglect certain sports and events. In short, televised sports broadcasts shape what viewers see and provide commentary on those images, helping viewers interpret what they see. In the case of legacy sports media, we might consider the agenda-setting function in terms of the dominance of men's professional (and college) football, baseball, and basketball in television broadcasts and televised sports news media. Research on legacy media in the United States has consistently found most of the coverage focuses on men's sports, and in particular the "big three" sports (basketball, baseball, and football).[19] The dominance of men's sports has been one of the long-standing trends in the research.

Corporate decisions on what to broadcast and when are based on assumptions about what viewers want, which in turn increases the audience, and profits from advertisers. This is a self-fulfilling prophecy, filling the programming with certain sports, leagues, and teams and providing commentary that hypes these events; and, lo and behold, that's what the people watch. Such has been the case with women's sports, where media decision-makers argue that they don't carry women's sports because there's presumably no interest and no audience. Researchers who study sports media have drawn attention to the ways in which sports media actively and purposively build and sustain audiences for sports, rather than passively meeting audience "demand." The "commonsense" assumptions regarding supply and demand are being challenged by the number of fans and viewers who are turning out and tuning in to women's sports events in record numbers. The 2024 NCAA women's basketball Final Four tournament had higher ratings than the men's Final Four that year. Moreover, the championship game between South Carolina and Iowa not only drew more viewers (18.9 million) than the men's championship game (14.8 million); more viewers tuned in to that game than every World Series game since Game 7 of the 2019 World Series and every NBA Finals game since Game 5 of the 2017 NBA Finals.[20] These fans of women's college basketball migrated to the WNBA, where the 2024 season witnessed record-breaking ratings, the highest in the league's history. The WNBA also had its highest attendance in twenty-two years (of the twenty-four total years of the league's existence).[21] Fans turned out in the millions to watch the games, selling out stadiums, and in the case of the Indiana Fever and Iowa basketball phenom, Caitlin Clark, causing their opponents, including the Las Vegas Aces and the Washington Mystics, to move games to larger stadium to accommodate the demand for tickets. The interest in women's sports is not confined to basketball. The expansion of a number of professional leagues for women, including the Professional Women's Hockey League, as well the University of Nebraska women's collegiate volleyball team, which in 2023 sold out the football stadium with over ninety-two thousand fans in attendance,[22] among other advancements have led many journalists to ask if we are in a new era of women's sports.

But prior to the record-breaking years of 2023 and 2024, historically sports media and specifically television networks had ignored most women's sports.[23] In professional basketball, in 2024, the NBA signed an eleven-year lucrative television contract worth $76 billion (or just under $7 billion a year),[24] whereas the WNBA's media rights deal signed in 2024 is valued at $2.2 billion (or $200 million annually).[25] While a significant increase over the last media deal (which was $12 million annually), the WNBA's deal pales in comparison to the NBA's media rights deal. Among the consequences of this disparity is that the average salary in the NBA is $12 million for the 2023–2024 season, while the average salary for the WNBA is just under $120,000 for the 2024 season. The highest salary in the WNBA is $252,000, well below the NBA league minimum salary of $1.4 million. Another consequence is that the WNBA is a shorter season, and fewer of its games are broadcast on television networks, if at all. Fans may now be able to watch WNBA games more than in seasons prior; however, they need to access several television and cable networks and streaming platforms to do so. An Indiana Fever fan, for example, would need subscriptions to ABC, ESPN, ESPN2, Amazon Prime, ION, NBA TV, CBS, and CBS Sports Network to catch the season's games.

Although the media landscape is shifting, men's sports continue to command much of the legacy sports media coverage and content. Consider the following:

- According to a longitudinal study, televised news and highlight shows' coverage of women's sports remains in the single digits. Research over a thirty-year span (at five-year intervals) found that (1) the three network affiliates in Los Angeles devoted only 5.1 percent of airtime to women's sports; and (2) ESPN's *Sports Center* apportioned only 5.7 percent of airtime to women's sports.[26]
- In 2010, ESPN produced a documentary series featuring thirty short sports films (*30 for 30*). Only two episodes featured women athletes.

ESPN would later produce *Nine for IX* in conjunction with the fortieth anniversary of Title IX in 2013, featuring nine films on women athletes. Subsequent seasons of *30 for 30* in 2011 and 2012 would feature women sports in only two documentaries. Over the course of the decade, additional "volumes" of *30 for 30* would be released. Between 2010 and 2020, a total of six documentary films out of 131 films produced featured women's sports, or just under 5 percent of all films. If we include *Nine for IX* in those numbers, the percentage increases to just over 10 percent. Certainly, this is not an accurate reflection of the worthy stories that could be told about women athletes and women's sports.

- The sports media, and in particular the legacy sports media marginalize and trivialize women athletes when they focus more on an athlete's appearance or attractiveness than on their performance and athleticism. Although this is beginning to shift,[27] gendered norms continue to shape the expectations we have for women athletes. For example, Olivia Dunn, a gymnast who competed for Louisiana State University (and her team won the NCAA championship in 2023, its first in the program's history), earned $9.5 million in "Name Image Likeness" deals, in part due to her social media following (nearly ten million on Instagram and five million on TikTok), driven in large part by her appearance and adherence to dominant beauty ideals.

This combination of relative invisibility, sexualized images, and trivialization, as Michael Messner asserts, "is not only about deeply sexist attitudes toward women but also about the sports media's continued focus on sport as a terrain by and for the elevation of men as a superior sex class."[28]

Television as a Game Changer

To enhance the spectator appeal of sports, the television industry, of which ESPN is the prime mover, has persuaded professional leagues and the NCAA to modify the rules and schedules to attract larger audiences, which will bring more income to broadcasters from advertisers and larger rights fees from the television industry to the leagues and school conferences. Here are some examples of how the media have changed sports:

- The NFL acknowledges how television has precipitated changes to the game in ways that allowed the league to "grow and flourish," including the use of instant reply, slow motion, and freeze frames. According to the NFL, "Replay made games more entertaining. It provided a

Conclusion

natural filler for the sport's many breaks in play and could be used to highlight hard hits, battles in the trenches, great runs and catches, and other key plays. Broadcasters also used replay to better explain the game's nuances, creating greater fan awareness, understanding and involvement."[29]

- In professional and college basketball, the point production potential was enhanced by using a shot clock, allowing dunks, and adopting the three-point shot. To accommodate television and advertisers, the number of time-outs was increased. During the game, these are referred to as "TV time-outs."

- Due to pressure by network television in the early 1970s, match play, where golfers compete head-to-head and the winner is determined by which golfer wins the most holes, was replaced by medal play, where the golfer with the lowest overall score against all competitors wins.

- Major League Baseball has implemented several changes recently to speed up the pace of the game, something the league believes appeals to both fans in the stadium and viewers at home. For the 2023 season, it established a pitch clock, limiting the amount of time a pitcher could prepare, and expanded the size of the bases, among other changes. The switch from afternoon games to night games for the World Series and All-Star Games has increased the number of fans who are able to watch on television.

- The sudden-death tie-breaking rule in football, ice hockey, and soccer has increased spectator interest. So, too, the playoff system where championships are won in a tournament style. Professional football and basketball have enhanced this by adding to the number of teams eligible to participate in the season-ending tournaments.

- Time-outs have increased and lengthened, grinding play to a halt. The NCAA men's basketball tournament, for instance, has stretched time-outs by thirty seconds to two minutes and thirty seconds.[30]

Conclusion

We have seen how the media are a force in sports, shaping the reality for sports consumers, preserving the dominance of men's sports, and changing sports rules and procedures to enhance its product. Most significantly, together these actions have a conservative bias—that is, while they entertain us, they reinforce the values and status hierarchy in society. As Mike Messner notes, "The sports media continues to play a large reproductive—rather than critical or disruptive—role in the politics of sport and problems grounded in social inequalities."[31] Yet, sports media also play a role in bringing to the fore necessary discussions around race, gender, and sexual inequality. Sports constitute a "platform" for social change in large part due to the expansive reach they have due to their broadcast and media distribution.

Notes

1. George H. Sage and D. Stanley Eitzen, *Sociology of North American Sport*, 10th ed. (New York: Oxford University Press, 2015), chap. 12, and D. Stanley Eitzen, "ESPN: The Force in Sports," in *Sport in Contemporary Society*, 10th ed., ed. D. Stanley Eitzen (New York: Oxford University Press, 2015), 72–80.
2. "Sports Media Racial and Gender Report Card," 2021, The Institute for Diversity and Equity in Sports, https://www.tidesport.org/.
3. Emily Tomasik and Jeffrey Gottfried, "U.S. Journalists' Beats Vary Widely by Gender and Other Factors," Pew Research Center, April 4, 2023, https://www.pewresearch.org/short-reads/2023/04/04/us-journalists-beats-vary-widely-by-gender-and-other-factors/.
4. "How Do Sports Fans in the U.S. Consume Sports?," YouGov, May 30, 2022, https://business.yougov.com/content/47133-how-do-sports-fans-in-the-us-consume-sports.
5. Sage and Eitzen, *Sociology of North American Sport*.
6. Eitzen, "ESPN: The Force in Sports," 74.
7. In fact, the recent college sports conference realignment that came into effect in the 2024 fall sports season, which saw the inevitable demise of the PAC-12 conference, the expansion of the B1G Ten conference to include UCLA and USC, as well as other colleges leaving or joining conferences, was driven primarily, if not solely, by media rights considerations and the potential gain of revenue generated by a conference through its television deals with networks like ESPN and ABC.
8. Jay Coakley, *Sports in Society: Issues and Controversies*, 9th ed. (New York: McGraw-Hill, 2007), 406.
9. Dave Zirin, "Joe Paterno: The God Who Fell to Earth," *Edge of Sports*, January 22, 2012, http://bit.ly/zxfDMN.
10. Zirin, "Joe Paterno: The God Who Fell to Earth," para 5. See also, Ken Reed, *How We Can Save Sports: A Game Plan* (Lanham, MD: Rowman & Littlefield, 2015), 157.
11. Those articles were then expanded and amplified in Jack Olsen, *The Black Athlete: A Shameful Story; the Myth of Integration in American Sports* (New York: Time-Life Books, 1968). A few other examples of important critiques of sport by the print media are: Murray Sperber, *College Sports, Inc: The Athletic Department vs. the University* (New York: Henry Holt, 1990); Jack Scott, *The Athletic Revolution* (New York: The Free Press, 1971); and John Feinstein, *A Season on the Brink: A Year with Bob Knight and the Indiana Hoosiers* (New York: Macmillan, 1986).

Notes

12 Bil Gilbert and Nancy Williamson, "Sport Is Unfair to Women," *Sports Illustrated*, May 1973.

13 Taylor Branch, "The Shame of College Sports," *Atlantic*, October 2011, 80–120.

14 Mark Fainaru-Wada and Steve Fainaru, *League in Denial: The NFL, Concussions, and the Battle for the Truth* (New York: Crown, 2013).

15 Andrew Jennings and Vyv Simson, *The Lords of the Rings: Power, Money, and Drugs in the Modern Olympics* (London: Simon & Schuster, 1992).

16 Eric Levenson, "How the Indy Star and Rachael Denhollander Took Down Larry Nassar," CNN, January 25, 2018, https://www.cnn.com/2018/01/25/us/larry-nassar-indy-star/index.html.

17 Fainaru-Wada and Fainaru, *League in Denial*.

18 Robert Lipsyte, "Inside the Church of Sports," *Slate*, June 1, 2011, http://www.slate.com/articles/sports/sportsnut/2011/06/inside_the_church_of_sports.html.

19 C. Cooky, L. D. Council, M. A. Mears, and M. A. Messner, "One and Done: The Long Eclipse of Women's Televised Sports, 1989–2019," *Communication & Sport* 9, no. 3 (2021): 347–71.

20 Cheryl Cooky, "Is This the Dawn of a New Era in Women's Sports," *The Conversation*, April 10, 2024, https://theconversation.com/is-this-the-dawn-of-a-new-era-in-womens-sports-227216.

21 "WNBA Delivers Record Setting 2024 Season," WNBA press release, September 27, 2024, https://www.wnba.com/news/wnba-delivers-record-setting-2024-season.

22 Madison Williams, "Epic Scenes Emerge from Nebraska's Volleyball Match in Football Stadium," *Sports Illustrated*, August 30, 2023, https://www.si.com/college/2023/08/31/nebraska-volleyball-epic-scenes-memorial-stadium.

23 Cooky et al., "One and Done."

24 Tim Bontemps, "What NBA's New TV Deal Means for the League, Players, Teams and Fans," ESPN, July 25, 2024, https://www.espn.com/nba/story/_/id/40635523/faq-nba-signed-new-deal-disney-nbc-amazon-prime.

25 Alexa Philippou, "WNBA Secures 'Monumental' Media Deal with Disney, Amazon, NBCU," ESPN, July 24, 2024, https://www.espn.com/wnba/story/_/id/40634341/wnba-secures-monumental-media-deal-disney-amazon-nbcu.

26 Cooky et al., "One and Done."

27 See Cooky et al., "One and Done"; T. Bruce, "New Rules for New Times: Sportswomen and Media Representation in the Third Wave," *Sex Roles* 74 (2016): 361–76. C. Cooky and D. Antunovic, *Serving Equality: Feminism, Media, and Women's Sports* (New York: Peter Lang).

28 Michael A. Messner, "Reflections on Communication and Sport: On Men and Masculinities," in *Sport in Contemporary Society*, ed. D. Stanley Eitzen (New York: Oxford University Press, 2015), 58.

29 NFL Operations, "Impact of Television: How Television Has Changed the Game," NFL, https://operations.nfl.com/gameday/technology/impact-of-television/.

30 Will Graves, "The 'Ills' of TV Breaks," Associated Press, March 27, 2015.

31 Messner, "Reflections on Communication and Sport," 61.

8
BIG-TIME COLLEGE SPORT: COMMERCIALIZED SPORT WITHIN ACADEMIA

We love sports, including big-time college sport. It provides great entertainment and drama wrapped in the exuberance of players and fans and all of it fueled by ritual displays, compelling rivalries, impressive athleticism, intense competition, "shining moments," and engaging media production and spectacle. At the same time, we feel conflicted by the intrusion of commercialism, scandals that involve players, coaches, and institutions, the exploitation of athletes by both universities and the NCAA, and the mythology and hypocrisy involved in organizing sport around the theme of the student-athlete—that is, big-time college sport is sold as an amateur activity that is part of the educational mission of universities.[1]

8 Big-Time College Sport: Commercialized Sport Within Academia

Sociology of sport scholar Jay Coakley notes the connection between colleges and athletics and the idea of school-sponsored sport is specific to the United States. Most developed countries around the world offer organized sports for young people and those programs are funded through community-based clubs and a combination of private and public funding. And while young people in secondary and post-secondary schools participate in organized athletics, the taken-for-granted expectation that high schools and colleges will fund athletic programs is unique to the United States.[2]

In this chapter, we focus on "big-time" college sport. Big-time college sport refers to the 128 men's football programs in the NCAA Division I Football Bowl Subdivision (FBS) and over 350 schools' basketball programs eligible for the NCAA men's basketball championship. NCAA women's basketball has witnessed record-breaking increases in attendance and viewership, generating higher ratings for the NCAA championship than the men's tournament in 2023.[3] Despite this recent trend, we focus on men's sports given that much of an athletic department's resources, mainstream media coverage and content, and cultural attention is dominated by big time men's sports programs. FBS programs make up slightly more than 10 percent of the total number of four-year colleges that have sports programs. In other words, most colleges and universities would not be considered to have "big-time" sports programs. Yet, the media attention focuses disproportionately on FBS schools; as such, our understanding of college sports is informed by what we see in those "big-time" programs. Moreover, research on the topic of the role of athletics on college campuses has historically focused on men's football and basketball programs. The overarching questions posed in this chapter are: Does big-time college sport complement or promote the academic goals of colleges and universities? What role does (or should) big-time college sport have in institutions of higher education?

Clearly, big-time college sport entertains, unites supporters of a given school, cultivates funding and development opportunities from donors and alumni, provides free publicity for the schools, gives talented athletes a mechanism to attend college, and serves as a training ground for the relatively few fortunate college athletes who make it to the professional level. In this chapter, we shall, as is our sociological inclination, examine the other side of big-time college sport, focusing on several contradictions, each of which is subsumed under the relationship of sport to the educational mission of higher education. But first, a little history.

A brief survey of the history of college sport reveals that the tension between the educational mission of universities and the role of athletics has been present since its origins. In 1852, the first intercollegiate sports contest occurred when the crews from Harvard and Yale raced against each other. In 1869, the first college football game was played, between Princeton and Rutgers, with several players taking the field who could have been ruled academically ineligible. Later, some schools used players who had no connection to their institutions. These early contests, for the most part, were organized by students. Faculties, administrators, friends of the school, and alumni were not involved. This was soon to change. In 1881, the first college faculty athletic committee was formed by Princeton and followed by Harvard a year later. In 1895, the first league (later known as the Big Ten) was established. The first national organization, later called the NCAA in 1910, was organized in 1905 to standardize rules and address problems associated with college sport (questions concerning the eligibility of athletes, the high rate of injuries, cheating, and the like).

The popularity of college sport was mostly localized during the first half of the twentieth century. Around 1970, the advent of televised athletics transformed college sport. Television focused on a few schools and funneled ever greater amounts of money into them. This was the beginning of big-time college sports as we know it today: hugely popular, national in scope, and highly commercialized. With the new source of funds flowing to a few schools, university athletic departments became quasi-separate entities, some boosters wielded extraordinary influence over athletic departments, and players were often abused and exploited.

What was once a student-run activity has been transformed, and now students, even those that participate, have virtually no voice in athletic policies, with control being vested in coaches, boosters, school administrators, leagues, national organizations, corporations, and television networks. In the process, college sport changed from an activity primarily for the participants (and it was almost exclusively male participants until the 1970s with the passage of Title IX; see chapter 3) and their fans, mostly fellow students, to full-scale commercial entertainment with national audiences, fanbases, and large monetary payouts. As the commercial stakes of big-time college sports exponentially increased over its history, so too have the economic incentives to "win-at-all-costs." At the extreme end of this "win-at-all costs" mentality are universities and athletic programs implicitly or explicitly endorsing academic or athletic cheating; covering up sexual violence perpetrated by athletes, coaches, and medical staff; ignoring credible allegations of child abuse; and other so-called "scandals." In the early 2020s, several lawsuits against the NCAA opened opportunities for athletes to garner commercial sponsorships, what are known as "Name, Image, and Likeness" (NIL) and possibly receive payment for their athletic participation. The impact of these cases, which made it all the way to the US Supreme Court, on the role of academics in athletics (and vice versa) have yet to be fully understood. Will the disparities in resources and attention between "big-time sports" and the so-called "non-revenue" or Olympic sports be further exacerbated? Will gender inequities between men's and women's sports expand in this NIL era of college sports, or will sponsorship opportunities help to bridge the gap?

The Case That Big-Time Sport Promotes Education

Contrary to a common (mis)perception of athletes prioritizing athletics over academics (e.g., the "dumb jock" stereotypes), many athletes thrive in an academic environment, receiving academic honors, graduating on time, and preparing for graduate or professional programs like medical school. Unfortunately, many athletes enter college ill-prepared for academia, particularly athletes from economically disadvantaged communities who attended underfunded high schools. Athletic scholarships provide an opportunity for students who might otherwise not be able to afford college. Athletes are provided academic support from tutors for each course they take. Academic advisors guide them in choosing majors and classes, helping students progress toward graduation. There are mandatory study sessions for athletes who are struggling academically. Most big-time programs have academic centers to facilitate learning that include computers and other teaching aids, as well as centralizing the learning experience for athletes.

Exposure to the college experience may open the mind to new possibilities for athletes, especially those who are the first from their families to attend college. This has the potential to motivate them to work hard at school and prepare them for life after sports.

The NCAA and individual schools devote considerable attention to the graduation rates of athletes. The NCAA has punished schools that have mediocre rates for their athletes. At the institutional level, some schools have stipulations in coaches' contracts, rewarding them monetarily when the graduation rates are above the acceptable level and reducing their pay if the rates are below the standard.

The Case That Big-Time Sport Compromises Educational Goals

Colleges and universities spend disproportionately more on athletes than on undergraduates with nonathletic abilities and accomplishments. A study from 2023 found that the sixty-nine universities in what was then called the Power 5 conference spend significantly more per athlete than they do on other students,

The Case That Big-Time Sport Compromises Educational Goals 155

and in some cases, schools spent 5 to 10 times more on student-athletes. For example, during the 2021–2022 season, Louisiana State University spent $381,724 per student-athlete, 10.4 times more than what it spent on a full-time student ($36,864). The University of Arkansas spent 9.2 times more on student-athletes, $315,490 vs. $34,171. And the University of Alabama spent nearly 9 times more or $274,710 per student-athlete than it spent per full-time student ($30,752).[4]

Not only do some schools spend more money on athletes than they do on students who do not participate in intercollegiate athletics, but often they also grant athletic scholarships that are considerably more than what full-time students receive. Athletes often aspire to a career in professional sports and as a result prioritize practice, training, and playing over studying, reading, and preparing for class. College admissions processes provide advantages for students who are being recruited that include support and assistance in filling out and submitting applications and financial aid forms as well as lower academic requirements, resulting in higher acceptance rates, even at universities that do not offer athletic scholarships, such as those in the Ivy League. A 2023 investigation by the Harvard Crimson[5] found students who were recruited for athletics had an 86 percent chance of acceptance into Harvard. This was compared to a 47 percent chance for children of faculty and staff, 33 percent for legacy applicants and a mere 6 percent for the average student applying to Harvard. At many schools, a certain number of admission slots are reserved for coaches to use for recruits. The implication is that student-athletes may be competing with other student-athletes for admission, rather than competing in the overall student applicant pool.[6]

Many argue that the special admissions criteria should be targeted to assist students from underprivileged and minoritized communities. This is a legitimate argument for students who come from violent neighborhoods, inadequately financed schools, and economically strapped communities. Coaches, scouts, and sports recruiters nurture athletes, identifying talented athletes and finding ways to enhance their talents. No similar infrastructure exists to coach similar students who either lack athletic talent or who do not aspire to participate in college sports.

What is troubling about this imbalance is not that athletes are undeserving or that helping them is wrong. The problem is that an opportunity to provide an education for academically talented students, and particularly those from minoritized and underrepresented backgrounds, is given much less priority than admission and scholarships for talented athletes, most of whom are white and from affluent families who live in suburban communities.[7]

Black athletes, and specifically Black men, are overrepresented as professional athletes. They make up 70 percent of players in professional basketball and

53 percent in professional football (see chapter 6). Some argue that the disproportionately high number of Black athletes in professional sport is an appropriate rationale for giving them scholarships to college—going to college allows them to hone their skills for a professional sports career. But only a small proportion of college athletes make it to the professional level (see chapter 6). When schools over-recruit students, and particularly minoritized students for their athletic skills and under-recruit for their academic skills, they contradict the fundamental purpose of education in a democratic society. Moreover, recruiting Black students primarily or solely for their athletic talents reinforces negative racial stereotypes regarding "natural" physicality and athleticism. While Black athletes represent over 55 percent of athletes at Power 5 schools, they represent less than 6 percent of the overall student-body.[8]

Avoiding Education

The education of inadequately prepared athletes is a daunting task. Many athletes are admitted to their schools even though they do not meet minimum admissions standards. How do the schools keep their inadequately prepared athletes eligible? Although the athletic departments hire tutors and academic counselors for their athletes, the athletic role, in the eyes of many coaches and athletes, supersedes the student role. Coaches who concur with this sentiment, coupled with the pressure to win, tend to diminish the student role. Athletes are counseled to take "easy" courses, to choose "easy" majors, and to sign up for courses from cooperative faculty members who are willing to give athletes "special" considerations in the classroom. Or they may be steered toward correspondence courses with few or no requirements.

Taking the Easy Route: Clustering in Easy Majors

While some athletes take a rigorous curriculum, others find majors or are guided to majors that are considered "easy" or as having "less academic rigor," thus keeping them eligible to play. The most common majors for student-athletes are: general/university studies, social sciences such as sociology or communication, business, and sports sciences/kinesiology/sport management. Researchers have also found that students with stronger athletic identities will have declared a less rigorous academic major and are more likely to be undeclared or undecided.[9] The percentage of student-athletes in STEM (Science, Technology, Engineering, and Math) majors is nearly half of the percentage of students who major in a STEM discipline. According to the NCAA's "diploma dashboard," 16 percent of student-athletes major in a STEM discipline compared to 28 percent of the overall student body. Interestingly, when breaking down the data by gender, women student-athletes were more likely to major in a STEM discipline than their nonathlete counterparts: 20 percent of women student-athletes majored in STEM compared to 13 percent of women in the overall student body.[10] This may be explained in part to the differing demands of athletes in big-time men's sports programs. It may also be due to gendered expectations and stereotypes; women athletes may be more comfortable in male-dominated STEM majors as a result of their participation in sports.

The Excessive Time Demands of Big-Time Programs Diminish the Student Role

To accentuate the athlete role, the coaches demand incredible amounts of time (practices, meetings, travel, studying videotape and playbooks). Athletes are required to lift weights and engage in other forms of conditioning as well as "informal" practices during the off-season, including summers.[11] The NCAA has attempted to control the excesses of these demands but has met with little success. Sport sociologists, Nathan Kalman-Lamb and Derek Silva interviewed twenty-five former college athletes and raise important questions regarding the "compensatory education on offer to student-athletes." Historically, the NCAA had claimed student-athletes are compensated through scholarships and other educational benefits that athletes receive (as we noted earlier in the chapter) and thus do not need additional forms of compensation. Yet the demands on student-athletes' time often impose limits on how engaged they can be when it comes to learning. Consider the following experience a former student-athlete shared:

> Our first four games were all night games. So they decided the best thing to do was to have night practice. So we would get out there around 6:15 and we wouldn't leave that facility till around 11:00. And so we would get our late, late dinner and while we were at dinner, I would see these athletes after going out and banging heads for an hour try to finish homework, try to turn something in before midnight, and I was like, "I have no idea how any of these players are going to graduate." And the sad fact of the matter is a lot of them won't. . . . They will not meet the GPA, they will not get the classes. Their eligibility will expire before they get the degree.[12]

In addition to the time constraints of big-time college sport, the athletes must also cope with physical exhaustion, mental fatigue, media attention, and demanding coaches. Athletes in these commercialized, professionalized programs have trouble reconciling the roles associated with their dual status of athlete and student.

The "Jock" Subculture

A now-classic study of one basketball program by sociologists Patricia and Peter Adler found that the pressures of big-time sport and academic demands resulted in the gradual disengagement of athletes from their academic roles.[13] The Adlers found that most athletes entered the university feeling idealistic about the academic side of their college performance. This idealism lasted about one year and was replaced by disappointment and a growing cynicism as they realized how difficult it was to keep up with their schoolwork. The athletic role came to dominate all facets of their existence. The athletes received greater positive reinforcement for their athletic performance than for their academic performance. They became increasingly isolated from the student body as a result of segregated living arrangements, and their racial and socioeconomic differences isolated them culturally from the rest of the students. They were even isolated socially from other students by their physical size, which many found intimidating. They interacted primarily with other athletes, and these peers tended to put down academics. First-year athletes took courses from "sympathetic" professors, but this changed as they moved through the university curriculum. The athletes were unprepared for escalating academic expectations. The typical response of these athletes was distancing themselves from the student role. The Adlers say that for these athletes, "it was better not to try than to try and not succeed."[14] This attitude was reinforced by the peer subculture. Thus, the structure of big-time programs works to maximize the athlete role and minimize the academic role—clearly opposite the goals of higher education.

Scandals Involving the Education of Athletes

Among the problems of big-time athletic programs is keeping their athletes eligible academically. Several tactics are used. One is the fake class. An egregious case occurred at the University of North Carolina–Chapel Hill where for nearly eighteen years between 1993 and 2011 the Department of African, African American, and Diaspora Studies offered more than two hundred lecture courses that never met and sponsored hundreds of independent study classes. Students who enrolled in these phantom classes were disproportionately football and basketball players.[15] All that was required of the students was a twenty-page paper, which always received an A or B grade.[16] The hypocrisy is compounded when the paper is plagiarized or written by someone other than the student. North Carolina is not alone in such fraudulent activities. Academic irregularities relating to athlete eligibility have been unearthed at such big-time programs as Auburn, Florida, Florida State, Georgia, Michigan, Minnesota, Stanford, Notre Dame, Tennessee, and USC.

"One and Done"

An NCAA rule prohibits young basketball players from going immediately from high school to the professional level until they are at least nineteen years old and at least a year removed from high school graduation.[17] This ruling reduces the options for those athletes who are just out of high school to play professionally overseas or, as most do, play in college for a year. The NBA wins in this arrangement by having big-time programs develop players by providing coaching and experience at no expense to NBA teams. The schools in the NCAA benefit by having excellent athletes for at least a year. The athletes in this "one and done" environment are, for the most part, uninterested students, just putting in their time. They take one "serious" semester (although steered to easy courses), enrolling for the second semester but not having to show up after a few weeks. The universities use these poorly compensated workers to win games and produce revenue. Their college education is irrelevant. This is the height of educational hypocrisy.[18]

Diverting Education Funds to Subsidize College Sports

According to estimates, most big-time sports programs' total expenses exceed total revenues, with the exception of the top twenty-five to thirty FBS programs.[19] The NCAA reports that a vast majority of programs operate at a deficit. To make up for this discrepancy, schools subsidize athletic departments with direct and indirect institutional support. For example, according to NCAA data compiled by the Knight Commission on Intercollegiate Athletics, in 2023 of the $10.9 billion in revenue generated by FBS schools, $1.35 billion comes from institutional/government support and $625 million comes from student fees.[20]

The Resulting Educational Performance of Athletes

Athletes in big-time sports are often underprepared for higher education. Poor preparation for college and depreciation of the student role has historically resulted in a lower graduation rate for big-time college athletes compared to their nonathlete peers, tracking them six years after entering college. Prior studies noted important racial disparities between the graduation rates of Black and white male athletes in big-time sports. There are indicators this is changing. Graduation rates have increased overall for student-athletes over a twenty-year period, according to the NCAA, with 90 percent of student-athletes successfully earning a degree. Examining graduation rates between 2002 and 2022, the graduation rates for Black FBS football student-athletes increased from 54 percent to 81 percent, and for Black men's FBS basketball student-athletes from 46 percent to 81 percent.[21] Although the upward trend in graduation rates may indicate positive changes, researchers call into question how well athletes, and in particular Black athletes, are being prepared through their coursework for a career outside of sports.[22] This is particularly so for students who are "clustered" into majors that may not align with their professional interests, but are considered easier, thus ensuring they maintain eligibility.

The inescapable conclusion is that providing a free education to athletes, while expecting more from them as athletes than as students, as well as creating a situation that moves them away from academic pursuits, is contrary to the lofty goals of higher education.

NIL and Pay-to-Play

In 2021, the US Supreme Court rendered a 9–0 unanimous decision in *NCAA v. Alston* that the NCAA's restrictions on "education-related benefits" violated anti-trust law. Of course, what constitutes "education-related benefits" is up for debate. As *Sports Illustrated*'s Andrew Brandt explains,

> Who is to say whether an athlete should have a $2,000 computer or a $10,000 computer? A $1,000 video monitor or a $20,000 video system that has high-quality streaming of lectures, which can also serve as a gaming device and home entertainment system? A $5,000 internship or a $50,000 internship? The NCAA may still enforce any "no Lamborghini" rule, as the court put it, but there are a lot [of] steps between spartan education-related benefits and a Lamborghini.[23]

While high-profile athletes are now able to generate sponsorship deals with major corporate brands, such as former University of Iowa women's basketball super star, Caitlin Clark (e.g., State Farm Insurance, Gatorade) and University of Southern California's Heisman Trophy winner, Caleb Williams (e.g., Dr. Pepper), many lower-profile athletes begin cultivating followers on social media to generate sponsorship deals with lesser-known brands or local and community-based companies. For example, during the 2023–2024 season, Purdue men's basketball players appeared in commercials for a local car dealership that aired during game time-outs on the stadium's jumbotron.

College Sport as Big Business

Since 2021, universities have also established NIL "collectives." NIL collectives are third-party entities, not officially associated with a university or athletic program, which fundraise from large and small donors and direct the fundraising dollars to student-athletes through NIL deals, such as signing autographs, attending donor functions, appearances in commercials, or other public or private activities organized by the collective. According to the NCAA's policies, athletic programs and collectives are prohibited from discussing player recruitment or acquisition strategies Yet, universities are setting up NIL deals for athletes who have yet to commit to the school. For example, in 2022, the University of Tennessee successfully recruited Nico Iamaleava with an at-the-time unprecedented $8 million NIL deal, generated through the university's collective. As part of the deal, Iamaleava agreed to make appearances and take part in social media promotions.[24]

Further complicating the issue, student-athletes may become eligible for direct compensation from their school should the *House v. NCAA* settlement be approved. *House v. NCAA* is an anti-trust class-action lawsuit filed in 2020 by former Arizona State swimmer Grant House and TCU/Oregon basketball player Sedona Prince. House and Prince sued the NCAA for barring name, image, and likeness (NIL) payments for athletes prior to 2021 (the year the NCAA allowed for NIL payments).[25] A settlement is currently being negotiated.

In May of 2024, the NCAA and Power 5 conferences agreed to allow Division I college athletes to receive pay directly from the universities they compete for, a significant departure from the NCAA's historical stance on amateurism. Also part of the settlement, the NCAA will pay "$2.75 billion to former Division I athletes who were unable to profit on their NIL rights, as well as a future revenue sharing model between the Power Five conference schools and athletes."[26] In early September 2024, the judge declined to rule on the settlement and has asked both sides to "go back to the drawing board."[27] Anticipating the change to compensating athletes, the University of Tennessee announced it would add a 10 percent "talent fee" starting in 2025 to season-ticket prices. The "talent fee" would provide additional funds for the NIL collective, as well as compensate athletes directly,[28] should the *House v. NCAA* settlement be approved. In mid-September 2024, South Dakota's attorney general filed a new lawsuit against the NCAA claiming that the back-pay plan proposed in the settlement would place "undue burden" on women athletes and non-Power 5 conferences, making them "responsible for a disproportionate share of settlement costs."[29]

College Sport as Big Business

As the Supreme Court case and other class action antitrust lawsuits most recently illustrate, big-time college sport is organized in such a way that separating the business aspects from the play on the field is impossible. The intrusion of money into collegiate sport is not new to the NIL era, and it is evident in the following representative examples:

- In 2019, Division I athletics generated $15.8 billion in revenue according to the NCAA. "Men's basketball and football generate the vast majority of revenues with media rights, bowl revenues, ticket sales, royalties and licensing, donor contributions and other sources accounting for more than half of these revenues. Institution and government support as well as student fees accounted for the remaining 44 percent of the cash inflows."[30]
- In 2022–2023, the NCAA generated $1.3 billion in revenue. Most of this revenue, $945 million, came from media rights deals and marketing of championship events.[31]
- In 2022, forty-nine schools generated $100 million or more, and five schools generated $200 million or more. The Ohio State University was the revenue leader, generating over $250 million. Texas was not far behind with $240 million.[32]
- In thirty-nine of the fifty states, the highest-paid public official is a college coach, either the men's football or men's basketball coach.[33] The median salary for an FBS head football coach is $3.5 million. The highest-paid men's football coach in 2023 was Nick Saban of Alabama, whose total pay from the school was $11,407,000 (not including other non-school compensation from endorsement deals, for example). The highest-paid men's basketball coach in 2023 was Bill Self of Kansas, whose total pay from the school was $9,625,642. (The highest-paid women's basketball coach was Kim Mulkey of Louisiana State University, $3,264,000.)
- In January 2024, the NCAA agreed to an eight-year, $920 million media rights deal with ESPN, triple the value of the previous deal.[34] The contract pays out $115 million annually. The NCAA also has an eight-year deal with CBS/Turner for the men's basketball tournament, set to end in 2032, and is valued at $8.8 billion.[35]
- Under Armour, the sporting goods company, has the exclusive rights to equip athletes at several universities. Notre Dame, for example, re-signed another ten-year deal with Under Armour worth $10 million a year.[36] Nike, the largest supplier of athletic equipment, had sponsorship deals with 79 of the 130 FBS schools in 2023.
- ESPN signed a $300 million contract over twenty years with the University of Texas to form the Longhorn Television Network to televise mostly Texas athletics, airing about two hundred live events. Texas has

College Sport as Big Business

the right to fire LTN announcers who do not "reflect the quality and reputation of UT."[37]

- The 2024 conference realignment primarily benefits the Big Ten and the SEC, which will see increased revenue through media rights deals. The College Football Playoff contract with ESPN is worth $7.8 billion through the 2031 season. The Big Ten and SEC are expected to receive roughly $21 million per school, while Big 12 and ACC schools will take home around $12 to $13 million.[38]

- The top ten most expensive college football tickets for the 2024 season will cost on average $200+ for two tickets.

Consequences of Money in College Athletics

Clearly big-time college sports are all about money. This has serious implications. First, college athletic programs are not amateur athletics (we will return to this point later in the chapter). Second, the system creates economic imperatives that lead college administrators, athletic directors, and coaches to make business decisions that supersede educational considerations. Tulane law professor Gary Roberts argues that this emphasis results in what he calls an "athletic arms race" among the schools, which involves increasing revenue and expenditures. To make money, an athletic department must spend money on increasing the recruiting budget, hiring more fundraisers and marketing personnel, improving practice facilities, adding new seating in the stadiums and arenas (especially skyboxes), purchasing the latest equipment, and building expensive new sports annexes with lavish locker rooms, weight rooms, training rooms, meeting rooms, lounges, and offices for the coaches and athletic administrators. In short, this "arms race" is an attempt to improve the school's overall image, impress alumni, and especially wow recruits. The spiraling costs result in most schools losing money.

Big-time programs generate many millions of dollars in donations from booster clubs, fans, and wealthy benefactors. In the latter case, oil tycoon T. Boone Pickens has donated about a quarter of a billion dollars to the Oklahoma State athletic department, and Phil Knight, founder of Nike, has donated more than $300 million to athletics at the University of Oregon. Most of the donations to athletic departments go for capital expenditures and funding scholarships. But this sports fund-raising success comes at a cost—while the athletic departments benefit, the overall giving to the universities has remained flat.[39] In effect, the more the athletic program gets, the less there is to support the academic programs.[40]

Coaches and athletic department administrators are paid handsomely. Added to this ever-accelerating cost is the cost of buying out highly paid coaches when they fail to deliver enough victories. According to an analysis by *USA Today*, major college athletic departments will have spent approximately $200 million on football coaching and staff changes during the 2023 season.[41] Head coach of Texas A&M Jimbo Fisher had more than $76 million remaining on his guaranteed contract when he was fired in November of 2023, in his sixth season with the school.

The bloated salaries of coaches and athletic administrators are a source of friction with the faculty. Is it appropriate to pay a coach five or ten times more than the president of the university or twenty times what a full professor is paid? This is especially galling to faculty members during difficult economic times when salaries and hiring are frozen, yet coaches, often regardless of whether they produce a winning season, receive generous salaries.

Another consequence of an athletic department's quest for money is that decision-making tends to leave the university and flow toward the sources of revenue. Television money dictates schedules. Booster organizations that supply funds may influence the hiring and firing of coaches. Do big donors have the final say in the selection of a new coach? As Professor Murray Sperber says, these practices "undermine one of the fundamental tenets of colleges and universities—their independence."[42]

Still another consequence of the athletic money chase is that students are, for the most part, left out. The irony is that students, who subsidize the athletic department through student fees that are folded into the cost of "tuition and fees" preventing students who are not interested in athletics from opting out, have no influence over how their money is spent. In some cases, these fees can be well over $1,000 per year. Of all the categories of contributors to athletics, only students are ignored in the power equation. Students are often left out in the distribution of the relatively scarce seats available in the arenas of successful teams or are allotted tickets in the "student section," often in less-than-ideal areas of the stadium. Premium seats go to big-spending boosters, depriving some students of the chance to watch their teams play. The situation worsens during tournament time, when schools are allotted relatively few tickets. These scarce tickets are typically given to the greatest benefactors of the athletic department. This common practice raises a serious question: shouldn't school sports be primarily for the enjoyment of students? The answer is that money makes the difference in the allocation of tickets.

Another consequence is the lure to schools at lower levels to become "big-time," despite the problems associated with big-time college sports, including the long odds against financial success. This desire creates major fiscal problems for them. They must upgrade their facilities. They must launch special fundraising campaigns that siphon money that might otherwise be donated to the academic side of the university. They need increased subsidies from the university administration. They require more money from student fees. They may also seek subsidies from various levels of government.

College Sport as Big Business

To raise the needed money, schools typically schedule away games with established powers for big payouts. This is evident in the first games of the college football season where Associated Press Poll "Top 25" teams will pay to play non-conference opponents. On the surface, this is a win-win situation for the two schools. The big-time school presumably adds a win to its record (as non-conference opponents tend to be "easier" competition for the top-ranked football programs), fills its arena or stadium, and keeps its place in the polls. Conversely, although there is a high probability the non-conference program will incur a loss on its season win-loss record, the school itself gets money to float its program, an acceptable compromise given many non-conference schools do not have the wealthy donor or alumni bases, do not generate revenue through television contracts, and may have fewer dollars from student tuition to support athletics.

Finally, the monetary rewards from television and other revenue streams are not distributed evenly, resulting in an uneven playing field. As mentioned above, the 2024 conference realignment primarily benefits the B1G Ten and the SEC conferences. In effect, the rich get richer and more successful, while the have-nots, with a few exceptions, lose money and fail on the field. That is, the best high school athletes tend to gravitate toward the dominant athletic programs because they will be on the "big stage" of television, large crowds, and national championships. Moreover, under the new NIL rules, NIL collectives can generate multimillion-dollar deals for high profile athletes while athletes in non-revenue sports or athletes in non-big-time sports programs will continue to struggle. The changes precipitated by the NIL deal and possible "pay-to-play" changes in NCAA policies can be easily covered by the schools in the power conferences, but schools in the less-endowed conferences are not able to keep up, making them less able to attract the best athletes. Attracting the best athletes increases the likelihood of winning, which brings in more money to the athletic department, which, in turn, is spent on larger recruiting budgets, building better facilities, increasing publicity, all of which increase the allure of these programs for the most talented recruits. This cycle perpetuates advantage, making it difficult for teams without winning traditions and leaving those schools in mediocre conferences at a distinct disadvantage.

Winning programs attract money. Corporations pay handsomely to have their logos displayed in the arenas and to have the stadiums named for them. Shoe/equipment companies provide subsidies to the most successful, amounting to several million dollars annually, to be the exclusive supplier. Royalties from the sale of merchandise generate millions to the elite schools. Proud supporters attend games, buy season tickets, pay for the right to purchase tickets, contribute to the athletic programs, and subsidize athletic scholarships. Schools like Michigan, Ohio State, Tennessee, and Penn State attract over one hundred thousand spectators to each home football game, and other schools with elite programs (for example, Nebraska, Florida, Florida State, Texas, Michigan, Ohio State) sell out at eighty thousand or more per game at high ticket prices. Similarly, schools such as Kentucky, Syracuse, and North Carolina sell out their stadium for men's basketball games with twenty-thousand-plus fans. The power conferences, with their television contracts and other revenue streams, provide their member schools with huge payouts. While the elite programs flourish, the majority of Division I athletic programs grapple with financial losses. And the financial gap widens.

Summary: The Contradictions of Big-Time Sport in Academia

Big-time college sport confronts us with a fundamental dilemma. On the one hand, college football and basketball offer entertainment, spectacle, and excitement, while bringing together the student-body, alumni, and community members in a shared ritual. On the other, the commercialization of big-time college sport has impacted the education mission of higher education in concerning ways. Educational goals have been superseded by the quest for big money. Because winning programs receive huge revenues from television, gate receipts, bowl and tournament appearances, boosters, and even legislatures many sports programs are guided by a win-at-any-cost philosophy.

The enormous pressures to win result sometimes in scandals. Sometimes there are illegal payments to athletes. Education is demeaned by recruiting athletes unprepared for college studies, by altering transcripts, by using surrogate test-takers, by providing phantom courses, and by not moving the athletes toward graduation. In addition, there are problems associated with the exploitation of athletes, gender inequality, and—in the case of college football—the maintenance of a male-segregated athletic subculture that, compared to its nonathletic counterpart, can promote anti-intellectualism, sexism, homophobia, and embrace the more toxic elements of masculinity. What role, then, does big-time sport play on college campuses?

Several contradictions further delineate the dilemma that big-time college sport presents.[43] The overarching contradiction is that we have organized a commercial entertainment activity within an educational environment, one that compromises educational goals. Ernest L. Boyer, former president of the Carnegie Foundation for the Advancement for Teaching, puts it this way: "I believe that the college sports system is one of the most corrupting and destructive influences on higher education. It is obscene, and there is no way to put an educational gloss on this enterprise."[44] In short, as currently structured, big-time sport is not compatible with education.

A fundamental problem is that athletes are recruited as students. Yet demanding coaches, as well as the athletic subculture, work against the student role. At the heart of this contradiction is the fact that institutions of higher learning allow the enrollment and subsidization of ill-prepared and uninterested students solely for the purpose of winning games, enhancing the visibility of the university, and producing revenue.

The third contradiction is that although big-time sports are revenue producing, for most schools they actually drain money away from academics. This occurs when scholarship money is diverted from students with cognitive abilities to students with athletic abilities, and when athletic budgets are supplemented with generous sums from student fees and subsidies from the academic budgets.

A final contradiction involves the issue of whether or not participation in sport is educational. University administrators often advance this as a rationale for college sport. But such administrators are caught in a contradiction because most of them willingly accept the present maldistribution of resources, scholarships, and opportunities for women's sport. Sociologist Allen Sack argues:

> If one accepts the notion that student-athletes are the prime beneficiaries of college sport, how in the world can women's programs receive less financial support than men's? If sport is educational, what possible academic justification can there be for denying this aspect of education for women? Wouldn't the denial of equal athletic opportunities be tantamount to saying that men should have more microscopes, laboratory facilities and library privileges than women?[45]

And, we would add, if sport is a useful, educational activity, why limit these benefits to the athletic elite? Why should the best athletic facilities be reserved for their exclusive use? Why are we limited to one team in each sport, rather than several teams based on differences in size and skill? If sport is justifiable as an educational experience, why limit the number of so-called minor sports? Should they not be expanded to meet the wishes of the student body? In our view, participation in sport is one that should be available to each student who is interested, and should be maximized instead of limiting its benefits to the few.

Notes

1   See, for example, Nathan Kalman-Lamb and Derek Silva, *The End of College Football: On the Human Cost of an All-American Game* (Chapel Hill: University of

North Carolina Press, 2024); Gilbert M. Gaul, *Billion-Dollar Ball: A Journey Through the Big-Money Culture of College Football* (New York: Viking, 2015).

2. Jay Coakley, *Sports in Society: Issues and Controversies*, 13th ed. (New York: McGraw-Hill, 2021).

3. Vanessa Romo, "Women's NCAA Championship TV Ratings Crush the Men's Competition," National Public Radio, April 10, 2024, https://www.npr.org/2024/04/10/1243801501/womens-ncaa-championship-tv-ratings.

4. Michael T. Nietzel, "Power Five Universities Spend Much More Per Athlete Than for Other Students, Finds New Study," *Forbes*, January 13, 2024, https://www.forbes.com/sites/michaeltnietzel/2024/01/13/power-five-universities-spend-much-more-per-athlete-than-for-other-students-finds-new-study/.

5. Crimson Editorial Board, "For Athlete Admissions, Something's Gotta Give," *Harvard Crimson*, November 2, 2023, https://www.thecrimson.com/article/2023/11/2/editorial-athletes-fair-admissions.

6. Christopher Rim, "Athletic Recruiting Offers Greater Odds of Ivy League Admissions Than Legacy Status," *Forbes*, February 15, 2024, https://www.forbes.com/sites/christopherrim/2024/02/15/athletic-recruiting-offers-greater-odds-of-ivy-league-admissions-than-legacy-status/.

7. Kirsten Hextrum, *Special Admission: How College Sports Recruitment Favors White Suburban Athletes* (New Brunswick, NJ: Rutgers University Press, 2021).

8. Nathan Kalman-Lamb and Derek Silva, "The Case to End College Football," *Sportico: The Business of Sports*, May 22, 2024, https://www.sportico.com/leagues/college-sports/2024/case-to-end-to-college-football-1234779221/.

9. S. J. L. Foster and M. R. Huml, "The Relationship Between Athletic Identity and Academic Major Chosen by Student-Athletes," *International Journal of Exercise Science* 10, no. 6 (2016): 915–25.

10. Kayci Mikrut, "NCAA Diploma Dashboards Provide Academic Insight," *NCAA News*, March 7, 2022, https://www.ncaa.org/news/2022/3/7/media-center-ncaa-diploma-dashboards-provide-academic-insight.

11. Natalie Meisler, "College Football Has Almost Become a Year-Round Sport," *Denver Post*, June 11, 2007.

12. Nathan Kalman-Lamb and Derek Silva, "College Athletes Are Being Robbed of an Education," *Chronicle of Higher Education*, August 26, 2024, https://www.chronicle.com/article/college-athletes-are-being-robbed-of-an-education?sra=true.

13. Patricia A. Adler and Peter Adler, *Backboards and Blackboards: College Athletes and Role Engulfment* (New York: Columbia University Press).

14. Adler and Adler, 247.

15. Sarah Lyall, "A's for Athletes, but Charges of Tar Heel Fraud," *New York Times*, January 1, 2014, 1A; S. L. Price, "How Did Carolina Lose Its Way?," *Sports Illustrated*, March 16, 2015, 64–65.

16. Paul M. Barrett, "New Headaches for UNC: Fake Classes Scandal Won't Go Away," *Bloomberg*, November 10, 2014, https://www.bloomberg.com/news/articles/2014-11-10/new-headaches-for-unc-fake-classes-scandal-wont-go-away.

17. The NCAA in collusion with the NFL requires that a player must have spent at least three years playing for a college team before being eligible for the NFL.

Notes

18 George H. Sage and D. Stanley Eitzen, *Sociology of North American Sport*, 10th ed. (New York: Oxford University Press, 2016).

19 Coakley, *Sports in Society*.

20 "Knight-Newhouse College Athletics Database," Knight Commission on Intercollegiate Athletics, https://knightnewhousedata.org/fbs.

21 Saquandra Heath and Massillon Myers, "Student-Athletes Continue to Graduate at Record rates," *NCAA News*, November 15, 2022, https://www.ncaa.org/news/2022/11/15/media-center-student-athletes-continue-to-graduate-at-record-rates.aspx.

22 Patrick Hruby, "'They Don't Feel Adequately Prepared': How Schools Struggle to Ready Athletes for Success after College Sports," *Global Sports Matters*, September 21, 2021, https://www.globalsportmatters.com/research/2021/09/21/schools-struggle-ready-athletes-success-after-college-sports-ncaa-eddie-comeaux/.

23 Andrew Brandt, "Business of Football: The Supreme Court Sends a Message to the NCAA," *Sports Illustrated*, July 29, 2021, https://www.si.com/nfl/2021/06/29/business-of-football-supreme-court-unanimous-ruling.

24 Stewart Mandel, "Five-Star Recruit in Class of 2023 Signs Agreement with Collective That Could Pay Him More Than $8 Million," *The Athletic*, March 11, 2022, https://www.nytimes.com/athletic/3178558/2022/03/11/five-star-recruit-in-class-of-2023-signs-agreement-with-collective-that-could-pay-him-more-than-8-million/.

25 "Billion-Dollar Settlement to Resolve Antitrust Litigation Will Impact Student-Athletes and NCAA Enforcement," Duane Morris LLP, June 6, 2024, https://www.duanemorris.com/alerts/billion_dollar_settlement_resolve_antitrust_litigation_impact_student_athletes_ncaa_0624.html.

26 "Billion-Dollar Settlement."

27 Justin Williams, "House v. NCAA Settlement On Hold as Judge Sends Parties 'Back to the Drawing Board,'" *The Athletic*, September 5, 2024, https://www.nytimes.com/athletic/5749342/2024/09/05/house-ncaa-settlement-college-sports-nil-boosters/.

28 Joe Rexrode, "Tennessee Includes 10 Percent 'Talent Fee' in Raising 2025 Football Season Ticket Prices," *The Athletic*, September 17, 2024, https://www.nytimes.com/athletic/5773813/2024/09/17/tennessee-football-ticket-prices-talent-fee/.

29 "Pop Speaks the Truth," *The Gist*, September 11, 2024, https://ca.thegistsports.com/newsletter/college/b0e2bb7b-5f04-4935-8e56-bd65b0c0a917/.

30 Andrew Zimbalist, "Analysis: Who Is Winning in the High-Revenue World of College Sports?," *PBS News Hour*, March 18, 2023, https://www.pbs.org/newshour/economy/analysis-who-is-winning-in-the-high-revenue-world-of-college-sports.

31 "NCAA Generates Nearly $1.3 Billion in Revenue for 2022–23," Associated Press, February 1, 2024, https://apnews.com/article/ncaa-revenue-mens-basketball-tournament-d721a558bed2cdcd7b5539173b454945.

32 "NCAA Finances: Revenue and Expenses by School," *USA Today*, March 14, 2024, https://sportsdata.usatoday.com/ncaa/finances.

33 Reuben Fischer Baum, "Infographic: Is Your State's Highest Paid Employee a Coach? (Probably)," *Deadspin*, May 9, 2024, https://deadspin.com/infographic-is-your-states-highest-paid-employee-a-co-489635228/.

34 Jessica Golden, "NCAA and ESPN Ink 8-Year, $920 Million Media Rights Deal," *CNBC Sports*, January 4, 2024, https://www.cnbc.com/2024/01/04/ncaa-and-espn-ink-8-year-920-million-media-rights-deal.html.

35 Andrew Lisa, "The Money Behind the March Madness NCAA Basketball Tournament," *Yahoo Finance*, March 20, 2023, https://finance.yahoo.com/news/money-behind-march-madness-ncaa-173857122.html.

36 Pete Sampson, "Notre Dame Re-signs with Under Armour on Ten-Year Contract," *The Athletic*, August 4, 2023, https://www.nytimes.com/athletic/4737881/2023/08/04/notre-dame-under-armour-new-contract/.

37 Michael Hiestand, "How Texas Is Steering College TV Sports," *USA Today*, August 12, 2011, 1C–2C.

38 Lilly Umana, "The Cost of College Conference Realignment," *NBC News*, September 14, 2024, https://www.nbcnews.com/news/sports/cost-college-conference-realignment-are-student-athletes-re-also-human-rcna170960.

39 Both T. Boone Pickens and Phil Knight are exceptions, having given generously to both the athletic department and academics.

40 Jeffrey L. Stimson and Dennis R. Howard, "Athletic Success and Private Giving to Athletic and Academic Programs at NCAA Institutions," *Journal of Sport Management* 21 (April 2007): 235–64; Brad Wolverton, "Growth in Sports Gifts May Mean Fewer Academic Donations," *Chronicle of Higher Education*, October 5, 2007, A1, A34.

41 Steve Berkowitz, "Schools Set to Pay at Least $200 Million in Buyouts to Hire and Fire College Football Coaches," *USA Today*, January 18, 2024, https://www.usatoday.com/story/sports/ncaaf/2024/01/18/college-football-coaches-buyouts-schools-200-million/72174164007/.

42 Murray Sperber, *College Sports Inc.: The Athletic Department vs. the University* (New York: Henry Holt, 1990), 65.

43 This section is largely from D. Stanley Eitzen, "College Sport," *Blackwell Encyclopedia of Sport* (Malden, MA: Blackwell, 2006), 4665–68.

44 Quoted in Michael Goodwin, "When the Cash Register Is the Scoreboard," *New York Times*, June 8, 1986, 27–28.

45 Allen L. Sack, "College Sports Must Choose: Amateur or Pro?" *New York Times*, May 3, 1981, 2S.

9

PROFESSIONAL SPORTS FRANCHISES: PUBLIC TEAMS, PRIVATE BUSINESSES

Most public address announcers at professional sports events, when introducing the teams, refer to the home team as "your" team, as in "your Denver Broncos," "your New York Yankees," or "your Atlanta Hawks."[1] The home fans do identify, often passionately, with the home team, the team representing their city or region. The team is their team in this respect. The fans also have a financial stake in these teams by purchasing the high-priced tickets and subsidizing the stadiums and arenas in which the professional teams play.

But the professional team to which they give their allegiance is not really theirs. Except for only one major league franchise in the four major (men's) sports—the Green Bay Packers—every professional team is owned by an individual, a family, a small group of business partners, or a corporation. For the NFL, Green Bay may remain the only franchise with public ownership. The NFL's current constitution is written to ban teams from pursuing a public ownership model: "No corporation, association, partnership, or other entity not operated for profit nor any charitable organization or entity not presently a member of the League shall be eligible for membership."[2] Private ownership of sports teams and clubs is not universal. Many clubs in professional soccer in Europe are publicly owned, including Spain's Real Madrid and FC Barcelona. Why does it matter whether a team is publicly or privately owned? As sports journalist R. J. Anderson of *CBS Sports* explains,

> The main difference between the private and the public ownership models can be surmised as such: Under one, teams are run like businesses; under the other, they're run like public goods. Private owners demand profit. They're willing to do whatever it takes to make the number go up, even if that means fielding a poor product or threatening the community with relocation. Public ownership does away with the unchecked profiteering, as well as with the relocation threats—the team is owned by the municipality it resides in, after all. That is not to say that profit is not a goal, it is merely not the only priority; besides, the public model demands greater transparency and democracy when it comes to a team's finances.[3]

In other words, the owner can sell and trade players, including so-called franchise players. The owner determines the ticket prices. The owner can move the team to another city. Examining professional sport as a monopoly, ownership for profit, and public subsidies to professional team franchises raises a question: Who profits and who loses in the way professional sport is organized?

Professional Sport as a Monopoly

Each major professional league is an unregulated monopoly.[4] Each league regulates itself, unfettered by government oversight and government rules against monopolies that apply to other industries. Each league operates as a cartel—as competitors joined together for mutual benefit. This means that the teams making up each league make agreements on matters of mutual interest such as rules, schedules, promotions, expansion, and media contracts. In professional sport, cartels exist to restrict competition for athletes, to limit franchises, and to divide markets among the league's teams.[5] Such arrangements are illegal in

Professional Sport as a Monopoly

most other businesses because they lead to collusion, price fixing, and restraint of trade.

Being a cartel gives each league enormous advantages. The cartel limits competition in several ways. Competitive bidding among teams for players is controlled through player drafts, contracts, and trades. A cartel keeps competition among the teams at a minimum by restricting the number of teams in the league and where they can locate. The owner of the Kansas City Royals, for instance, is protected from a rival team locating in his or her territory. There are some metropolitan areas with two major league baseball teams, but these exceptions occurred before baseball agreed to territorial exclusivity. Even for the few exceptions (Chicago White Sox and Chicago Cubs; the New York Yankees and the New York Mets; and Los Angeles Angels and Los Angeles Dodgers), the teams are in different leagues (National vs American). This protection from competition eliminates price wars. The owners of a franchise can continue to charge the maximum without any fear of price cutting by competitors.

The league cartel also controls the number of franchises allowed. The number of franchises is not determined by the number of players with sufficient talent and skills to play in the professional leagues. According to the NCAA, the probability that a college baseball player will go pro is about 5 percent; about 1 percent for men's basketball; less than 1 percent for women's basketball; 1.5 percent for football; and less than 1 percent for women's soccer and softball.[6] What this means is that there are more athletes who can compete at the professional level than there are opportunities to play. The surplus of talent could be used in league expansions; however, it is not. It is not always in the best interest of a league to expand the number of teams as this dilutes the resources distributed among the teams in the league and creates more competition among teams. Instead, leagues are often incentivized to limit the number of franchises.

In writing about Major League Baseball, sport sociologist George Sage asserts that this is clearly the result of the MLB's reluctance to expand because the owners do not want to "diminish their political and economic power by adding new franchises. It seems obvious that expansion has little to do with the availability of capable baseball players."[7] When it does expand, it does so to benefit the league. The last four additions reveal why. In 1993, the Florida Marlins and the Colorado Rockies were admitted because neither Florida nor the Colorado Mountain time zone had a major league team. These additions tapped new fan and media markets, which would benefit the other league members. So, too, did the $95 million that each team paid to join. Neither team was allowed a share in television revenues for two seasons, which had the effect when the initiation fee was added of totaling to $106 million. In 1998, the Arizona Diamondbacks and the Tampa Bay Devil Rays played their first seasons, each having paid $125 million to become members of the cartel. Both teams were added for reasons like the ones dictating the addition of the Marlins and Rockies—the

Southwest: Arizona/Utah/New Mexico/Nevada had no major league baseball team and Tampa Bay was located in a large, heretofore untapped market that did not infringe on Miami, 275 miles away.

Each league is generally reluctant to add new teams because scarcity permits higher ticket prices, more beneficial media arrangements, and continued territorial purity. In short, the value of each franchise increases by the league's restriction on the number of teams. This monopolistic situation enables a league to negotiate television contracts for the benefit of all members of the league. The 1961 Sports Broadcast Act allowed sports leagues to sell their television rights as a group without being subject to antitrust laws. Antitrust laws prohibit anticompetitive agreements and unfair monopolies. As a result, national and cable networks along with streaming platforms may bid for the right to televise the games of a league. The league itself collects the "rights fees" and then determines how to distribute the revenue to the franchises in the league. For example, the NFL distributes its revenue equally among its teams. This limits competition in that a franchise that generates higher television ratings would be more valuable to a television or streaming network than a franchise that either operates in a smaller media market (i.e., a smaller city/town) and/or has lower ratings. Before the 1961 Act, the New York Giants, for example, earned ten times as much revenue from television rights fees than the Green Bay Packers. Earning more revenue would give individual franchises a competitive advantage in recruiting and hiring talent, would decrease parity among the franchises in the league, leading to a possible situation where only a handful of teams consistently win while the rest suffer given the disparity in revenue. The NFL's ability to negotiate the television contracts for all the franchises prevents such competition and ensures parity across the league, which benefits all the teams as more competitive parity draws in a wider fanbase, audience, and viewership across the league, rather than concentrating it in the hands of a few teams. For successful franchises, such revenue sharing depresses the value of the franchise. The NBA has adopted the NFL's model of revenue sharing although the league has proposed an 8 percent "league office cut" of the new (as of 2025) nearly $75 billion television and streaming deal it's set to sign. Such agreements also box out regional and local television networks who cannot compete with the offers of major media corporations like ESPN and Amazon, and then are unable to broadcast games.

The following are the "televised" rights deals with the major professional leagues in the United States.[8]

- National Football League (NFL): Earned a combined $100 billion over eleven years (through 2033) for the primary broadcast deal split among Amazon, CBS, ESPN, Fox, NBC, and NFL Network. Netflix paid about $400 million for three years' worth of exclusive Christmas Day games,

Professional Sport as a Monopoly 175

and YouTube pays the league $2 billion per season for Sunday Ticket. The NFL receives $6 billion a year from five broadcast partners.

- National Basketball Association (NBA): Earned $24 billion for a nine-year deal with ESPN, TNT Sports, and NBA TV that ends in 2025. The NBA received $2.7 billion annually from its broadcast partners. The NBA is currently negotiating its next rights deal.

- Women's National Basketball Association (WNBA): Part of the NBA negotiations, its current $60-million-per-season deal (with Amazon, CBS, ESPN, and Scripps Sports) is expected to increase given the recent growth in viewership, attendance, and fan engagement (see chapter 3).

- Major League Baseball (MLB): ESPN, Fox, and TNT are paying a combined $12 billion over seven years, ending in 2028. Apple has a separate seven-year deal, running through 2029 and worth a total of $595 million. Roku's newly inaugurated Sunday afternoon games are worth $10 million per season to MLB.

- National Hockey League (NHL): ESPN, TNT Sport. About $4.4 billion for a seven-year deal through the 2027–2028 season.

- US Soccer: Amazon, Apple, CBS, ESPN, Fox, NBC, Scripps, Telemundo, TNT Sports. The terms of soccer's media rights contracts are "complicated," given the domestic and international competitions for both the men's and women's leagues; however, the combined contracts are worth $3 billion.

The leagues also negotiate advertising and other ancillary sources of revenue to be shared among league members, such as being the "official" beer of the league or the "official" sponsor of the Super Bowl Half-Time show (Apple pays the league $50 million a year for that designation), and the sale of merchandise and licensing. In 2022, each of the thirty-two teams in the NFL brought in $372 million from national media rights, league sponsorships, merchandising and licensing.[9] Another advantage of the monopoly enjoyed by the professional leagues is that the players are drastically limited in their choices and bargaining power. The league cartel holds down wages because the athletes have few options besides playing in the league. In football, players are drafted out of college. If they want to play in the NFL, they must negotiate with the team that drafted them. Their other choices are to play in the Arena Football League or the Canadian Football League, for example. These other options offer much less pay, and Canadian teams limit the number of Americans allowed per team. Zach Collaros, who plays quarterback for the Winnipeg Blue Bombers is the highest-paid CFL player of 2024. Collaros earns $600,000 annually.[10] The CFL's average salary is $73,200. Compare this with the highest-paid NFL players in 2024: Green Bay Packers quarterback Jordan Love, Cincinnati Bengals quarterback Joe Burrow, and Jacksonville Jaguars quarterback Trevor Lawerence will each make $55 million in salary alone, according to the NFL. A final advantage of the cartel controlling of the number and location of franchises is that the owners prosper. Since the owners rarely add teams to the cartel, the teams are scarce commodities, which means that their worth appreciates much faster than other investments.

The fifty most valuable teams in 2023 were worth a combined $256 billion, which is 15 percent more than the combined value in 2022. Consider these examples of the growth curve in professional team franchise value:[11]

- NFL: The Dallas Cowboys franchise was purchased in 1960 for $600,000; in 1984, it was sold for $60 million and in 1989 for $150 million. In 2023, its value was estimated at $9.0 billion.[12]
- NFL: The Washington franchise (now the Commanders) was purchased in 1999 for $750 million. The value for the franchise rose to $2.85 billion in 2015. The franchise was sold again in 2023 for $6.05 billion.
- NBA: The Miami Heat was purchased for $33 million in 1988. The franchise was valued at $425 million in 2011, $1.175 billion in 2015, and $5.7 billion in 2023.
- MLB: The New York Yankees, purchased in 1973 by George Steinbrenner for $8.8 million, was worth $1.7 billion in 2011, $3.2 billion in 2015 and $7.55 billion in 2024.
- MLB: In 1977, the Boston Red Sox was worth $18.7 million. In 2002, the franchise was sold for $660 million. The value in 2015 was $2.1 billion. In 2024 it was valued at $4.5 billion.
- NBA: Mark Cuban purchased the Dallas Mavericks of the NBA for $285 million in 2000. In 2015, it was valued at $1.15 billion. In 2024, it was valued at $4.5 billion.

To summarize, the major professional sports leagues in the United States are monopolies, and therein lies the problem. Two economists, James Quirk and Rodney Fort, argue that many problems of the professional team sports business arise from the monopoly power of professional leagues. Eliminate the monopoly power of leagues and you transfer power from the insiders—owners and players alike—to the outsiders—fans and taxpayers. Eliminate the monopoly power of leagues and you eliminate the problem of lack of competitive balance in a league due to the disparity in drawing potential among league teams. Eliminate the monopoly power of leagues and you eliminate the blackmailing of cities to subsidize teams.[13] Owning a professional team is, except in rare instances, a very profitable endeavor because of the advantages of belonging to a cartel, the sale of media rights, and, as discussed in the following section, the public's subsidization of arenas.

Public Subsidies to Professional Team Franchises

The scarcity of professional teams (the consequence of league monopoly) and the tremendous fan interest in having a major sports franchise in their city lead to large public subsidies for the relatively few teams. The subsidies to franchise owners take two forms—tax breaks and the availability of arenas at very low cost.

The tax code benefits team owners in two ways. First, the typically enormous profits from the sale of a team are counted as capital gains for team owners (as with the sale of other American businesses) and thus are taxed at a lower rate than other sources of income such as salaries and wages. Consider this example from a *ProPublica* investigative report:[14]

> At a concession stand at Staples Center in Los Angeles, Adelaide Avila was pingponging between pouring beers, wiping down counters and taking out the trash. Her Los Angeles Lakers were playing their hometown rival, the Clippers, but Avila was working too hard to follow the March 2019 game. When she filed taxes for her previous year's labors at the arena and her second job driving for Uber, the 50-year-old Avila reported making $44,810. The federal government took a 14.1 percent cut.
>
> On the court that night, the players were also hard at work. None more so than LeBron James. The Lakers star was suffering through a painful strained groin injury, but he still put up more points and played more minutes than any other player. In his tax return, James reported making $124 million in 2018. He paid a federal income tax rate of 35.9 percent. Not surprisingly, it was more than double the rate paid by Avila.
>
> The wealthiest person in the building that night, in all likelihood, was Steve Ballmer, owner of the Clippers. The evening was decidedly less arduous for the billionaire former CEO of Microsoft. He sat courtside, in a pink dress shirt and slacks, surrounded by friends. His legs were outstretched, his shoes almost touching the sideline. Ballmer had reason to smile: His Clippers won. But even if they hadn't, his ownership of the team was reaping him massive tax benefits.
>
> For the prior year, Ballmer reported making $656 million. The dollar figure he paid in taxes was large, $78 million; but as a percentage of what he made, it was tiny. Records reviewed by *ProPublica* show his federal income tax rate was just 12 percent. That's a third of the rate James paid, even though

Ballmer made five times as much as the superstar player. Ballmer's rate was also lower than Avila's—even though Ballmer's income was almost 15,000 times greater than the concession worker's.

This might seem shocking that someone making over half a billion dollars a year would pay a lower percentage in taxes than a middle-income worker. Owners of major professional sports win, however, even when the team may not. As explained in the *ProPublica* investigation:

Ballmer pays such a low rate, in part, because of a provision of the U.S. tax code. When someone buys a business, they're often able to deduct almost the entire sale price against their income during the ensuing years. That allows them to pay less in taxes. The underlying logic is that the purchase price was composed of assets—buildings, equipment, patents and more—that degrade over time and should be counted as expenses. But in few industries is that tax treatment more detached from economic reality than in professional sports. Teams' most valuable assets, such as TV deals and player contracts, are virtually guaranteed to regenerate because sports franchises are essentially monopolies. There's little risk that players will stop playing for Ballmer's Clippers or that TV stations will stop airing their games. But Ballmer still gets to deduct the value of those assets over time, almost $2 billion in all, from his taxable income.

A second tax benefit is indirect but bountiful, nonetheless. This financial advantage accrues to team owners as companies or corporations purchase luxury suites, skyboxes, tickets, and food. The businesses are permitted to write off 50 percent of these costs as business expenses. This tax subsidy to businesses and corporations makes the high cost of attending sports events more palatable, which helps to keep the price of tickets and skyboxes inflated and profits steady. All other taxpayers, however, are left holding the bag.

Despite these advantages, team owners today paint a bleak picture of team finances. They do this to get the fans on their side in salary disputes with players, to keep the players' salary demands as low as possible, and to secure support for further subsidies in renovating existing stadiums or building new ones. The negative financial picture painted by the owners is misleading because it refers usually to accounting losses (expenses exceeding income) that are not really losses.

The second type of public subsidy of professional sport is the provision of sports facilities to most franchises at very low cost. These arenas and stadiums are essential to the financial success and spectator appeal of professional sports. Team owners seek new and improved sports facilities, mostly, but not always, at taxpayer expense, and typically they get them. If not, they move. This threat to move (some would call it blackmail or a shakedown), real or implied, has resulted in a construction boom. Economists estimate that taxpayers have spent approximately $30 billion in stadiums over the past thirty-four years.[15] A research study published by economists[16] found an increase in the direct government subsidies for the construction of professional sports venues over the last fifty-plus years, from around $10 billion in the 1960s–1980s to more than $23 billion in the 1990s–2010s (adjusted for inflation). The researchers attribute this increase in part to sports stadiums becoming more extravagant over time, including the increase in the number of luxury suites and skyboxes, which did not exist when many stadiums were originally built. It is important to note that owners of professional sports teams are not in need of these subsidies. The top twenty professional sports team owners on the 2023 *Forbes* 400 list of the world's wealthiest people are worth a collective $382 billion. And according to *Forbes*, "For most, the NFL, the NBA and MLB remain a very lucrative side hustle."[17] Yet, stadiums are financed by the taxpayers. So, too, are new roads and overpasses to access these stadiums. Let's examine a few examples of how team owners over the past few decades have received enormous benefits from local taxpayers.

Case Study: Two Stadiums, One for the Cincinnati Bengals and One for the Cincinnati Reds; a Sweetheart Deal for the Owners and "the Worst Stadium Deal" for the Taxpayers

In the mid-1990s, under threat by the Cincinnati Bengals to relocate if they did not get a new stadium, Hamilton County agreed to finance the building of two stadiums: one for the Bengals and the other for the Cincinnati Reds. The county agreed to what turned out to be a "sweetheart deal" for the teams by issuing $1 billion in bonds, to be paid off with a sales tax hike of 0.5 percent.[18] The county agreed to pay for the new fields, including all cost overruns, pick up nearly all operating and capital improvement costs (about $8 million a year), and give the teams all of the parking revenue, while the county would pay for all security costs. This one-sided arrangement soon became even more of a burden to the county.

The overarching problem was that a single county took on this economic liability rather than sharing the risk across nearby counties or with the state. The financing for the Denver Broncos' new stadium, for example, was shared by six counties. When the Pittsburgh Steelers and the Philadelphia Eagles got new stadiums, the state of Pennsylvania was responsible for part of the financing.

The county's financial woes began when the initial cost for the Bengals stadium of $280 million escalated to $454 million. As the financial burden increased, sales taxes decreased with the advent of the Great Recession and heightened joblessness. The annual debt payments were steep—$34.6 million in 2010, equal to 16.4 percent of the county budget. As a result, the county had to cut funds for schools, the sheriff's department, the juvenile court, and youth programs. Moreover, this is a county where one out of seven residents live below the poverty line.

So, while the teams presumably prosper (at the time the Bengals had only two winning seasons in over a decade since moving into the stadium in 2000), the county is left "holding the bag." As Neil deMause, expert on the ills of the public financing of sports arenas puts it: "One hopes this will be a cautionary tale for other local governments negotiating leases, but it probably won't be."[19]

Indeed, just a few years shy of the end of their lease in 2026, the Bengals asked the county for an additional $300 million for stadium renovations.[20] The county asserted their goal of a "multi-faceted approach" to funding the renovations. In December 2023, Hamilton County commissioners voted to approve $39 million in funds.[21] The Bengals were able to acquire $100 million in funds through an "NFL-G5 loan program" to pay for the renovations and $40 million in private funds. According to ESPN, the money will be spent on "updating audio and video systems, renovating suites and club lounges, concession upgrades and other projects aimed at improving the fan experience. The franchise has also invested $40 million in private funds for the team's indoor practice facility, training room and locker room, with the latter currently under construction."[22]

This case study is an egregious example of the price that even nonfans are required to pay for sports arenas, seemingly in perpetuity. Although it appears Hamilton County learned some lessons from the "worst stadium financing deal ever,"[23] other franchises have not. In 2022, the New York legislature's approval of $850 million in public subsidies for a new stadium for the Buffalo Bills was described by economist Victor Matheson as one of the "worst stadium deals in recent memory—a remarkable feat considering the high bar set by other misguided state and local governments across the country."[24] Over 60 percent of the costs of the new stadium will be paid for by taxpayers, a dramatic departure in recent trends in stadium funding, suggesting a return to an overreliance on public funding for a private stadium.

Case Study: Dallas Cowboys Stadium, an Ostentatious Edifice Subsidized in Part by Taxpayers Who, for the Most Part, Have Limited Access to the Excess

In the early 2000s, owner Jerry Jones wanted a new stadium in Arlington (midway between Dallas and Fort Worth) for his Dallas Cowboys.[25] In 2004, the cost was estimated at $650 million. Arlington's contribution was capped at $325 million and was to come from a half-cent increase in the city's sales tax and increases of 2 percent on the hotel occupancy tax and 5 percent on car rentals. Jones was responsible for the rest, which was paid with commercial loans, a league loan of $150 million, and proceeds from a ticket and parking tax. The final cost to build the stadium doubled from the original estimate to $1.3 billion.

The stadium, completed in 2009, was at the time the largest domed stadium in the world with the world's largest column-free interior in the world. The stadium had a retractable roof. It also had the world's largest high-definition two-sided video screen, which hung from twenty-yard line to twenty-yard line, measuring more than 11,500 square feet (160 feet wide and 72 feet high) and weighing 1.2 million pounds. This video marvel alone cost $5 million more than the entire cost of construction for the previous arena for the Dallas Cowboys ($35 million). There were an additional 2,900 television screens installed throughout the facility. The seating capacity is 80,000 and expanded to 110,000 with standing room. There were 270 suites when the stadium was built in 2009, today there are 380. Suites average about $20,000 per game. When the stadium was first built, club seats cost $340, today those tickets go for between $3,700 and $4,500. The average cost of a non-premium ticket in 2009 was $110.20, today it is $348. Season ticket holders must buy "personal seat licenses," which are multiyear commitments that in 2009 cost from $2,000 to $150,000 (this license does *not* include the ticket). The lowest-priced ticket at the time the stadium opened was $29 for the "party-pass option"—standing room on platforms in the end zone. Tickets for "standing-room options" for the 2024 season range from $25 for preseason tickets to $65–$100 for the regular season. The Fan Cost Index in 2023 (tickets for a family of four, parking, drinks, and a souvenir) was $665.60 per game.[26] In 2023, team sponsorship revenue was $2.35 billion dollars, the highest in the NFL. When the franchise sold the stadium naming rights to AT&T in 2013, it received $1.2 billion dollars. Clearly, this stadium is a financial windfall for owner Jones.

The new Cowboys Stadium represents a trend in professional sports: bigger and ever more expensive entertainment, which is affordable to only the wealthiest fans. Evidence of this new "gilded age" of sport is found throughout the professional leagues, not just the NFL. When the New York Yankees moved their stadium in 2009, the new Yankee stadium generated controversy as the $2.3 billion stadium, one of the most expensive ever built, was subsidized with $1.2 billion in public funds. The construction also came at a loss for the city as public park lands were used in the development. The stadium opened in 2009 and was criticized at the time for its high ticket prices. For example, the 1,800 seats circling the infield cost $500 to $2,500 per seat and provide concierge service and access to a private club, private entrance, private elevator, and private concourse.[27] And then there are the luxury suites, which rented for $600,000 to $850,000 a year, where, in the words of journalist Bill Moyers, "The fat cats gather, safely removed from the sweaty masses."[28] Moreover, the price for attending has skyrocketed with these new arenas. Even the "sweaty masses" at Yankee stadium would pay more than other baseball fans, as the Yankees had the highest average ticket price in the league, $63 a ticket. The irony, of course, is that these stadiums are built, in large part, with taxpayer subsidies. The team owners of the Yankees and Mets promised to pay all $1.7 billion in construction costs of the stadiums that opened in 2009. It was revealed later that the owners were collecting a combined $1.8 billion in lease and tax breaks against the construction costs.[29] What appeared at first that the owners were generous turned out to be a hoax on the taxpayers.

Case Study: The Funding of the Milwaukee Bucks Basketball Arena: The Business-Politics Nexus

In 2014, two billionaire hedge fund owners, Wesley Edens and Marc Lasry, bought the Milwaukee Bucks for $550 million. A year later, the value was estimated at somewhere north of $1 billion (a doubling of their investment). The new owners insisted that the team would leave Milwaukee unless the public would pay half the cost of a $500-million arena. The resulting deal included a $35-million parking garage paid for by the city with half the revenue going to the Bucks, along with all the revenue from naming rights for the arena. Even more lucrative to the owners was that a development company owned by Edens and Lasry was sold ten acres of vacant publicly owned downtown land—appraised at $8 million—for $1.[30]

There is a political side to this shakedown story. Real estate tycoon Jon Hammes was given ownership shares in the Bucks, presumably for his political influence. He was the national finance co-chair for Wisconsin governor Scott Walker's 2016 presidential campaign where he pledged to work to meet the campaign's goal of as much as $3 billion. He was also connected to a political action committee that contributed $150,000 to Walker. In advance of the deal being consummated, Hammes purchased an acre and a half of property around the area where the Bucks arena was to be built. All of this is a form of political money laundering—where billionaire owners take public funds for stadiums and donate their newfound wealth to the very politicians who facilitated their stadium grab.[31] The story ends with Governor Walker signing a bill to subsidize the arena for $250 million. This occurred just one month after the governor and legislators cut $250 million from the budget of the University of Wisconsin system.

Other Examples of Egregious Subsidies to Team Owners

The Montreal Expos were transplanted to Washington, D.C., for the 2005 season. For three years they played in the old RFK stadium. In 2008, they moved into a publicly financed new stadium that cost the taxpayers 97 percent of the total cost of $674 million. The owners were obligated to pay only $20 million of the construction costs, and in return they would receive all of the money received from tickets, parking, concessions, and naming rights.[32] Critic Dave Zirin points out that this subsidy occurred at the same time that the city was set to close down twenty-four public schools; the city's libraries shut down early for lack of funds; and the African American unemployment in the city was 51 percent. As Zirin described, "It's a monument of avarice that will clear the working poor out of the Southeast corner of the city as surely as if they just dispensed with the baseball and used a bulldozer. This is sports as ethnic and economic cleansing."[33]

After a threat in the early 2000s to move the Chicago Bears to the suburbs or to Northern Indiana, the city of Chicago agreed to finance its share of the $632 million project to renovate Soldier Field (the Bears were to pay $200 million) with a 2 percent city hotel tax. At the time, estimates were that the renovated stadium had at least doubled the value of the Bears' franchise.[34] Almost two decades after the renovations were completed, in 2021 the Bears owners purchased Arlington Race Track for $197 million dollars. Over three hundred acres of land in a suburb of Chicago were set to be used for a new stadium. Residents of the suburb and surrounding communities raised concerns regarding cost and impact on the community of such a move. The Bears franchise began seeking alternative sites when estimates of the property value and the proposed settlement with Arlington Park's original owners (Churchill Downs) were higher than anticipated, leading the Bears to determine the property was not "commercially viable."[35] After several years of negotiation, the Bears struck a deal with the City of Chicago in March of 2024 to build a new stadium just south of Soldier Field. The Bears state they will invest $2 billion of private funds for the project, which includes park space and year-round community amenities, and "owner George McCaskey said the Bears would 'seek no public funding for direct stadium structure construction,' but would need assistance to complete the rest of the multibillion-dollar project." It is unclear what that "assistance" would be, and public funding estimates for the new stadium are not yet known, according to ESPN.[36]

There will be more examples to add to this list. As journalist Dan Moore notes in a May 2024 article published in *The Atlantic*,

> You would think that three decades' worth of evidence would be enough to put an end to the practice of subsidizing sports stadiums. Unfortunately, you would be wrong. America finds itself on the brink of the biggest, most expensive publicly-funded-stadium boom ever, and the results will not be any better this time around.[37]

This boom includes proposed stadium and arenas in Las Vegas, with more than $1.1 billion in public funding, not counting tax breaks for a baseball stadium;

Chicago White Sox owners seeking $1 billion for a baseball stadium and $2.4 billion for a football stadium (as noted above); Cleveland ($600 million for football); Buffalo ($850 million for football); and Nashville ($1.26 billion for football).[38]

You may live in or near one of the cities described above or be fans of the franchise. Cheryl grew up in the Chicago suburbs and as an adult once lived a few blocks from Wrigley Field. When the Bears suggested possibly moving from Soldier Field to (gasp!) the outlying suburbs, as a lifelong Bears fan, she found this quite upsetting. As a sports sociologist, she is ambivalent about the outcome, the Bears are staying in their home stadium in the city—but at what cost? And is it really worth it? As fans and as critics, one question for us to consider is who benefits when the public subsidizes the construction or renovation of sports stadiums? Are these benefits equally distributed across the various groups and communities impacted? What does it say about American society when taxpayers support public subsidies for billion-dollar owners while also voting for budget cuts for education and health care?

The Rationale for Public Subsidization of Professional Sports Teams

Citizens have, for the most part, been willing to underwrite these subsidies to teams for four reasons. First, conventional wisdom holds that the presence of major league sports teams enhances a city's prestige. Image is important, at least to civic boosters, and having a major league team gives the impression of being a first-class city. A professional team housed in a stadium downtown restores the image and prosperity of the downtown area with the gentrification of stadium environs (e.g., warehouses are converted into upscale lofts; trendy restaurants, nightclubs, and boutiques locate nearby).[39] Tourists and television viewers now see the city in a new, more positive light.

Second, the presence of a major league team representing a city means a lot to the sports fans in that city and nearby environs. These fans can now identify with that team instead of watching a televised game between opponents from other places. This collective rooting for a major league team is believed to provide some social glue holding together a sprawling metropolitan area by bringing people together with a common identity.

Third, fans want to see games in person, to feel the excitement, and to see not only the heroics of the home team but also sports stars from the visiting team. Attending a major league game is a noteworthy event for many. It is also a costly event, as noted throughout this book, which makes attendance increasingly an event for the affluent. Fourth, it is commonly asserted that a major league team creates substantial economic growth. This is an important issue:

The Rationale for Public Subsidization of Professional Sports Teams

Does a major league sports franchise generate a significant investment return for the community? And if there are economic benefits, who benefits and who does not?

Let's consider the claim that having a major league team and building a bigger and better stadium benefit the community economically. The following eight points represent a summary of the evidence from academic research refuting the myth of professional sport as an economic force in the community. Since the 1990s, economists who have studied sports stadium and its impact on local economies have found "overwhelmingly, no long-term increases in employment or incomes for local citizens."[40]

1. Professional sports teams are relatively small firms, when compared with the corporations and universities in a locality. Urban scholar Mark Rosentraub concludes, "Sports is just too small a component of any community's economy to be the engine that propels jobs and growth."[41] Rosentraub also observes, "Professional sports may be the 'icing on a region's or city's economic cake,' but it is not an 'engine' that drives any economy."[42]

2. A common belief is that the presence of a professional sports team increases expenditures in restaurants and hotels, thereby stimulating growth and creating jobs. To a degree this is true—restaurants and hotels do locate near the stadium, revitalizing the area and bringing jobs. But most of this activity, about 80 percent of it, is just a transfer of spending from some parts of the metropolitan area to a more focused location. There is also less spending on other forms of recreation as attention is directed at the professional team. For example, on game days there is a decline in movie attendance, skiing on the nearby ski slopes, and even shopping in brick and mortar stores. Economists refer to this as the "substitution effect." The substitution effect has increased as newer stadiums have expanded and upgraded their food and beverage options and incorporated fan shops and other vendors in the stadium, which, given the proximity, incentivizes fans to spend their money in the ballpark rather than in the community. There are some jobs that are created, including in ticketing and hospitality, as well as white-collar jobs within the franchise (coaches, trainers, etc.) however, stadium employment is seasonal and part-time, such as beer vendors, maintenance workers, and concession stand workers. These jobs pay at or around minimum wage. As Victor Matheson, an economist who has studied the impact of stadiums on urban communities, says, "Sure, you have 2,000 workers, but you have 2,000 workers working ten days a year for six hours, and that's just not many full-time equivalent jobs."[43]

3. Corporations do not move to an area because of a sport team or teams but primarily because of such factors as a suitable workforce, a positive (for management) labor climate, good schools, and relatively low taxes.

4. Economists have a concept called the "multiplier effect," which refers to the money paid in profits or wages that is then spent (recirculated) in the community. The common argument by the proponents of civic growth is that the regional multiplier for any tourist industry is three. Rosentraub, however, makes the case for a multiplier effect of two when it comes to professional sports teams. Consider, for example, the money paid to the players. About half of the money earned by sports teams is paid to affluent players. At least half of this money, however, is spent elsewhere (e.g., agent fees, investments, permanent home, vacation home, purchase of luxury items not produced in the local economy).

5. When teams relocate, there is some economic gain to the community (no more than $10 to $15 million in new economic activity), but that gain is another community's loss, again, a transfer of economic activity rather than the creation of new economic activity. Similarly, when teams build stadiums in the community, they "crowd out" locals and tourists who would not be attending the sporting events at the stadium. In other words the normal economic activity of a city is crowded out by the fans and tourists coming in to the city for the game, so there's no net increase.

6. Despite claims by public relations firms and civic boosters to the contrary, scholarly analyses of the economic impact of a stadium and a professional team show consistently that sport has a negligible impact on metropolitan economies. In short, "Professional sports have been oversold by professional sports boosters as a catalyst for economic development."[44] Economist Robert Baade concludes, "Using economics as a justification for the subsidy is a political expedient, perhaps necessity, but it is inconsonant with the statistical evidence."[45]

7. Although sports teams may not have a tangible economic impact on a metropolitan community, they do have intangible benefits. Rosentraub says, "It may be important to attract millions of visitors to a downtown if only to remind them of the vitality and creativity contained in America's cities. If sports teams and their facilities accomplish that goal and establish pride in central cities, they may well be . . . 'major league'. . . . Further, if cities are to remain integral components of American life, then keeping sports in cities is important. Sport is too important a part of Western society for us to think that cities can exist without the

teams and the events which define essential dimensions of our society and life."[46]

8 Although sports are an important part of a community's quality of life, the citizens of every community must decide whether the public subsidization of professional sports enhances the quality of life enough to warrant the investment and, more important, whether there are other areas that are better community investments. As Rosentraub wonders, "What are we to say to the residents of Cleveland, Indianapolis, and St. Louis who need better schools, health care, and neighborhoods when we refuse to raise some taxes but consent to give sports owners and athletes hundreds of millions of dollars in support?"[47]

We want to elaborate on this last point because it presents an interesting but disturbing inconsistency—US society approves a welfare system to wealthy team owners and affluent athletes while condemning the social welfare system for the poor.[48]

From 1935 to 1996, the United States had a minimal welfare safety net for those in need (minimal when compared to the more generous welfare states of Western Europe and Scandinavia). Beginning in the 1980s with the Reagan administration, this welfare program has gradually been dismantled. This dissolution accelerated in 1996 during the Clinton administration when the federal government made welfare assistance to families temporary and withdrew $55 billion in federal aid to the poor. At federal and state levels, politicians from both major political parties favored doing away with welfare and substituting programs that would provide market-based solutions. The leaders of both political parties sought to reduce taxes or at least resist tax increases. This significant reduction of welfare for the poor occurred at a time (2005) when some thirty-seven million Americans (12.6 percent) were living below the government's poverty line, one out of every six American children was poor, and forty-five million Americans had no health insurance. Urban schools were desperately behind suburban schools in resources, and only one-third of those children who qualified for Head Start Programs, which support children's growth from birth to age five through services centered around early learning and development, health, and family well-being, received it. In short, the politicians, with the apparent support of the populace, embarked on a social experiment that, at least in the short run, would make life much more difficult for the economically disadvantaged. This inhumane approach was rationalized as necessary to rid the nation of a welfare system that was contrary to the American values of individualism, competition, and self-reliance.

At the same time, many of these same politicians have encouraged a welfare system for team owners (wealthy individuals or corporations) and their high-paid athletes. The system of subsidies to emerge has, as economist Robert A. Baade described it, created a reverse "Robin Hood" effect—taking from the poor, the near poor, the working class, and the middle classes and giving to the rich.[49] This welfare to owners takes several forms, some of which we've discussed in previous sections. Federal law allows cities to issue tax-exempt bonds to finance the building of stadiums and arenas. The Congressional Research Service estimates that the cost to the federal treasury of such exemptions is $100 million in lost tax revenue. The 50 percent deductions of the cost of luxury suites and the like for businesses amount to a 17 percent federal subsidy for wealthy people to watch games.[50] The resulting lost tax revenues to the federal treasury come from other sources, which we all pay.

When the stadiums are built and paid for by taxpayers, there is a clear transfer of wealth from the taxpayers to the owners and the players. Urban scholar Mark Rosentraub says: "Sales taxes paid by lower-income people produce excess profits that are divided between players and owners, all of whom enjoy salaries about which the taxpayers can only dream. A subsidy spread across hundreds of thousands of people amounts to a small charge each year. It is still, however, a transfer of wealth from the lower and middle classes to the upper class."[51]

This transfer occurs as the new stadium increases the value of the team. When it is sold, the owner reaps greater capital gains. The transfer of wealth also occurs when luxury suites and club-level seats are built, and the additional revenues generated go to the owners. So, too, with revenues from parking and concessions. Sometimes cities provide owners with moving expenses, practice facilities, office space, land, and special investment opportunities to entice them to stay or to move their team to the city.

Even though the public votes on raising taxes for a stadium, the obligation is not finite. The public sector ends up with the responsibility for any cost overruns, which are common. Most telling, stadiums are generally built with the owner investing some money but the public providing most of funds. The asymmetrical nature of this relationship is revealed in the division of the revenues generated from the operation of the stadium—the owner who puts up about 20 percent (on average) receives 100 percent of the proceeds! The public, which invested most of the money for construction and maintenance of the facility, receives none of the proceeds.

To summarize, the professional team owner–city relationship entails several related contradictions. First, the mayors, governors, and legislators who work against social welfare programs that benefit children, elderly, unhoused, un/underinsured, and un- or underemployed citizens are more than generous with their subsidies to uber rich sports franchise owners. Second, the wealthy owners who favor private enterprise and marketplace solutions in their other business activities insist on public subsidies to maintain their lucrative professional teams. Paul Allen, for example, one of the wealthiest Americans (worth some $17 billion in 2015), insisted that he would move the Seattle Seahawks unless the residents of Seattle voted to build a stadium for his team (which they did). Third, team owners faced with what they consider inadequate subsidies will move their franchise to a locality that provides more generous subsidies. Fourth, the citizens of cities put up with this hypocrisy. In addition, the public, which underwrites the largesse to the wealthy, ends up being less likely to be able to afford to see the games in person. The cost of tickets, tending to increase anyway, escalates with a new stadium. Some stadium commissions require the purchase of a "personal seat license." As a result of these practices, the crowds in these new arenas are becoming more and more affluent.

Finally, as Mark Rosentraub observes, "If It Quacks, It Is Still a Duck," meaning that no matter what the spin, the subsidies that owners receive constitute welfare.[52] Ironically, it is a reverse type of socialism that redistributes wealth upward. Yet owners, civic boosters, editorial writers, and politicians who spend much of their time defending capitalism and the free market support it unabashedly and uncritically.

An Alternative Structure

There is another way—a fairer way—to structure professional sport. Teams could be owned by local governments (cities, counties, or region) or by community stockholders rather than individuals, families, or corporations, as is now the case. Localities already subsidize the teams but do not own them, which allows the owner to insist on more and better subsidies with the threat of moving the team to a more lucrative situation. The Green Bay Packers football team is the only major professional team that is owned by the people. Author Jim Hightower provides a description of this unique type of team ownership:

> Some 1,900 of the locals, including truckers, barkeeps, merchants, and bus drivers, own a piece of the Pack, organized back in 1923 as a community-owned, nonprofit company. The stockholders draw no profit, and the locally elected board of directors that operates the team is unpaid, but all concerned draw great pleasure from knowing that the Packers are theirs.
>
> What a difference ownership makes. Not a dime needs to be spent to hype up fan support, since the team literally belongs to them. The town [of 112,000] built Lambeau Stadium, owns it, operates it, and fills each of the 60,790 seats in it for every home game—forty straight years of sellouts, whether the team

is winning or not. As of February 2024, if you were to add your name to the waiting list for season tickets, your estimated wait is sixty years! There are 148,000 names currently on the waiting list.

Green Bay fans and citizens never have to worry that some pirate of an owner is going to hijack the Pack and haul their team to Los Angeles or any other big-city market, because Green Bay is their team. It stands as a shining model of how fans in other cities could get control of their teams and stop corporate rip-offs.[53]

Shifting team ownership to community ownership is relatively easy. Each locality could buy the local team at its market value, which would amount to something less than what they now pay to build the owner a new stadium. There is only one catch: the owners in each league have passed a rule specifically banning any future team from being community owned! In other words, the teams will continue to be owned by individuals and corporations but financed by the public. This maintains a situation in which each team may claim that it is *yours*, but it is really *theirs*.

Notes

1. George H. Sage, "Stealing Home: Political, Economic, and Media Power and a Publicly Funded Stadium in Denver," *Journal of Sport and Social Issues* 17 (August 1993): 110–24.
2. R. J. Anderson, "Public Ownership Works for Some of World's Best Sports Teams—Is There a Future for the Idea in America?," *CBS Sports*, June 12, 2024, https://www.cbssports.com/mlb/news/public-ownership-works-for-some-of-worlds-best-sports-teams-is-there-a-future-for-the-idea-in-america/.
3. Anderson.
4. Jay Coakley, *Sport in Society: Issues and Controversies*, 13th ed. (McGraw-Hill, 2021); James Surowieki, "The Financial Page: Scrimmage," *New Yorker*, March 21, 2011, 25.
5. Roger G. Noll, "The U.S. Team Sports Industry," in *Government and the Sports Business*, ed. Roger G. Noll (Washington, DC: Brookings Institution, 1974), 2.
6. "Estimated Probability of Competing in Professional Athletics, National Collegiate Athletics Association, April 1, 2024, https://www.ncaa.org/sports/2015/3/6/estimated-probability-of-competing-in-professional-athletics.aspx.
7. George H. Sage, *Power and Ideology in American Sport*, 2nd ed. (Champaign, IL: Human Kinetics, 1998), 199.
8. Rick Porter, "Sports TV's Multibillion-Dollar Rights Race: Where the Leaderboard Stands Right Now," *Hollywood Reporter*, July 2, 2024, https://www.hollywoodreporter.com/business/business-news/sports-tv-rights-race-mlb-nfl-nba-1235937583/.

Notes

9 Mike Ozanian, "NFL National Revenue Was Almost $12 Billion," *Forbes*, July 11, 2023, https://www.forbes.com/sites/mikeozanian/2023/07/11/nfl-national-revenue-was-almost-12-billion-in-2022/.

10 Rodney Reeves, "The Highest-Paid CFL Players," *Front Office Sports*, May 22, 2024, https://frontofficesports.com/highest-paid-cfl-players/.

11 *Forbes* provides franchise valuations for all teams in the four major leagues annually, at various times during the year.

12 The estimated value of sport franchises in 2023 that are listed here are from "The World's Most Valuable Teams," *Forbes*, September 8, 2023, https://www.forbes.com/sites/mikeozanian/2023/09/08/the-worlds-50-most-valuable-sports-teams-2023/. The 2023 valuations of NFL teams are from "The NFL's Most Valuable NFL Teams 2023," *Forbes*, August 30, 2023, https://www.forbes.com/sites/mikeozanian/2023/08/30/the-nfls-most-valuable-teams-2023-dallas-cowboys-remain-on-top-at-a-record-9-billion/.

13 James Quirk and Rodney Fort, *Hard Ball: The Abuse of Power in Pro Sports* (Princeton, NJ: Princeton University Press, 1999), 9.

14 Robert Faturechi, Justin Elliott, and Ellis Simani, "The Billionaire Playbook: How Sports Owners Use Their Teams to Avoid Millions in Taxes," *ProPublica*, July 8, 2021, https://www.propublica.org/article/the-billionaire-playbook-how-sports-owners-use-their-teams-to-avoid-millions-in-taxes.

15 Dan Moore, "Taxpayers Are About to Subsidize a Lot More Sports Stadiums," *Atlantic*, May 8, 2024, https://www.theatlantic.com/ideas/archive/2024/05/sports-stadium-subsidies-taxpayer-funding/678319/.

16 J. C. Bradbury, D. Coates, and B. R. Humphreys, "The Impact of Professional Sports Franchises and Venues on Local Economies: A Comprehensive Survey," *Journal of Economic Surveys* (January 31, 2022), http://dx.doi.org/10.2139/ssrn.4022547.

17 Justin Birnbaum, "America's Richest Sports Team Owners 2023," *Forbes*, October 3, 2023, https://www.forbes.com/sites/justinbirnbaum/2023/10/03/americas-richest-sports-team-owners-2023/.

18 The following is from Reed Albergotti and Cameron McWhirter, "A Stadium's Costly Legacy Throws Taxpayers for a Loss," *Wall Street Journal*, July 12, 2011, A1, A12.

19 Neil deMause, "Bengals Stadium: Worst. Deal. Ever?" *Field of Schemes*, July 28, 2011, https://www.fieldofschemes.com/news/archives/2011/07/4607_bengals_stadium.html.

20 Christopher Wood, "No More Public Money for the Bengals. It's Time for Them to Pay Their Own Way," *Cincinnati Enquirer*, April 30, 2024, https://www.cincinnati.com/story/opinion/contributors/2024/04/30/bengals-stadium-lease-has-long-been-an-economic-black-hole/73498606007/.

21 John London, "Hamilton County Commissioners Approve $39 Million Toward Paycor Stadium Upgrades," WLWT5, December 14, 2023, https://www.wlwt.com/article/hamilton-county-commissioners-paycor-stadium-upgrades/46133095.

22 Ben Baby, "Bengals to Invest $100M in Renovations amid Stadium Talks," ESPN, May 21, 2024, https://www.espn.com/nfl/story/_/id/40193066/bengals-invest-100m-renovations-amid-stadium-talks.

23. Dashiel Bennett, "The Worst Stadium Financing Deal Ever Is Still Crippling Cincinnati's Taxpayers," *Business Insider*, July 12, 2011, https://www.businessinsider.com/worst-stadium-deal-cincinnati-2011-7.

24. Victor Matheson, "I've Studied Stadium Financing for Over Two Decades—and the New Bills Stadium Is One of the Worst Deals for Taxpayers I've Ever Seen," *The Conversation*, April 15, 2022, https://theconversation.com/ive-studied-stadium-financing-for-over-two-decades-and-the-new-bills-stadium-is-one-of-the-worst-deals-for-taxpayers-ive-ever-seen-180475.

25. For sources on the Cowboys Stadium, see, for example, "Cowboy Stadium," Ballparks, 2011, http://football.ballparks.com/NFL/DallasCowboys/newindex.htm; Sally Jenkins, "Does Football Cost Too Much?" *Parade*, November 29, 2009, http://www.parade.com/news/2009/11/29-does-football-cost-too-much.htm; Jeff Mosier, "The Cost of Cowboys Stadium Has Escalated to $1.2 Billion," *Dallas News*, April 1, 2010, http://stadiumblog.dallasnews.com/archives/2010/04/the-costo-of-cowboys-stadium.htm.

26. Christina Gough, "Fan Cost Index of National Football League Teams in 2023," Statista, March 21, 2024, https://www.statista.com/statistics/202584/nfl-fan-cost-index/.

27. Josh Levin, "Shake Me Down at the Ball Game," *Sports Illustrated*, June 23, 2008, 14–15.

28. Bill Moyers, "Transcript," *Bill Moyers Journal*, Public Broadcasting System, September 19, 2008, http://www.pbs.org/moyers/journal/09192008/transcript3.html.

29. Neil deMause, "Why Do Mayors Love Sports Stadiums?" *Nation*, August 15–22, 2011, 17.

30. Michael Powell, "Bucks' Owners Win, at Wisconsin's Expense," *New York Times*, August 15, 2015, D1.

31. Dave Zirin, "Scott Walker Is Trolling Us," *Nation*, July 22, 2015.

32. S. L. Price, "Going Against the Percentages," *Sports Illustrated*, March 31, 2008, 130.

33. Dave Zirin, "Washington DC's Sporting Shock Doctrine," *Edge of Sports*, April 1, 2008.

34. Andrew Martin, Liam Ford, and Laurie Cohen, "Bears Play, Public Pays," *Chicago Tribune*, April 21, 2002, 1, 16.

35. Courtney Cronin, "Source—Chicago Bears Plan New Stadium South of Soldier Field," ESPN, March 11, 2024, https://www.espn.com/nfl/story/_/id/39704677/source-bears-planning-new-stadium-south-soldier-field.

36. Cronin.

37. Moore, "Taxpayers Are About to Subsidize."

38. Scott Lincicome, "Sports Are Great, but Stadium Subsidies Stink," Cato Institute, May 15, 2024, https://www.cato.org/commentary/sports-are-great-stadium-subsidies-stink.

39. See David Whitson and Donald Macintosh, "Becoming a World-Class City," *Sociology of Sport Journal* 10 (September 1993): 221–40; and Keith Law, "The

Imbalance Sheet: The New Stadium Fallacy," interview with economist Brad Humphreys, Baseball Prospectus, April 12, 2001, www.baseballprospectus.com/news/20010412imbalance.html.

40 Jessica Luther and Kavitha A. Davidson, *Loving Sports When They Don't Love You Back: Dilemmas of the Modern Fan* (Austin: University of Texas Press, 2020).

41 Mark S. Rosentraub, "Does the Emperor Have New Clothes? A Reply to Robert J. Baade," *Journal of Urban Affairs* 18, no. 1 (1996): 23.

42 Mark S. Rosentraub, *Major League Losers* (New York: Basic Books, 1999), 140.

43 As cited in Luther and Davidson, *Loving Sports*, 220.

44 Robert A. Baade, "Professional Sports as Catalysts for Metropolitan Economic Development," *Journal of Economic Affairs* 18, no. 1 (1996): 1–17; Roger G. Noll and Andrew Zimbalist, eds., *Sports, Jobs, and Taxes: The Economic Impact of Sports Teams and Stadiums* (Washington, DC: Brookings Institution, 1997); C. C. Euchner, *Playing the Field: Why Sports Teams Move and Cities Fight to Keep Them* (Baltimore: Johns Hopkins University Press, 1993); Dean Baim, *The Sports Stadium as a Municipal Investment* (Westport, CT: Greenwood, 1992); Mark S. Rosentraub, "Sport and Downtown Development Strategy: If You Build It, Will Jobs Come?" *Journal of Urban Affairs* 16 (1994): 221–39; Rosentraub, *Major League Losers*.

45 Robert A. Baade, "Stadium Subsidies Make Little Economic Sense for Cities," *Journal of Urban Affairs* 18, no. 1 (1996): 37.

46 Rosentraub, "Does the Emperor Have New Clothes?" 29.

47 Rosentraub, 30.

48 The following is taken primarily from Rosentraub, *Major League Losers*, 3–17; D. Stanley Eitzen, "Dismantling the Welfare State," *Vital Speeches of the Day* 62 (June 1996): 532–36; D. Stanley Eitzen and Maxine Baca Zinn, "New Welfare Legislation and Families," paper presented to the American Sociological Association, San Francisco, August 1998; and D. Stanley Eitzen, "Welfare for Owners, but Not for Poor," *Coloradoan* (Fort Collins), April 2, 1998, A10.

49 Robert A. Baade and Alan Sanderson, "Field of Fantasies," Heartland Institute, Intellectual Ammunition website, quoted in Jon Morgan, *Glory for Sale: Fans, Dollars and the New NFL* (Baltimore: Bancroft Press, 1997), 315.

50 "How You Pay $$$ for Stadiums Far, Far Away," *USA Today*, June 5, 1997, 14A.

51 Rosentraub, *Major League Losers*, 447.

52 Rosentraub, 447.

53 Hightower, *There's Nothing in the Middle of the Road but Yellow Stripes and Dead Armadillos* (New York: Harper Perennial, 1998), 22–23. See also Sue Halpern, "Home Field Advantage," *Mother Jones* 27 (November/December 2002): 30–33; Dave Zirin, *Bad Sports: How Owners Are Ruining the Games We Love* (New York: Scribner, 2010), 181–88; Dave Zirin, "Non-Profit Packers Win," *Progressive*, March 1, 2011, 21; Jeff Bercovici, "The Power of the Packers," *Forbes*, September 26, 2011, 86–90; and Neil deMause, "The Radical Case for Cities Buying Sports Teams, Not Sports Stadiums," *Vice Sports*, December 29, 2014, https://sports.vice.com/article/the-radical-case-for-cities-buying-sports-teams/.

10
THE CHALLENGE: CHANGING SPORT

This book is titled *Fair and Foul: Beyond the Myths and Paradoxes of Sport* because sport is both elevating and deflating, appealing and appalling, inspiring and disillusioning. Although we have tried to present some of the ways *sport is fair*, our emphasis has leaned strongly toward how *sport is foul*. Our goal is to engage readers in an analysis of sport that leads them to reflect on how sport really works based on what we know from academic research and empirical evidence and how it might be improved. To do this, we ask: Who benefits from sports the way they are currently arranged, and at what cost?

Is Change Possible?

Several factors make sport difficult to change. Foremost, those who are in decision-making, ownership, or leadership positions in sport have disproportionate power, control, and influence. Next, the money generated by sport is enormous—between 2022 and 2023, the five major sports leagues collectively earned just under $50 billion. This does not account for collegiate sports and other aspects of the sports industry, such as the sporting goods industry, which was estimated to generate nearly $115 billion in 2023. Those who benefit from the way sport is organized have a vested interest in maintaining the status quo. In other words, those who benefit have little incentive or motivation to change sport.

Despite these dynamics, there are guiding principles that make change possible. First, sport, as it is practiced in the United States, is not fated by nature or even by the "invisible hand" of the market; it is a social construction, the result of historical actions and choices. Americans have created the organization of sport that now exists, and Americans maintain it.[1] This means, then, that because sport is created by people, it can be changed by them as well.

Second, historically, sport has occasionally changed for the better because of the deliberate acts of individuals and the collective, organized efforts of social movements and organizations. Three well-known examples illustrate this point. In these and other significant challenges to the status quo, change did not occur without a fight. Individuals and groups confronted the powerful and succeeded. We discuss several historical examples here that illustrate how social change in sport is possible.

The Racial Integration of Baseball

Baseball was rigidly segregated before World War II. But, in 1947, Branch Rickey, the owner of the Brooklyn Dodgers, brought talented Jackie Robinson into the major leagues against the vehement opposition of his fellow owners (the owners voted fifteen to one in 1946 to maintain segregation) and most major league players.[2] Rickey's bold move was not entirely altruistic, since he saw Black athletes as a reservoir of untapped talent and believed that racial integration would increase attendance by tapping into the Black fan base.

Black players soon achieved prominence in Major League Baseball, and after decades of struggle against racism, the eradication of segregation and Jim Crow laws, a racially integrated sports league gained popularity and acceptance among the (white) fan base. Many people were involved behind the scenes in effecting this extraordinary transformation. In 1944, Albert "Happy" Chandler, who was sympathetic toward the goal of racial integration, became the commissioner of Major League Baseball, replacing a strict segregationist, Kenesaw Mountain

Landis. During the war and after it, Black newspapers, most prominently in New York and Pittsburgh, argued for racial integration in baseball. Their argument (used also by a few white sportswriters) was that Black men fought in World War II to protect freedom, yet American society denied Black athletes the freedom to compete on a level playing field with white athletes. The logic of that argument, the decisiveness of Branch Rickey, and the courage of Jackie Robinson changed baseball (and other sports) forever.

There were unintended consequences of this change. As sports journalist Dave Zirin and other sports historians have pointed out, Major League Baseball only recruited players from the Negro Leagues. What would Major League Baseball look like today, if owners had not only integrated Black players into Major League Baseball, but also managers and coaches, front office employees and staff into the league? The process by which professional baseball was racially integrated required Black players to assimilate into the MLB, however, the MLB did not have to assimilate or accommodate the Negro League, in terms of its leadership, ownership, and management. It was in 2024, seventy-seven years after Jackie Robinson integrated Major League baseball that the league adjusted its baseball statistics and records to reflect the accomplishments of players in the Negro Leagues.[3]

Free Agency for Athletes

Before the landmark court cases of the mid-1970s, professional athletes in team sports were trapped by the reserve clause in their contracts. Once a player signed a contract with a club, that team had exclusive rights, and the player was no longer free to negotiate with other teams. In the succeeding years, the player had to sell his services solely to the club that owned his contract unless it released, sold, or traded him, or he chose to retire. The reserve clause specified that the owner had the exclusive right to renew a player's contract annually. Thus, a player was bound perpetually to negotiate with only one club. The player was the club's property and could be sold to another club without the player's consent. In effect, this clause kept the salaries of players artificially low and restricted the players' freedom. As one observer put it, "After the Civil War settled the slavery issue, owning a ball club was the closest one could come to owning a plantation."[4]

The late 1960s was a period in American history when various marginalized communities (racially minoritized individuals, women, members of LGBTQ+ communities) engaged in mass social movements in attempts to change existing power relationships. Within this society-wide framework, athletes, too, began to recognize their common plight and organized to change it. Most fundamentally, they felt that because the owners had all the power, the players did not receive their true value in the marketplace. The result was that athletes, as individuals and as player associations, began to assert themselves against what they considered an unfair system.

Several cases were instrumental in modifying the reserve clause in baseball. Most important was Curt Flood, who was traded by the St. Louis Cardinals in 1969 to the Philadelphia Phillies but refused to play for them, sitting out the 1970 season. He sued organized baseball, alleging that the reserve system constituted a system of peonage. The US Supreme Court ruled five to three against Flood but recognized that the system should be changed by congressional action.

Although Flood lost his struggle, he opened the way for the eventual destruction of the reserve clause.[5] Flood's heroic stand, coupled with the decisions of arbitrators releasing three major league baseball players from their contracts (teams then bid for their services, offering many times what they had been paid by their owners under the reserve clause, indicating their "true" market worth) led to an agreement between the owners of professional baseball and the Players Association in 1976. This agreement killed the reserve clause by permitting free agency (after a specified time, a player was free to negotiate with all teams, not just his original team).

Gender Equity

As part of the social movements of the 1960s, the National Organization of Women (NOW) gathered data at the national and local levels on discrimination against girls and women in community and school sports. Armed with this information, the organization lobbied Congress, which ultimately passed Title IX (in 1972), which prevents educational institutions that receive federal funding from discriminating on the basis of sex. Although Title IX applies broadly to educational programs and opportunities, the law requires schools to provide equal athletic opportunities for boys and girls, men and women. This landmark decision precipitated a dramatic increase in the number of girls and women who play sports. Prior to Title IX, one in twenty-seven girls played sports; today, that number is one out of every three. Similarly, girls and women athletes went to court to successfully challenge the male sports structure in various youth sports programs, school districts, state associations, and colleges. As a result, Little League baseball is no longer exclusively for boys; over 1.7 million girls play youth soccer, and girls participate in sports once exclusive to boys, such as wrestling and football.

Although Title IX dramatically shifted the landscape of sports offered in educational institutions, gendered cultural ideologies that link athleticism and masculinity are deeply entrenched in American culture. Girls and women may have access to sports, but gendered forms of discrimination continue.

Consider that although there has been a dramatic increase in the number of girls and women playing sports, that has been accompanied by increases in the number of boys and men participating in sports. In other words, there is a gender gap in participation. And as noted in chapter 3 and elsewhere in the book, at the college level, women's athletics continue to struggle to receive the same resources, scholarship dollars and quality of facilities and equipment as men's athletic programs. The changes to collegiate sports in the "Name Image and Likeness" era are seemingly exacerbating disparities between men's and women's programs, and the opportunities for men and women collegiate athletes to monetize their athletic participation.

Should We Change Sport?

Sport is important because it is a microcosm of society. Sport reinforces societal class, race, and gender inequities. At the same time, it also provides opportunities for racially minoritized communities; women, LGBTQ, and nonbinary athletes; and for those from impoverished communities. Sport can be at the forefront of social change, as when Major League Baseball racially integrated before many other social institutions in the United States. Sport matters because it affects each of us, sometimes profoundly. It clearly has an impact on the interests and values of children. Family life is disrupted by practice and game schedules as well as the cost of coaching, equipment, travel, and camps. Our taxes and the tax code subsidize professional teams, owners, and players. The tuition and fees of college students subsidize athletic programs. Many of the products we purchase cost more because their producers have invested heavily in sports-related advertising. Corporations intrude in high school and college sports. Money drives big-time college sport, influencing the lives of student-athletes.[6] Large sums of money distort the original intent of sport—the participants' joy and pleasure in the activity. Thus, play becomes work, and the outcome supersedes the process.

As sociologists, our understanding of sport leads us to seek change in the problem areas we discussed throughout the book. First, striving to win, which is the essence of sport, sometimes leads to unethical behaviors by players, coaches, fans, and others associated with sport. Clearly, establishing new and improving existing third-party institutional oversight, enforceable policies, and accountability are critical to ensuring the health, safety, and well-being of athletes and participants. Such change would also help to ensure equity for all participants.

Second, youth sport has moved from peer control to adult control. With this change, play has become work. Participation for its own sake has become a public activity, with winning often becoming all-consuming for the children, their parents, and their coaches. The games that children play mirror elite-level competition. Although adult-structured activities might make sense as children get older (perhaps at the middle- or high-school level), we question their utility and purpose for four- and five-year-olds, and, perhaps, nine-, ten-, and eleven-year-olds as well.

Third, our youth and school programs are elitist. They provide too few resources for most young people and too many for gifted (usually male) athletes.[7] If sport is a benefit to participants (and we believe that it is), then it should be provided for everyone—skilled and unskilled, able-bodied and other-bodied people, and for affluent and poor communities. Maximum participation should be a major goal of youth and school programs.

Fourth, college sport at the big-time level has become too big, too dominated by money concerns, too controlled by those outside the university (television networks, bowl and tournament administrators, alumni and donors—individual and corporate) to make sense educationally. Big-time college sport, if anything, undermines educational goals by demanding too much from the athletes in time and commitment. Moreover, the system is unfair to the college athletes in big-time programs. These athletes create the wealth in college sports; however, it was only since the early 2020s that athletes have had some success in getting their share of the pie.

Fifth, girls and women have not achieved full equality in sport, although considerable progress has been made since the 1970s when Title IX was passed. The enforcement of Title IX needs to be more rigorous. Fundamentally, the interpretation of Title IX needs to be unequivocal in its insistence on gender equity.

Sixth, athletes from racially minoritized backgrounds, once denied participation, now dominate the major team sports (except for baseball) in the United States. And although they dominate numerically as players, they rarely appear as head coaches, general managers, owners, athletic directors, trainers, or sports publicists. Athletes of color must receive the experience necessary for consideration for these positions, and those who have the requisite experience and skills must be considered seriously. Both league and public acceptance of individuals from racially minoritized communities in positions of power is crucial.

Seventh, we believe that it is egregious for cities and regions to use public money to build and maintain stadiums and provide other subsidies for the profit of privately owned professional teams. Cities should own these teams.[8] Although the leagues have rules against city ownership, these rules can be superseded by Congress, since professional sport involves interstate commerce. If Congress does not act, there are other options; for example, voters may refuse to subsidize owners (as has happened in a quarter of recent elections).

Eighth, attending big-time college and professional sports events, even when these enterprises are subsidized by the public, has become too costly. Anyone other than the affluent, for the most part, is shut out, and only the very wealthy experience the thrill of watching collegiate or professional sports in person. This is unacceptable. One idea would be a "cheap-seat" section of every major arena, every ballpark, every football stadium operating in professional sports. Not bad seats. Not nosebleed seats. Cheap seats. That means reasonably priced. Sport as entertainment should be available for all fans of the sport.

How Do We Go About Making Changes?

We can make changes in sport by making changes in social arrangements. We do not have to be passive actors who accept society's arrangements as inevitable. To the contrary, we can be actively engaged in social life, working for the improvement or even the radical change of faulty social structures. This notion that human beings construct and reconstruct society implies another idea—that the personal is political. As individuals, we make choices— to participate or not, to accept a coach's dehumanizing behavior or not, to pay outrageously expensive prices or not, to support or undermine a (racial-, gender-, or sexual-)minority head coach, to encourage or discourage ethical behaviors, to place winning above all other considerations or not, to choose or reject the dominant sports—choices that promote the status quo or that envision something different.

Individuals would have an enormous impact if they would join others to boycott sports that exploit them. Fans are the ones who spend more than many billions a year on sports (equipment, memorabilia, tickets, and the like). Fans shell out great sums of money to pay the seat tax for the right to buy tickets. Colleges extract student fees for their athletic departments whether a student is interested in sports or not. And even if they are, the schools may not allot enough seats for them to attend games. Voters are the ones who have approved spending billions of dollars in public money for building new stadiums. Fans are the ones who continue to forgive and forget irresponsible behavior by players, coaches, and owners. If enough fans withdrew their financial support of professional sports (we include big-time college sports in this category) in protest of the way things are, meaningful changes might occur. It depends on leadership of such a movement and a commonly held belief that they are being exploited.

Fans can make a difference. They can campaign against the subsidization of team owners who want newer and better stadiums and arenas. Voters occasionally have rejected public funding for sports arenas in places like Minneapolis–St. Paul, Pittsburgh, San Diego, South Florida, and North Carolina.

Legislatures, tuned to citizen resistance, have rejected subsidization of sports facilities in New Jersey, Philadelphia, San Diego, and St. Louis.

Despite the problems in sport, most fans continue to support the sports establishment uncritically. Sports fans passively watch twenty-four-hour sports channels or spend hours following social media accounts. Many sports fans are critical of the behavior of athletes and the high cost of sport across the country, but they still root wholeheartedly for their home teams. The 1960s liberation efforts by racial minorities, women, LGBTQ+ and other marginalized and oppressed communities required not only mobilization and action but also a "raising of consciousness" to bring the formerly unconvinced into the cause. This needs to happen in the sports sphere as well. We need more education and awareness of the problems, with a keen understanding of who benefits and who does not under the current system and how their actions maintain the status quo.

There are three additional ways to initiate change.[9] First, people can work within the system, volunteering to coach youth sports teams or serving on the board of directors of a sports league. Teachers can become coaches or move into athletic administration. College professors can serve on athletic committees or serve as their institution's athletic representative to a league and the NCAA. But as people become insiders and move into positions of increasing power, they must resist the tendency to develop a vested interest in the status quo.

A second way to effect change is to become involved in opposition groups. Only rarely can an individual make much of a difference. A better strategy is to become involved in collective action—joining with others to seek a solution to some problem by putting pressure on power wielders. This may be a group opposed to tax-subsidized construction of a stadium or a group promoting the construction of a community playing facility such as a new ice arena, baseball field, or soccer field to accommodate growing demand. Students at Duke University and others have organized and have successfully pushed administrators to adopt rules requiring that all campus athletic gear be produced in compliance with labor and human rights standards.

These same activists should insist that corporate advertising be banned from all arenas; that universities cap athletic budgets for football and basketball and put an end to the "arms race" for bigger facilities and more amenities; and that the influence of big-money donors be limited so that students and fans can continue to attend athletic events at reasonable prices. Activists might also find unexpected common ground with coaches and fans concerned about how the integrity of the game has been subordinated to the media networks, or how corporations are colonizing and poisoning the high school recruiting scene.[10]

A third option is to financially support existing organizations that show promise in bringing about change. The Center for Study of Sport in Society at Northeastern University is an organization that works within the system to make it more inclusive and to make colleges and universities more responsive to the needs of student athletes. It engages athletes in after-school tutoring programs for disadvantaged primary and secondary students in schools and community centers, and it promotes public awareness on such issues as men's violence against women and human rights.[11] Another important organization is the Women's Sports Foundation. This organization sponsors research, lobbies politicians, mobilizes pressure on decision-makers, and provides information to the public—all with the goal of attaining gender equity in sports.[12] The Knight Commission on Intercollegiate Athletics is an independent group of scholars, educators, lawyers, and executives who "develop, promote, and lead transformational change in collegiate athletics that prioritizes the education, health, safety and success of college athletes."[13]

Sport has an incredible grip on most people. It is compelling; it can be a magical, wonderful illusion. But even as sport excites and inspires, it has problems. Let's not get rid of sport. Let's make it better. For us, that means sport should be more fun, more inclusive, more humanized, and more ethical. Our hope is that you will join us not only to understand these complex social arrangements called sport but also to work for their improvement. As journalist/activist Dave Zirin says: "If we challenge sports to be as good as they can be—a force to break down walls that divide us, a motor for inclusion—they can propel us toward a better world, a world worth playing in—and worth fighting for."[14]

Notes

1. Paraphrased from Claude S. Fischer et al., *Inequality by Design: Cracking the Bell Curve Myth* (Princeton, NJ: Princeton University Press, 1996), 7.
2. For the history of the Branch Rickey/Jackie Robinson integration experiment, see Jules Tygiel, *Baseball's Great Experiment: Jackie Robinson and His Legacy* (New York: Oxford University Press, 1983); Jackie Robinson, *I Never Had It Made* (New York: Putnam, 1972).
3. Juliette Arcodia and Colin Sheeley, "Negro Leagues Statistics to Be Officially Incorporated into MLB Historical Record," *NBC News*, May 28, 2024, https://www.nbcnews.com/news/sports/negro-leagues-mlb-baseball-records-rcna154409.
4. Alex Ben Block, "So, You Want to Own a Ball Club," *Forbes*, April 1, 1977, 37. See also, Bob Costas, "Baseball's Free Agency Revolution," *Bloomberg Businessweek*, December 4, 2014, 14–15.
5. Dave Zirin, *A People's History of Sports in the United States: 250 Years of Politics, Protest, People, and Play* (New York: The New Press, 2008), 205–08.
6. The Power 5 conference realignment in 2023 and 2024 has raised concerns about the impact on student-athletes' academics, mental health, and overall well-being

of traveling over two thousand miles during an academic semester for an athletic competition (as would be the case when Big Ten West coast schools such as UCLA and USC compete against East Coast schools such as Rutgers and the University of Maryland).

7 Ken Reed, "Nader Calls for Sports and Physical Education for All Students," League of Fans, August 11, 2011, http://leagueoffans.org/2011/08/11/nader-calls-for-sports-and-physical-education-for-all-students.

8 Ken Reed, "Nader Announces Push for Community Ownership in Professional Sports," League of Fans, July 13, 2011, http://leagueoffans.org/2011/07/13/ralph-nader-announces-push-for-community-ownership.

9 Adapted from Jay J. Coakley, *Sports in Society: Issues and Controversies*, 8th ed. (New York: McGraw-Hill, 2004), 590–91.

10 Thad Williamson, "Bad as They Wanna Be: Loving the Game Is Harder as Colleges Sell Out Themselves, the Fans, the Athletes," *Nation*, August 10–17, 1998, 40–41.

11 See, for example, the following publications by the Center for the Study of Sport in Society (Northeastern University): *Sport in Society Annual Report*, *National Consortium for Academics and Sports Quarterly Newsletter*, and *Sport in Society News*.

12 Women's Sports Foundation, Eisenhower Park, East Meadow, NY, https://www.womenssportsfoundation.org/.

13 See "About the Knight Commission," Knight Commission on Intercollegiate Athletics, https://www.knightcommission.org/about-knight-commission/.

14 Zirin, *A People's History of Sports*, 268.

PHOTO CREDITS

page 1: Photo by Mike Carlson on Getty Images

page 29: Photo by Kent Nishimura on Getty Images

page 55: Photo by Tim Nwachukwu on Getty Images

page 77: Photo by Visual China Group on Getty Images

page 103: Photo by Krista Long on Getty Images

page 119: Photo by Maddie Meyer on Getty Images

page 137: Photo by Chris Parent/LSU on Getty Images

page 151: Photo by Matthew Holst on Getty Images

page 171: Photo by Greg Fiume on Getty Images

page 195: Photo by Michael Steele on Getty Images

INDEX

ABC 63, 113; and Indiana Fever 145; Monday Night Football on 140; streaming platform of 140
abuse, sexual 93–95
academic success, girls' and women's sports 68, 79
academics: athletes in "one and done" environment 159; avoiding education 156; clustering in easy majors 156–57; college sport as big business 161–63; compromising educational goals 154–56; consequences of money in college athletics 163–66; contradictions 166–67; excessive time demands of big-time programs 157–58; "jock" subculture 158; NIL and pay-to-play 160–61; overview 151–54; promoting education 154; resulting education performance 159–60; scandals involving athletes' education 158–59
ACL. *See* Anterior Cruciate Ligament
ACLU. *See* American Civil Liberties Union
Adderall 89
additive drugs 88–89
"Adjusted Games Lost" (statistic) 83
Adler, Peter 158
adult-centered play, dark side of 108–9
adult-organized sports, for children: adult-centered play and dark side 108–9; analysis of differences 107–8; beginning too early 109–10; costs 110–11; excessive parental demands 113–14; forms of play for young children 103–5; organization 105–6; organization intrusion on children's sport 112–13; out-of-control parental behavior 111–12; process 106–7; specialization 110
advertising, negotiating 175–76
African Americans: athletes 31, 44, 49, 60, 123–25, 127, 143, 155–56, 196–97; backlash against activism of 31; coaches 125–26; and "color-blind" society 120–21; encouraging 35; and forms of stratification 120; in Major League Baseball 123–24; in MLB 123–24; and Negro leagues 79; NFL player percentage 7, 10–11; overrepresentation as professional athletes 155–56; participation and opportunity 60; progress in race relations 43–45; racial bias 121–22; resulting academic performance 159–60; scandals involving athletes' education 158–59; segregation among 122–23; underrepresentation among 125–27; unifying 35–36; and unity achieved through sports 49–50; and violent sports 81–82; and examples of egregious subsidies to team owners 182–83
agenda setting 144–46
agent of change, sport as 8
AHA. *See* American Heart Association
Ali, Muhammad 44
All-Star Games 147
Allen, Paul 189
amateurism 5, 20, 40–41, 70, 161
Amazon Prime 145
American Civil Liberties Union (ACLU) 47
American Heart Association (AHA) 85
anabolic, term 89
analysis of differences, youth sport 107–8

Index

and COVID-19 30
Anderson, R. J. 172
Anterior Cruciate Ligament (ACL) 87
Arizona State University 86
Armstrong, Lance 90–91
Asian Americans 122, 132
Aspen Institute 104–5, 112
Aspen Institute Report 111
Associated Press 165
athletes 15–20, 69–71; academic irregularities relating to eligibility of 152–53; amateur 40–41, 156; arms race 163–66; avoiding education 156; barriers to 61–66; cheating 153–54; class inequities 127–29; clustering in easy majors 156–57; college sport as big business 161–63; college sport as big business 161–63; commercial interests 141–44; competitiveness of 6–7; compromising educational goals 154–56; consequences of money in college athletics 163–66, 163–67; dark-side of adult-centered play 108–14; destructive aspect of sport 80; developing friendships 42; drug use by 88–91; education funds diversion for college sports subsidy 159; excessive time demands of big-time programs 157–58; exploitation of 151–53; free agency for 197–98; gender inequities 129–33, 198–99; and health benefits of sport 78–79; and homophobia 47–48; ill preparation for academia 154; impact on society of 68; "jock" subculture 158; male dominance as norm 7–8; media and sport 137–38; media coverage of 66–67; and #MeToo movement 95–96; mental health of 91–93; NIL and pay-to-play 160–61; in "one and done" environment 159; physical injuries 80–87; professional sport as monopoly 172–77; promoting goodwill 33–36; public subsidies to professional team franchises 177–79; pushback on activism of 31; racial inequalities 120–27; racially marginalized backgrounds 44; and RED-S 87–88; resulting education performance 159–60; scandals involving athletes' education 158–59; segregation of 45; sexual abuse of 93–95; sport as male preserve 144–46; on "sport is fair" side 4; on "sport is foul" side 5; televised sports 141; and television 146–47; and Title IX 56–60; unity achieved through sports 49–50; us vs. them attitude 36–38; as winners because of achievements 120
Athletic, The 138
Atlanta Braves 124
Atlantic, The 183

B1G Ten Conference 141
B1GTen Network 138
Baade, Robert A. 186, 188
bad apples. See Great American Sports Myth
Baltimore Sun 70
Barnes, Katie 48
barriers, girls' and women's sports: cultural 64; policy 66; political 64–66; structural 61–63
baseball: establishing pitch clock in 147; major league baseball 42, 126, 173–74; 198; players 13, 109, 123, 173, 198; and race 43–44; racial inequities 123–24; racial integration of 196–97; sexuality in 47–48; and social class 41–42; teams 42, 173; as variation of "sport as microcosm of society" theme 11–14, 114; young children playing 106–7, 109–10
basketball: arena funding case study 182; and college sport as big business 161–63; men's basketball 38, 62–63, 123–24, 147, 152, 160, 162, 166, 173; players 159–60; professional basketball 131, 145, 155; women's basketball 63, 78, 126, 144, 152, 160, 162, 173
beginning too early, youth sport 109–10
Berlin, Germany, Olympic Games in 34, 49
Biden, Joe 5
big business, college sport as 161–63

Big Ten 153
big-time college sport: athletes in "one and done" environment 159; avoiding education 156; as big business 161–63; compromising educational goals 154–56; consequences of money in 163–66; contradictions 166–67; education funds diversion for college sports subsidy 159; excessive time demands of big-time programs 157–58; "jock" subculture 158; NIL and pay-to-play 160–61; overview 151–54; promoting education 154; resulting education performance 159–60; scandals involving athletes' education 158–59
Biles, Simone 5, 92
bin Laden, Osama 32
Black Lives Matter (#BlackLivesMatter), 4, 7, 30, 43
Black people. *See* African Americans
Bleacher Report 138
Boston Red Sox 176
boxing 36, 41, 128; injuries in 86–87
Boyer, Ernest L. 166–67
Brackenridge, Celia 95
Brady, Tom 10
brain, injury of 81, 83–84
brake drugs 89
Brandt, Andrew 160
Brazil, Olympic games in 38
Brees, Drew 110
Brooklyn Dodgers 196
Brown, Michael 4
bull riding 82
bureaucracies, domination of individual by 8
Burrow, Joe 176
Butkus, Dick 84
Butler, Jimmy 124

California Interscholastic Federation (CIF) 112
Cantu, Robert 83–84
Carlos, John 49
Carnegie Foundation for the Advancement for Teaching 166–67
case studies. *See* public subsidies to professional sports franchises

Castro, Fidel 34–35
Cavenaugh, Gerald 13–14
CBAs. *See* collective bargaining agreements
CBS 139–40, 145, 162, 174–75
CBS Sports 62, 172
CBS Sports Network 145
Center for Study of Sport in Society 202–3
Chandler, Albert "Happy" 196–97
changing sport: free agency for athletes 197–98; gender equity 198–99; going about making changes 201–3; overview 195; possibility of 196, 199–201; racial integration of baseball 196–97
Chastain, Brandi 67
Chataway, Christopher 36
Chauvin, Derek 122
cheating 4, 17, 91, 142, 153
Chicago Bears 84, 183
Chicago Bulls 124
Chicago Cubs 173
Chicago White Sox 173, 184
children, physical injuries to 80–82. *See also* peer play and adult-organized sports for children; youth sport
China, Goodwill Tour in 38
China, tensions with 38
chronic traumatic encephalopathy (CTE) 81, 83
CIF. *See* California Interscholastic Federation
Cincinnati Bengals 85, 176, 179–80
Cincinnati Reds 179–80
Clark, Caitlin 133, 145, 160
class inequalities 127–29
Clinton, Hillary 121
coaches 1, 4–5; and #MeToo movement 95–96; in adult-organized sports for children 105–12; barriers 61; big-time college sport 151, 153, 155; class inequities 127–29; college sport as big business 162; commercial interests 141–42; consequences of money in college athletics 163–64, 163–66, 167; dealing with excessive parental demands 113; destructive aspects of sport 80, 84, 86; drug use 89–90;

Index

education avoidance 156; excessive time demands of big-time programs diminishing student role 157–58; football 75–77, 135, 137, 143, 146, 168, 182, 192; gender inequities 129–33; gender pay gap 46; intrusion of organizations on children's sport 112–13; male dominance 7–8; mental health and sports 91–93; "one and done" environment 159; orientation to change 13–14; participation and opportunity 59–60; and pervasive racism 7; possibility of change 197–202; professional sports franchises 185; racial inequities 120–27; sexuality of 46–47; sexual abuse by 93–95; and social class 40–41; in Super Bowl 9–11; televised sports 141; underrepresentation among 125–27; unity and division 39–40; and unity in sports 34–35; untrained coaches 112
Coakley, Jay 3–5, 107–8, 141–42, 152
Cobb, Ty 123
Collaros, Zach 175
collective bargaining agreements (CBAs) 69
collectives (NIL) 160–61
College Football Playoff 163
college sport: athletes in "one and done" environment 159; avoiding education 156; as big business 161–63; compromising educational goals 154–56; consequences of money in 163–66; contradictions 166–67; education funds diversion for college sports subsidy 159; excessive time demands of big-time programs 157–58; "jock" subculture 158; NIL and pay-to-play 160–61; overview 151–54; promoting education 154; resulting education performance 159–60; scandals involving athletes' education 158–59
Collins, Jason 47
Colorado Rockies 173
commercial interests 141–44
competitiveness, high degree of 6–7
concussions, in football 81–84
concussions, rates of 81

Cooky, Cheryl 55–56
costs, youth sport 110–11
COVID-19 29–30, 79, 131
Crenshaw, Kimberlé 120
Cronkite News 86
CTE. *See* chronic traumatic encephalopathy
Cuba, sport in 34–35
Cuban, Mark 176
Cullors, Patrisse 122
cultural barriers, girls' and women's sports 64
Curry, Stephen 4, 124, 131

Dallas Cowboys 176; stadium case study 180–82
Dallas Mavericks 176
dark side, adult-centered play 108–9
Davidson, Kavitha A. 3
Deford, Frank 39–40
deMause, Neil 180
Denhollander, Rachel 95
destructive aspects, of sport: #MeToo movement 95–96; conclusion 96; dietary dangers 87–88; drug use 88–91; injuries and 82–86; mental health 91–93; overview 77–78; physical injuries to children and youth 80–82; sexual abuse 93–95
dietary dangers 87–88
division (through sport in United States) 36–38; gender 45–46; intense identification with "nation" 39; race 43–45; sexuality 46–48; social class 40–43; strong case 39–40
Division I (NCAA) 47, 57, 63, 85, 126, 132, 161, 166
Douglas, Gabby 95
Drake, Michael 96
drug use 88–91
Dunn, Olivia 146

EADA. *See* Equity in Athletics Disclosure Act
easy majors, clustering in 156–57
eating disorders 87–88
economics: alternative structure 189–90; Cincinnati Bengals and Cincinnati Reds case study 179–80; Dallas

Cowboys stadium case study 180–82; Milwaukee Bucks basketball arena case study 182; other examples of egregious subsidies 182–84; public subsidies to franchises and 177–79; public subsidization rationale and 184–89
Edens, Wesley 182
education: avoiding 156; compromising goals 154–56; education funds diversion for college sports subsidy 159; promoting 154; resulting education performance 159–60
El Salvador, sport in 37
EPO. *See* erythropoietin
equality of opportunity, sports and 13
Equity in Athletics Disclosure Act (EADA) 59
erythropoietin (EPO) 89–90
ESPN 5, 138; and college sport as big business 161–63; commercial interests of 142–43; intrusion of organizations on children's sport 113; professional sport as monopoly 174–75; reporting on "worst stadium deal" 180; shifts in media landscape 140; social class 40–41; sport as male preserve 145–46; television as game changer 146–47
ESPN2 145
excessive time demands of big-time programs 157–58

Fair Play: How Sports Shape the Gender Debates (Barnes) 48
fair-foul debate: girls' and women's sports 55–75; unity and division 29–53
fair, sport as being 3–5, 17–18. *See also* fair–foul debate
Fan Cost Index 42
fans 1, 125, 138, 151, 153, 190, 199, 201–2; and athletes from racially marginalized backgrounds 44; big-time programs 163, 166; dispersing 63; experiencing paradox 3; franchises 171; full-scale war between El Salvador and Honduras 37; and fundamental myths 14–17; of hockey 106; intellectual ability of 45; intense identification with "nation" 39; at Israel-Turkey game 37; male dominance 132; manipulation of 49; and media 139–45; and mental health 92–93; misperception of 67; negative reaction of 127; power over 2; professional sport as monopoly 176; public subsidies to professional team franchises 178, 184; rational for public subsidization of professional sports teams 184–89; television as game changer for 147; televised rights fees 42; ticket prices 10; wealthiest fans 181–82; and women athletes 48; zeal of 32–33
FBS. *See* Football Bowl Subdivision
female athlete triad 80, 87–88
50 Years of Title IX (report) 69–71
Finland, sports n 22n12
Fisher, Jimbo 164
Flake, Jeff 49
Flood, Curt 198
Flores, Brian 125–26
Florida Marlins 173
Floyd, George xiii, 30, 122
food 9–10, 62, 86, 178, 185
football: avoiding education 176; clustering easy majors 156–57; coaches 96, 111, 123, 126, 162, 164; college football 41, 47, 85–86, 144, 152, 165–66; college sport as big business 161–63; concussions in 81–84; educational performance of athletes in 159–60; high school football 85; injuries 82–86; player size 85–86; players 13, 18, 39, 81–87, 143, 175; professional football 13, 18, 44, 56, 71, 82–86, 147; programs 94, 146, 152, 161; scandals involving education of athletes 158–59; sudden-death tie-breaking rule in 147; as variation of "sport as microcosm of society" theme 9–14
Football Bowl Subdivision (FBS) 57–58, 126, 152
Forbes 124, 179
foul, sport as being 3–5, 17–18. *See also* fair–foul debate

Index

FOX 140
Fox Sports 138
Front Office Sports 138
"Frontline" 84
Fubu 138
funds diverting 159

Garza, Alicia 12
Gaza, sport and 37–38
gender: equity 198–99; gender bland sexism 67; inequalities 129–33; male dominance as norm 7–8; unity and division 45–46
Georgetown University 38
Germany 90
Gill, Emmitt L., Jr. 93
girls' health and sports 78–79
girls' and women's sports: barriers to 61–66; gender inequalities 129–33; impact on society of 68; and #MeToo movement 95–96; media coverage 66–67; NIL and pay-to-play 160–61; overview 55–56; participation and opportunity 56–60; sexual abuse 93–95; shifts in landscape of 68–71; and youth sport 103–5
Gist, The 138
Gobert, Rudy 29–30
Goodhart, Phillip 36
Gordon, Derrick 47
Great American Sports Myth 3–5
Great Recession 179
Green Bay Packers 85, 172
gridiron football 83. *See also* football
Gu, Eileen 131

H&R Block 70
Hamilton County, Ohio 179–80
Hamlin, Damar 85
Hammes, Jon 182
Harvard Crimson 155
HBCUs. *See* historically Black colleges and universities
Head Start Programs 187
healthy aspects, of sport: overview 77–78. *See also* destructive aspects, of sport
heterosexuality 48

historically Black colleges and universities (HBCUs) 79
Ho, David 29–30
hockey 41, 47–48, 82, 89–90, 106, 142, 147
homophobia 46–48
Honduras, sport in 37
HoopScoop Online 113
House, Grant 161
Howard Center for Investigative Journalism 59
Howe, Jonathon 45
Hulu 138
hyper-segregation 45

impetus, youth sport 107
India, sport in 33–34
Indianapolis Star 143
individualism 13–14
individuals, domination of 8
injury: of brain 81, 83–84; to children and youth from sport 80–82; football 82–86; in other sports 86–87; painkillers for 84; in professional football 82–86; serious 81–82
Institute for Sport and Social Justice 126
International Olympic Committee (IOC) 87–88, 141, 143
intersectionality 19, 56, 120, 132
IOC. *See* International Olympic Committee
ION 145
Israel, basketball in 37
issues of race, class and gender: class inequalities 127–29; gender inequalities 129–33; overview 119–20; racial inequalities 120–27
Ivy League 155

James, LeBron 4, 124, 131
"jock" subculture 158
Johnson, Magic 124
Jordan, Danny 36
Jordan, Michael 44, 124

Kaepernick, Colin 4, 30–31, 49–50
Kansas City Royals 173
Kelley, John 40

Khatami, Mohammed 33
King, Billie Jean 109, 130
Kirby, Sandra 95
Knight Commission on Intercollegiate Athletics 159, 203
Knight-Newhouse College Athletics 131
Knight, Phil 163

L.A. Dodgers 44
L'Equipe 91
Landia, Kenesaw Mountain 196–97
landscape (of media) shifts in 138–40
Lapchick, Richard 127
Lasry, Marc 182
Latinos 44; in MLB 123–24; racial divides and 122; racial inequities 125
legacy media 138–40
Lenskyj, Helen 94
LGBTQ+ 47–48, 64, 197, 202
Longhorn Television Network 162
Los Angeles Angels 173
Los Angeles Dodgers 173
Los Angeles Lakers 124
Louisiana State University 155, 162
Love, Jordan 176
Loving Sports When They Don't Love You Back (Luther) 3
LPGA (Ladies Professional Golf Association) 130
Luther, Jessica 3

Major League Baseball (MLB) 49, 140; Black players assimilating into 197; and COVID-19 30; growth curve 176; injuries in 83; professional sport as monopoly 175–76, 179; professional sports as monopoly 173; racial inequities 123–24; racial integration of baseball 196–97; rights deal of 175; rule changes in 12, 147; and shifts in media landscape 140
Major League Soccer (MLS) 130
males: dietary dangers 87–88; and gender inequalities 129–33; male dominance as norm 7–8; in media landscape 138–40; in professional football 82–86; sexual abuse by 93–95; sport as male preserve 144–46. *See also* girls' and women's sports; women
Mandela, Nelson 35
Mandell, Richard D. 34
Manilow, Paul 32
March Madness 63
Maroney, McKayla 95
Martin, Trayvon 4
materialism, emphasis on 7
Matheson, Victor 185
McCain, John 49
McCartney, Paul 32
McCaskey, George 183
McDonald's 113
McKee, Ann 81
media: commercial interests 141–44; and consequences of money in college athletics 163–66; overview 137–38; rights deals 174–75; shifts in landscape 138–40; televised sports 141; television as game changer 146–48
media coverage, barriers, girls' and women's sports 66–67
mental health 91–93
Messi, Lionel 131
Messner, Michael 55–56, 66–67, 95, 104, 132, 146
Meta 9
#MeToo movement 95–96
Miami Dolphins 125–26
Miami Heat 176
Micheli, Lyle 80
Michigan State University 95
Michigan, reduced sports participation in 129
Middle East, sport in 37–38
Middle School Elite 113
mifepristone 121
Milwaukee Bucks basketball arena case study 182
Monday Night Football 140
money, consequences of 163–66
monoculture. *See* Super Bowl
monopoly, professional sports as 172–77
Montreal Expos 182–83
Moore, Dan 183
Mountjoy, Margo 88
Mulkey, Kim 162

Index

multiplier effect 185
Murphy, Kyle 86

Name, Image, and Likeness (NIL) 70, 113–14; big-time college sport 153–54; and pay-to-play 160–61
NASCAR 49
Nassar, Larry 95–96, 143
Nassib, Carl 4, 47
National Alliance for Youth Sports 112
National Association for the Advancement of Colored Peoples (NAACP) 122–23
National Athletic Trainers Association 110
National Basketball Association (NBA) 4, 9, 16; and COVID-19 29–30; gender inequities in 129–30; "one and done" environment 159; professional sport as monopoly 174–76; racial inequities in 124–26; revenue of 69; rights deal of 175; sexuality in 47; shifts in media landscape 140; and social class 42; sport as male preserve 144–45; unity achieved through sport 49
National Collegiate Athletic Association (NCAA) 30, 41, 57, 141; athletes in "one and done" environment 159; on avoiding education 156; and college sport as big business 161–63; diploma dashboard of 156–57; education funds diversion for college sports subsidy 159; and excessive time demands of big-time programs 157–58; *NCAA v Alston* 160–61; and professional sports as monopoly 173; promoting education 154; resulting academic performance 159–60; and structural barriers 61–63
National Committee for Accreditation of Coaching Education 112
National Federation of State High School Associations 57, 59
National Football League (NFL) 4, 18, 49, 141, 179; baseball *versus* 11–12; caveats 49; commercial interests 141–44; Dallas Cowboys stadium case study 180–82; and duality of sports 30–32, 39; franchise with public ownership 172; growth curve 176; NFL-G5 loan program 180; pervasiveness of racism in 7; professional sport as monopoly 174–76; racial inequities in 124–27; rights deal of 174–75; sexuality in 47–48; and shifts in media landscape 140; social class in 40–42; specialization 110; sports injuries 83–86; and Super Bowl 9–10; on television 146–47
National Hockey League (NHL) 49; rights deal of 175
National Organization of Women (NOW) 198–99
National Public Radio (NPR) 64
National Women's Soccer League Players Association 65
nations, role of sport among: division 36–38; unity 33–36
Nazi Olympics, The (Mandell) 34
NBA 130, 140; adopting NF model of avenue 174; growth curve 176
NBA TV 145
NBC 140, 174
NCAA v. Alston 22n0, 160–61
NCAA. *See* National Collegiate Athletic Association
Negro League 197
Netflix 138
New England Patriots 10, 32
new media 138–40
New York Giants 174
New York Mets 173
New York Times 43
New York Yankees 173, 176
Neymar 131
Nike 9, 113, 162–63
NIL. *See* Name, Image, and Likeness
Nine for IX 146
Nixon, Richard 71n2
Nocetti, Ron 112
non-revenue sports 165
nonprofit organization 10
NOW. *See* National Organization of Women
NPR. *See* National Public Radio

O'Brien, Jeff 126
Obama, Barack 120–21

Obama, Michelle 120
obesity epidemic 104
OCR. *See* Office of Civil Rights
Ohio State University 96, 162
Oklahoma State University 163
old media 138–40
Olsen, Jack 143
"one and done" environment 159
opportunity, girls' and women's sports and 56–60
organization, youth sport 105–6
organizations: intrusion of 112–13; unequal distribution of power in 8
Oriard, Michael 40
orientation to change, differences in 13
Osaka, Naomi 92, 131
out-of-control parental behavior 111–12
Outside the Lines 142

pain principle 87
Pakistan, sport in 33–34
Palestine, sport in 37–38
Pan American Games 34–35
Pantani, Marco 90
paradox, experiencing: sport as microcosm of society 6–14, 19–21; sport is fair-sport is foul debate 3–5, 17–18
Paramount+ 140
parents: commitment of 110–11; excessive demands of 113–14; out-of-control behavior of 111–12. *See also* peer play and adult-organized sports for children; youth sport
Parkinson's disease 83
participation, girls' and women's sports and 56–60
Paterno, Joe 96
patriotism, expressions of 49
pay-to-play 160–61, 165
peer play and adult-organized sports for children: adult-centered play and dark side 108–9; analysis of differences 107–8; beginning too early 109–10; costs 110–11; excessive parental demands 113–14; impetus 107; organization 105–6; organization intrusion on children's sport 112–13;

out-of-control parental behavior 111–12; process 1067; specialization 110; untrained coaches 112
Penn State, football at 142–43
pervasiveness of racism 7
Pew Research Center 124
PGA 130
PGA. *See* Professional Golf Association
Phelps, Michael 92
Philadelphia Eagles 179
Philadelphia Phillies 198
physical health, girls' and women's sports 68, 79
physical injuries, to children and youth 80–82
Pickens, T. Boone 163
Pittsburgh Steelers 179
Planned Parenthood of Southeastern Pennsylvania v. Casey 66
players (in football) size of 85–86
Playmakers 143
policy barriers, girls' and women's sports 66
positive deviance 80–81
Povich-Howard Centers 62
Power 5, 131, 161
Power 5 conference 154–56
power, unequal distribution of 8
predominantly white institutions (PWIs) 45
Price, S. L. 34
Prince, Sedona 62, 161
Princeton University 152–53
process, youth sport 106–7
Professional Golf Association (PGA) 124–25
Professional Women's Hockey League 130, 145
professional sports: alternative structure 189–90; Cincinnati Bengals and Cincinnati Reds case study 179–80; Dallas Cowboys stadium case study 180–82; Milwaukee Bucks basketball arena case study 182; as monopoly 172–77; other examples of egregious subsidies 182–84; overview 171–72; public subsidies to franchises of 177–79; public subsidization rationale 184–89
proportionality test 56–58

Index

ProPublica 177–78
Public Broadcasting System 143
public subsidies to professional sports franchises 177–79; Cincinnati Bengals and Cincinnati Reds case study 179–80; Dallas Cowboys stadium case study 180–82; Milwaukee Bucks basketball arena case study 182; other examples of egregious subsidies 182–84
public subsidization rationale 184–89
PWIs. *See* predominantly white institutions

race, unity and division 43–45
Racial and Gender Equity Report Card 127
racial inequities 120–27; African Americans 121–22; differentials in incarceration rate 12–23; Latinos 122; Latinos and 123; limits placed on Black athletes 124–25; sport as exception 123–24; stacking 125; in Super Bowl 10–11; underrepresentation among coaches 125–27
racism, pervasiveness of 7. *See also* racial inequalities
Raducanu, Emma 131
rags to riches, narrative 128
Raisman, Ali 95
Rapinoe, Megan 4–5
Rasego, Zaack 36
RED-S. *See* Relative Energy Deficiency in Sports
Reese, Angel 133
Relative Energy Deficiency in Sports (RED-S) 80, 87–88
revenue sports of football and basketball 128–29
reverse "Robin Hood" effect 188
Rickey, Branch 196
rights deals 174–75
Ritalin 89
Roberts, Gary 163
Robinson, Jackie 44
Roe v. Wade 65, 121
Ronaldo, Cristiano 131

Rooney Rule 7
Rosentraub, Mark 185–89
Rutgers University 153
Ryan, Joan 94

Saban, Nick 162
Sack, Allen 167
Sage, George 110–11, 173
Sam, Michael 47
Sandusky, Jerry 96, 142
Sanger, Daniel 106
SB Nation 138
scandals involving athletes' education 158–59
Schlereth, Mark 84
Science, Technology, Engineering, and Math (STEM) 156–57
Seattle Seahawks 189
SEC. *See* Southeastern Conference
Self, Bill 162
September 11, 2001, sport following 31–32
sexual abuse 93–95
sexuality, unity and division 46–48
Shirley Povich Center for Sports Journalism 59
Silver, Adam 29–30
Smith, Tommie 49
soccer 4–5, 33–34, 37, 48–49, 65, 67, 69, 202; clubs in professional soccer 172; commercial interests in 142–43; gender equity in 198; gender inequities in 130–31; professional sport as monopoly 173, 175; racial inequities in 125; rights deals in 175; sudden-death tie-breaking rule in 147; women soccer 87
social class, unity and division 40–43
social/emotional well-being, girls' and women's sports 68, 79
society, sport as microcosm of 19–21; agent of change 8; common characteristics 6–8; domination of individual by bureaucracies 8; emphasis on materialism 7; football *versus* baseball 11–14; high degree of competitiveness 6–7; male dominance as norm 7–8; Super Bowl variation

9–11; unequal distribution of power in organizations 8
Soldier Field 182–84
South Africa, sport in 35–36
Southeastern Conference (SEC) 123
specialization, youth sport 110
Sperber, Murray 2, 164
sponsorship 160–61
sport: within academics 151–70; as agent of change 8; class inequalities in 127–29; gender inequalities in 129–33; as male preserve 144–46; media and 137–49; mental health and 91–93; paradoxes of 1–3, 14–17; professional sports 171–93; racial inequalities in 120–27; shifts in media landscape of 138–40; and women's health 78–79
Sports Broadcast Act of 1961, 174
Sports Illustrated 34, 35, 39, 47, 143, 160
SportsCenter 5, 142
Springboks (team) 35–36
stacking, race and 44–45, 125
stadiums 7, 10, 20, 30, 200–201; and male dominance 132; building stadiums in communities 186, 188; consequences of money in athletics 163–66; Dallas Cowboys stadium case study 180–82; increase in violence in 39; Milwaukee Bucks basketball arena case study 182; patriotic displays in 32; public subsidies to professional team franchises 178–79; and social class 42–43; and sport as male preserve 145; subsidizing 183–84; substitution effect 185; "worst stadium deal" case study 179–80
State of Play 2023, 104–5
STEM. *See* Science, Technology, Engineering, and Math
structural barriers, girls' and women's sports 61–63
subsidization, education funds and 159
substitution effect 185
Super Bowl: expenses involved in attending 10; following September 11, 2001, 31–32; glorifying violence in 10; high degree of competitiveness in 6–7; racism in 10–11; symbolizing fundamental sports paradox 11; as variation of "sport as microcosm of society" theme 9–11
Super Bowl Half-Time 175
Super Bowl LVII 11–12
Świątek, Iga 131
synthetic steroids 90

Tampa Bay Devil Rays 173–74
Taylor, Breonna 122
television, sports in: commercial interests 141–44; consequences of money in college athletics 163–66; television as game changer 146–48; as window on reality or social construction 141
tennis 19, 41, 69, 78, 80, 92, 109–11, 124, 128, 130–31
Texas Western 123
The Institute for Diversity and Equity in Sport (TIDES) 126–27, 132
Theberge, Nancy 78
therapeutic exemptions 89
30 for 30, 142
Thriving Through Sport (report) 79
TIDES. *See* The Institute for Diversity and Equity in Sport
TikTok 138
Time 92
time, orientation toward 12–13
Title IX 45–46, 153, 198–99; and gender inequalities 129–33; girls' and women's sports 55–60; and structural barriers 61–63
Tokyo Olympics 92–93
Tometi, Opal 122
track 41, 60, 81, 88, 90, 128, 183
Trevor Project 4
trigger laws 121
Trump, Donald J. 30, 121
Turkey, sport in 37
Turner Network 62

U.S. Supreme Court 121
UCLA 7, 148n7, 204n6
Ulrich, Jan 90
Underwood, John 43

Index

United States: class inequalities in 127–29; concussion crisis in 82–83; football popularity in 82–83; gender in 45–46; gender inequalities n 129–33; girls' and women's sports in 55–75; professional sports as monopoly in 172–77; race in 43–45; sexuality in 46–48; social class in 40–43; sports within academics 151–70; tensions with China 38; unequal distribution of power in organizations in 8; unity and division through sport in 39–48
unity and division: caveats 49–50; gender 45–46; overview 29–32; race 43–45; role of sport in unity/division among nations 32–38; role of sport in unity 33–36; sexuality 46–48; social class 40–43; through sport in United States 39–48; throughout sport in United States 39–48
University of Arkansas 155
University of Kentucky 58, 123, 162
University of Maryland 96
University of North Carolina-Chapel Hill 158
University of Notre Dame 162
University of Oregon 163
University of Southern California 160
US Census Bureau 122
US Golf Association (USGA) 124
US House of Representatives 129
US Senate 129
US Women's National Soccer Team (USWNT) 5, 69–70
US Women's World Cup Soccer 67
USA Today 32, 46, 57–58, 163–64
USC 7, 159, 204n6
USGA. See US Golf Association
USWNT. See US Women's National Soccer Team

violence, glorifying 10
virtual draft 30
Voting Rights Act of 1965, 121

WADA. See World Anti-Doping Agency
Wade, Dwayne 4
Washington Post 82, 113

Weinreb, Michael 31
Wertheim, Jon 6–7
Wiliams, Venus 41
Williams Institute 46–47
Williams, Caleb 160
Williams, Serena 41, 44, 131
Winnipeg Blue Bombers 175
Winter Olympics 78
wokeness 43
women: dietary dangers 87–88; health and sports 78–79; and male dominance as norm 7–8; in media landscape 138–40; sexual abuse of 93–95
Women's National Basketball Association (WNBA) 4–5, 30, 48–49, 69, 126, 130, 140; professional sport as monopoly 175; rights deal of 175; sport as male preserve 144–45
Women's National Basketball Players Association 65
Women's Sports Foundation 46, 57–5, 59, 65, 107; *Thriving Through Sport* report 79
Woods, Tiger 124, 125
World Anti-Doping Agency (WADA) 90
World Health Organization 29–30

X (formerly known as Twitter) 9
Xi, Jinping 38

youth sport: adult-centered play and dark side 108–9; analysis of differences 107–8; beginning too early 109–10; costs 110–11; excessive parental demands 113–14; forms of play for young children 103–5; organization 105–6; organization intrusion on children's sport 112–13; out-of-control parental behavior 111–12; process 106–7; specialization 110
youth, physical injuries to 80–82
YouTube 9
YouTubeTV 140

Zimmerman, George 122
Zirin, David 8, 32, 142–43, 183, 197, 203

ABOUT THE AUTHORS

D. Stanley Eitzen was professor emeritus of sociology at Colorado State University, where he taught for twenty-one years, most recently as John N. Stern Distinguished Professor. He was the author or coauthor of twenty-four books, including three on sport, as well as numerous scholarly articles and chapters in scholarly books. He was a former president of the North American Society for the Sociology of Sport and the recipient of that organization's Distinguished Service Award. Among his other awards, he was selected to be a Sports Ethics Fellow by the Institute for International Sport.

Cheryl Cooky is a professor of American studies and women's, gender, and sexuality studies at Purdue University. She is the coauthor of *Serving Equality: Feminism, Media and Women's Sports* (Peter Lang, 2022) and *No Slam Dunk: Gender, Sport and the Unevenness of Social Change* (Rutgers University Press, 2018), as well as numerous scholarly articles and book chapters. She is the editor of *Sociology of Sport Journal*, past president of the North American Society for the Sociology of Sport (NASSS), and recipient of its Distinguished Service Award. Committed to making research accessible, Dr. Cooky has written over a dozen op-ed articles and has appeared in over one hundred national and international news media outlets.